THE ISLE OF W

Feast of Food and Drink

JO RICHARDSON

PHOTOGRAPHY BY BEN WOOD

FORELAND BOOKS

Jo Richardson is a long-established book editor specializing in cookery and healthy lifestyle, and has worked on books by many leading contemporary chefs, cookery writers and food bloggers. She is also a cookery author in her own right and regularly develops and publishes healthy-eating recipes on her Island Cook website, www.islandcook.org.uk. Although an 'overner' (mainland migrant) rather than a 'caulkhead' (third-generation Islander), Jo was a frequent visitor to the Island over many years, enjoying in equal measure its breathtaking scenery and its wonderful produce, before finally settling permanently 15 years ago and living there blissfully ever since.

The location photographer **Ben Wood** moved from London to the Isle of Wight with his wife Anna in 2000. Best known for his marine photography and his book *The Island*, published in 2006, Ben has established an enviable reputation as one of the Island's most prolific and finest photographers. Having worked with numerous top food photographers as an assistant in London in the 1990s, the chance to collaborate with Jo Richardson on this book was too good an opportunity to miss, particularly as it combined two of Ben's abiding interests – The Isle of Wight and food.

©2017 Jo Richardson
First published in the UK by Foreland Books 2017
ISBN 978 1 52620649 7

Written and styled by Jo Richardson

Contributions by Professor Paul Richardson

Photography by Ben Wood
www.islandimages.co.uk

Design by Style of Wight Magazine
www.styleofwight.co.uk

Published by Foreland Books
Seascape Cottage
Forelands Field Road
Bembridge
Isle of Wight PO35 5TR

publisher@iowfeastoffood.co.uk
www.iowfeastoffood.co.uk

Distributed beyond the Isle of Wight by
Casemate UK Ltd
The Old Music Hall
106–108 Cowley Road
Oxford OX4 1JE
www.casematepublishing.co.uk

Printed in the UK by Short Run Press, Exeter

Contents

The perfect pastoral sweep up to the Island's high point of St Catherine's Down.

Introduction

understand why I was drawn to the Isle of Wight in the first place, with its natural seaside – anywhere that has woods and meadows running down to the sea has my vote – and quiet yet accessible countryside. What I don't understand is why I was positively driven to decamp to the Island, especially given that part of the pull can't have been memories of blissful childhood holidays, unlike for many other people, since I visited for just one day as a sullen youth. But having had the chance over the last decade and a half to ponder the matter, I now realize that a form of nostalgia could well provide the explanation.

My homeland is Kent, traditionally known as the Garden of England characterized by its abundance of orchards and hop gardens (one of the latter that supplied the Shepherd Neame Brewery providing me with game employment in the summer vacations of my college days), and more recently its reintroduced vineyards. So bells began to ring when I learned of the Island's rich apple- and hop-growing

heritage to add to its pioneering wine-growing, only to discover that the same 'Garden of England' title had been bestowed upon the Isle of Wight as long ago as 1781.

My beloved childhood home was on the fringes of the North Downs, so therein lies another connection to the Island – quite literally, geologically speaking, as the Wight's Downs and the Kent Downs form either end of one mighty chalk range.

My folks were not big on holidaying away from home, so much so that my dad's joke every summer was (again resonantly), 'We're going abroad for our holidays this year – the Isle of Wight!' We didn't even make it that far, as I've already pointed out, but with Kent being a coastal county, too, we were in easy distance of the seaside for 'days out' even in the old family jalopy that we had to will up and over the Downs. The term 'sea' was applied loosely here in that the closest of our regular destinations was Allhallows,

The view across the Solent to 'the other side' with a Palmerston Fort in the foreground.

onto whose name had been tacked '-on-Sea' in an effort to convince visitors such as us that we were indeed by the sea rather than the Thames estuary. Not that we cared a hoot either way, but it did mean that being able to see across to the other side when swimming or playing on the beach became implanted and imbued with connotations of carefree summer days. Small wonder then that on my first visit to the Island as a mature adult, lying on the beach at Springvale near Seaview gazing across the Solent to Portsmouth, I felt a curious sense of coming home. And so it has proved to be.

I count myself hugely fortunate in having been brought up on a diet of fresh seasonal produce grown by my parents and grandparents, who were committed to the ethos of cultivation without the use of chemicals long before the concept of organic had become mainstream. And in the heyday of battery hens, my folks were also leading the way in high-welfare farming by producing free-range eggs on a small, non-intensive basis. We also had our own supply of fresh unpasteurized milk from our resident Toggenburg goats, Emma and Jane (whom my dad would refer to adoringly as 'his girls', not including me). My dear mum was as good a cook as she was a gardener, with an instinctive flair for conjuring up tasty, satisfying offerings out of, well, not a lot to be honest, at least in terms of protein, as 'times wos 'ard'. But we never went short of nutritious versatile

veg, whether everyday greens and spuds or more exotic items such as asparagus and kohlrabi — it was a family tradition to make a wish in celebration of the first tasting of each crop of the year — and all manner of orchard and soft fruits were carefully stored or preserved to help ensure year-round self-sufficiency.

Which brings me back to the Isle of Wight and its strength and depth of natural resources, and the amazing array of fresh produce they deliver. And not least to the formidable agricultural expertise, enterprising spirit and artisanal skills, much of which building on a unique inheritance of historical experience, that have been brought together to harvest and harness the Island's bounty so successfully. My quest, and my privilege, has been to survey the spectrum of this dedicated activity as an outside observer and to explore its end results, both the packaged products and fresh produce, through the seasons over the course of a year in my humble Bembridge kitchen. And the more I have researched and sampled the Wight's food and drink, the more impressed I have been by its diversity, quality and creativity. My main concern is that I have merely scratched the surface, given the wide range and ever-evolving nature of this sphere of endeavour on the Island, so I can only apologize in advance for any unintended omissions. Nevertheless, I hope this book will help spread the word about the true wealth of the Wight.

A few notes for users

Seasonal options
Although the book is structured to reflect the seasons of the year, running sequentially from spring to winter, with appropriate seasonal ingredients featured for each chapter, the recipes can easily be adapted for other times of year and I've included suggestions for alternative seasonal ingredients accordingly.

Local ingredient substitutes
Where I've specified Island ingredients, you can of course substitute other similar ingredients should you not be able to source them (although many items can be ordered online), or if you are cooking in another context, in which case you can explore alternatives local to the area you are in.

As far as possible I have given easy adaptations where required to make the recipes gluten free or dairy free, in addition to there being a vegetarian (and occasionally vegan) main dish option for each dining scenario, bar the one devoted to fish and seafood.

Sourcing info
Where people, products or places are mentioned in the main body of the book, you will find any contact or location information you may need in the directory section at the back of the book.

Kitchen kit
I have been mindful that if you are cooking from this book in holiday accommodation you may not have access to a full *batterie de cuisine*, although in the case of the kitchens we were kindly given access to, and in my wider experience, good provision is generally made in that regard on the Island. Having said that, I don't by and large go in for sophisticated kit (space doesn't allow in my poky kitchen), but I have given some alternatives for particular tasks that I have personally found to be a stumbling block on occasions. In any case, should you relish the opportunity to cook when you go away free from the constraints of everyday routine and time (as I do), it's worth packing a few versatile, portable items of kit. Check ahead that kitchen scales and measuring spoons are to be had, as they are sometimes frustratingly absent.

The following are the other main specifics:

Crushing spices - I widely use toasted and crushed or ground whole spices, and a pestle and mortar, let alone an electric spice or coffee grinder (though you could pack one), may not be to hand. While you can always substitute ready-ground, the loss in flavour will be significant, but it's easy to improvise by enclosing the toasted spices in a resealable plastic bag and rolling over them with a glass bottle or rolling pin until roughly or finely crushed.

Blending ingredients for sauces – You may well expect to find a blender or food processor at your disposal, but blending small quantities of ingredients can present a problem in any kitchen, so the answer is to pack (or buy) a basic stick blender, both compact and inexpensive. However, you will also need a deep-sided receptacle for blitzing your ingredients to keep splattering to a minimum. A ½-litre/1-pint Pyrex measuring jug will provide you with two handy tools in one.

Whisking eggs, cream and sponge mixtures – Again small and cheap, a hand-held electric whisk is good enough for any of these tasks.

Fine straining of liquids – There is a bit of mucking about to be done if you're in the market for making syrups and so on for homemade concoctions, so ideally you will need a fine-mesh sieve and a muslin, but you can improvise for the latter with a large cotton hanky, freshly laundered of course, or a well-rinsed new J-cloth.

Baking recipes – A few basic baking tins are involved here, but there are also some freeform items that require only a baking sheet.

Oven temperatures – For the sake of simplicity, I have specified the temperature for conventional (static) ovens only if cooking on electric (along with the equivalent Gas Mark), so if using a fan oven, reduce the temperature by about 20°C, although individual ovens will vary, so consult the manufacturer's instructions if available. All ovens vary in any case, but precise temperatures aren't critical except when it comes to baking cakes.

A Slice of Wight

The Isle of Wight was granted its coat of arms almost a century ago with the pious motto 'All this beauty is of God', while the atheist author of the *Communist Manifesto* Karl Marx, an enthusiastic Island holidaymaker in his later life, had already written 50 years earlier to his collaborator Engels, 'This island is a little paradise'. The fact is that, whatever your faith or convictions, the Island is one of the most naturally blessed parts of the United Kingdom, with over half its area designated Areas of Outstanding Natural Beauty.

A diamond-shaped adjunct to the British mainland (sometimes known round here as 'the North Island') about four miles across the Solent, its 147 square miles in area and 140,000 residents (augmented by more than two and a quarter million visitors a year) make it the largest English island by area and the second largest by population, though vying with Rutland for the title of the smallest English county, apparently depending on whether the tide is in or out.

Aeons of rising and falling sea levels and tectonic shifts have produced an unusually varied geological structure that has been characterized as 'England in miniature'. They have also made it a wonderful source of dinosaur fossils and the remains of prehistoric crocodiles and molluscs, earning it the title 'Dinosaur Isle'. However, as an island it is really quite young in geological terms; the great river that drained much of southern England only finally encircled it to become the modern Solent 7,000 years ago, after the end of the last Ice Age.

The backbone of the Island is a chalk ridge with outriders, reaching a height of 240 metres on St Boniface Down behind Ventnor, leading Marx to declare, with some exaggeration, 'Here you can breathe sea and mountain air at the same time'. The Downs provide well-drained grazing for sheep and cattle, frost-free south-facing valleys with their own microclimates that are favourable locations for the Wight's two notable vineyards and apricot and cherry orchards, and rich pastures, such as the Rew Valley, which are the source of the Island's highly prized milk, cream and related dairy products.

The chalk aquifers deliver pure water for the local brewers and mineral water producers. Meanwhile, the river valleys, especially the Medina through the centre of the Island, provide fine, briny alluvial soil that is perfect for asparagus, sweetcorn and salad crops and the internationally acclaimed Wight garlic. In general, the climate is sunnier and warmer than the mainland, giving a longer growing season even than the neighbouring counties of Dorset and Hampshire.

The benign environment does not end on the beach. The warm, clean waters around the Island's rocky and sandy edges are rich with fish and crustaceans – notably crabs and lobsters, and that most exclusive delicacy the Bembridge prawn. And the predominant south-westerlies bring the wonderful air quality that led the Victorians to build the Royal National Hospital for Diseases of the Chest on the site of what is now the Ventnor Botanic Garden. As Tennyson said: 'the air here is worth sixpence a pint', then the price of two flagons of beer.

'…come to the Isle of Wight;
Where, far from the noise of smoke and town,
I watch the twilight falling brown
All round a careless-ordered garden
Close to the ridge of a noble down.'

ALFRED, LORD TENNYSON, POET LAUREATE

Wight Flavours

The Island's reputation as a foodie hub has mushroomed in recent times and in a highly competitive context, awash with such buzzwords as 'artisanal', 'heritage', 'locally sourced', 'sustainable' and 'traceability'. In reality, the Isle of Wight has long been diligently going about its core business of producing quality food and drink from its land and waters. For a start, it is much more rural than the rest of South East England; 84% of the land is classed as rural with 35% of its businesses and 36% of the population based in the countryside. Agriculture, fisheries and forestry account for around 3% of GDP and 4% of employment, as compared with less than 1% and 1.3% respectively for the country as a whole.

Although the Island's agriculture benefits from a mild climate that allows a longer growing season as well as its favourable geology, with well-drained grazing on the Downs and rich alluvial soils in the 'midlands', there are the higher transport costs involved in exporting to the mainland to contend with. The Island is also subject to all the wider market challenges, such as the drop in milk prices over recent years, which has led to a steady decline in its dairy herds from 150 in the mid-1980s to around two dozen today.

In response, there has been a shift away from general mixed farming towards specialized production including high-quality meat, crops that are especially suited to and extended in season by the local conditions like asparagus, sweetcorn, tomatoes and apricots, building on the Island's widespread fame for garlic, and more recently hand-crafted premium products such as small-batch gin and roasted coffee (see pages 17 and 97). So much so that the Royal Isle of Wight Agricultural Society has now introduced the Wight Marque food provenance scheme whereby a blue rosette logo of accreditation certifies those products that have been grown, reared or processed on the Island, whereas a gold logo denotes those retail outlets, eating places and accommodation providers that have been judged to use or sell at least ten Wight Marque products. This has helped support fruitful collaboration between local farmers, growers and food producers on one side, and retailers, wholesalers and the range of businesses in the hospitality sector on the other.

At the same time, many farms have diversified their income streams by providing holiday accommodation in converted barns, for instance Nettlecombe Farm near Whitwell, which offers everything from a petting farm with goats, pigs, lambs, alpaca and even reindeer to coarse fishing and yoga, or Tapnell Farm near Yarmouth with its restaurant and gift shop, glamping and eco pods, clay pigeon shooting and air-rifle range, adventure activities and farm theme-park experience.

Like the Downs in providing the backbone to the Island, there is a unique strong, deep structure underlying all these endeavours – a dependable, enduring and adaptable framework of family businesses, some going back generations, others relative newcomers. And not only does its connections hold good within the individual family networks, they reach out to inter-connect, cooperate and support other family enterprises for mutual benefit and for that of the Island as a whole.

All aboard in a strong swell on Captain Stan's Shooting Star out in the Channel.

Catch of the Day

The Island's waters give as generously as the land. Both the Channel and the Solent are blessed with shellfish and a wide variety of fish such as cod, pollack, whiting, plaice, Dover sole, flounder, dab, bream, mackerel, brill, turbot, ray, gurnard, red and grey mullet, huss, conger eel and bass, depending on the catch and the season, available responsibly caught by day boats from fishmongers across the Island, some of which have their own vessels. These include the Ventnor Haven Fishery, owned by the Blake family who have been fishing the local waters for decades; Captain Stan's Bembridge Fish Store and Ryde Fish Store, a member of the Seafish Responsible Fishing Scheme whose fish is caught from their boat *Shooting Star* but also sourced from other local fishermen; and The Best Dressed Crab, Bembridge, yet another family-run business who built their own top-class fishing boat *My Way*, now owned and operated by a fellow local fisherman.

The Island is particularly renowned for its wealth of fine-tasting crabs and lobsters, besides seasonal prawns, cockles and whelks. The many sunken wrecks around its coastline offer attractive habitats, as do the various rocky shelves like the extensive rocky ledge close to the shore at Bembridge where lobster pots can be dropped into the sea without the use of a boat. J & B Fisheries in Freshwater, which owns boats for catching crab and lobster, has its own smokehouse, while Phillips Seafood and Smokehouse in Cowes, established in the 1970s to smoke salmon, nowadays also offers a variety of lightly oak-smoked locally caught shellfish and fish.

In addition to fresh fish, cooked seafood specialities such as crab cakes, pâté and pasties are prepared by both Ventnor Haven Fishery (available from their Seafood Corner outlet in Newport as well as the Fishery itself) and Captain Stan's. Catch Isle of Wight, meanwhile, has won Great Taste Awards for its fish cakes, crab bisque and Soupe de Poisson, made using sustainable fish sourced along the South Coast and mostly sold through Hampshire farmers' markets or wholesale to restaurants and shops across the region.

The Isle of Wight's rivers, ponds, reservoirs and fishing lakes also yield a bounty of freshwater fish including carp, roach, rudd, perch, tench and trout, rainbow trout being available to buy fresh and smoked.

Choice Cuts

There is little to separate the Island's beef, pork and lamb in terms of quality, as it is superior stuff across the range, all carrying that now highly valued traceability tag.

In some cases, this means all the way from conception to consumption, as with Mottistone Manor Farm's Aberdeen Angus cattle – a familiar sight grazing on the Downs of West Wight – being bred and reared on the Island, the beef hung for up to 28 days and then prepared by their own butcher ready for sale in their farm shop and to top eating establishments. The slow-maturing traditional Ruby Red Devon is Brownrigg's breed of choice, which, unlike modern breeds, lays down intra-muscular fat in the meat to produce that sought-after marbling for succulence and flavour – available from their own farm shop near Godshill. Premium grass-fed beef from other farms across the Island, such as Kemphill near Ryde, encompassing a variety of British breeds like English Longhorn, Hereford and Highland as well as Aberdeen Angus, is on sale through other main outlets including the butchery at Farmer Jack's Farm shop in Arreton, Hamiltons Fine Foods based in Newport and its butchers' shops there and in Cowes, Briddlesford Lodge Farm near Wootton and Island Foods in Ryde. And speaking of Briddlesford, the bull calves of their herd of pedigree Guernsey cows (more on those later) are reared according to the highest welfare standards to around six months of age for the production of sweet and tender rose veal.

Grass-fed is the watchword for lamb in the same way as it is for beef, winning hands down over grain-fed meat for not only flavour but nutritional value, notably a higher percentage of omega-3 fatty acids, together with a lower overall fat content. An added bonus is that the Island's downland grazing is continually exposed to salty sea breezes, which also enhances the flavour and texture (think saltmarsh lamb), as in the case of the renowned lamb from Dunsbury Farm on Compton Downs (recently acquired by the National Trust in the interests of wildlife conservation, in particular the rare Glanville Fritillary butterfly), and Cheverton Farm near Shorwell. Brownrigg is again a major player with a flock of some 1,000 sheep that are lambed outside during April, while Duxmore Farm with its main holding to the north of Arreton Downs and tenanted land around Quarr Abbey near Ryde boasts a flock of pedigree Suffolks, and Jacobs and Black Welsh Mountain sheep besides their commercial flock, which they run alongside their Aberdeen Angus suckler herd.

On the subject of speciality breeds, you will be sure to spot the impressive horned black Hebridean sheep should you find yourself in the vicinity of one of their roving grazing sites around the Island, employed by the National Trust as heavy-duty lawnmowers, happy to browse on coarse vegetation to allow the Island's impressive show of orchids and other precious wild flowers to flourish. The dark woolly Galloway, another ancient Scottish breed but of cattle in this case, is likewise employed by the Trust

The green, green grass of Wight that sustains such wonderful meat and dairy produce.

to graze Compton Downs. And in summer, you are likely to see the Mottistone Fold of Highland cattle grazing on Mottistone Down, again used for conservation grazing besides pedigree sales and beef. Come the autumn, most of the herd is moved to the Downs at Wroxall, near the principal base of owner/breeder Michael Poland's Wight Conservation Estate at Wroxall Cross Farm, in order to trim the summer vegetation to length. The Garlic Farm has also reared a herd of Highlanders, which you can enjoy watching as you freely wander the farm or tour on a tractor trailer, and the beef is often served in their restaurant. Likewise, The Seaview Hotel sources its beef and other produce for its Michelin-awarded restaurant from its own Newclose Farm near Carisbrooke, home to another Highland herd along with pigs, Rhode Island Red hens and two herds of deer, red and fallow, providing both fine cuts of venison and meat for venison sausages.

When it comes to pork production, once again Brownrigg, incorporating the Isle of Wight Bacon Company, is a shining example, rearing all their animals free range on a diet of natural grains and pulses – you can see them happily rooting about outside their community housing from the footpath through Moor Farm near Godshill – without the use of antibiotics or growth-promoting additives and employing humane husbandry methods.

Available fresh from their farm shop, the farmers' markets in Ryde and Newport and online, also on offer are bacon, gammon and ham products, dry-cured and smoked at their Sheepwash Farm, also near Godshill. Prime Island pork is also to be had from Briddlesford Lodge Farm Shop and Farmer Jack's Farm Shop in Arreton, as well from the quality butchers across the Island, skilled in the traditional practice of properly maturing the meat to enhance flavour and eating quality. One exemplary case in point, Hamiltons Fine Foods/Hamiltons Butchers, does its own dry-curing and hardwood-smoking of premium local pork to produce traditional bacon and gammon. And at eatery and bakery Cantina in Ventnor, they use pork from Clifton Pigs, a pedigree rare-breed free-range pig enterprise, to produce a platter of mixed house-cured charcuterie.

Prize Poultry

The Brownrigg success story continues here, or rather returns to its beginnings as a small-scale turkey producer back in 1990, since when it has grown to become the largest free-range poultry business on the Island. Besides year-round production of chicken (plus c. 3,000 eggs a day, sold through Southern Co-operative stores Islandwide and other outlets) and duck, bronze and white turkeys are available for Christmas, prepared and matured on the farm, together with goose and a special range of three-bird

Low winter sunshine as the Kern Shoot ends a successful day.

'royal roasts'. Other Wight Marque-accredited free-range egg producers include Hazelgrove Farm Eggs at Ashey near Ryde and Medham Farm near Cowes (also home to sister business Tipsy Wight; see page 18), which both sell duck eggs as well as chickens' at the farm gate; and Quarr Abbey's kitchen and farm shop is well supplied with eggs from their comfortably rehoused ex-commercial hens. Other farm shops and local stores sell their own eggs, sometimes from specialist breeds as in the case of Delysia Farm near St Helens, or are supplied by other small egg producers, and honesty boxes for eggs from domestically reared poultry are to be found all over the Island.

Fair Game

The Isle of Wight is host to some 43 locally organized shoots for pheasant, partridge and duck, the most per square mile in the UK, with the Bowcombe Estate shoot regarded as one of the top ten in the country, plus there is plenty of rough shooting for rabbit and pigeon. Consequently, there is no shortage of game to be bagged locally, with most butchers carrying some, especially in the run-up to Christmas, while others are game specialists for wholesale and catering in addition to retail, as in the cases of Island Foods in Ryde, Hamiltons Fine Foods and its butchers' shops, P J Thorne in Freshwater, Paul Murphy in Shanklin and Brownrigg's near Godshill. John Day at Delysia Farm also sells local pheasant and partridge, both fresh and smoked on site in his Bradley smoker. Most of the aforementioned outlets also sell packs of mixed game for pies.

Milk and Much More

With favourable geological and climatic conditions underpinning the high quality of the Island's dairy produce, it is by playing to premium that the local industry has managed to survive the punishing recent times, although not without suffering casualties. The long-established Griffin family farm at Briddlesford Lodge, for example, sells milk just as it comes, unpasteurized, from their award-winning herd of Guernseys (besides pasteurized), make their own luxuriously rich double cream and clotted cream, halloumi-style cheese (plus other cheeses in the pipeline) and butter, and also supply famed family business Minghella next door with their surplus cream and milk, from which they make their renowned gourmet ice cream that has secured more than 80 Great Taste Awards. Similarly, raw milk from the Queen Bower Dairy's Guernsey herd goes to make, on the self same site, The Isle of Wight Cheese Company's Cheddar-type Gallybagger (Isle of Wight dialect for 'scarecrow') and Gallybagger Mature plus their special-edition Old Gaffer Blue, while a mix of the dairy's (J W Reed's) pasteurized milk together with that sourced from other local farms is used to produce Isle of Wight

Blue and Soft cheeses (see page 144). Likewise, Reads Farm in Carisbrooke supplies the nearby Isle of Wight Ice Cream Company in Newport with milk from its Holstein Friesian herd to whip up a range of dairy ice creams and sorbets, as well as Calbourne Classics to make their top-quality whole milk and Greek-style yogurts and flavoured ice creams along with other local milk. Completing the trio of dairies still very much in operation on the Island is Wight Milk of Coppid Hall Farm, Havenstreet, which delivers Islandwide including to the majority of schools and Southern Co-operative stores.

One notable casualty of the downward pressure on the milk industry, the Rew Valley Dairy near Ventnor, has taken on a new life as home to the Butter Vikings, suppliers of speciality butter to the world-renowned Noma restaurant in Copenhagen, Denmark among other top international eateries. They have relocated from Sweden to this verdant valley specifically in order to capitalize on the local superlative cream.

The Island also has a commercial goat dairy, The Green Garn at Bouldnor near Yarmouth, based on a 60-strong herd of mainly British Saanens with some Toggenburgs, Golden Guernseys and British Alpines. Here again, the milk is put to creative use in producing a mild-tasting, creamy soft goats' cheese available in different fresh herb flavours and delicious goats' milk fudge.

Top of the Crops

It is hard to overestimate the contribution that The Garlic Farm Boswell family business has made to the cultivation and popularization of garlic, and consequently the renown of the Isle of Wight across the UK, since the harvesting of their first crop in 1977 back when it was an alien ingredient to most Brits. Colin Boswell has since travelled the world researching and selecting rare varieties to nurture and develop, ensuring that its seed garlic can flourish beyond the particularly advantageous conditions of the Island with its high light intensity and well-balanced chalky soil.

The Garlic Farm's shop at Newchurch (and other outlets both nationwide and Islandwide and online) sells a wide range of varieties, including rare heritage ones, in seed form (bulbs or cloves) for growing, as well as all you need for cooking, depending on the season, such as green or 'wet' garlic, garlic scapes (flower stalks of hardneck varieties; see page 39), garlic spring onions, the oversized elephant garlic, oak-smoked garlic, black garlic, whole garlic bulbs, garlic plaits and grappes (bunches) and garlic butter. Also on offer is their famous range of garlic-based products including sauces, condiments, preserves and snacks. The Garlic Festival, first sponsored by the Boswells in 1983, has mushroomed into a major event on the Island's packed calendar, with garlic remaining at the heart of it but also showcasing the depth and diversity of the Island's other food and drink products (see page 158).

Elephant garlic in spectacular full bloom on The Garlic Farm.

Another standout crop is asparagus, which thrives in the Island's sunny, saline, sandy coastal conditions, also cultivated by The Garlic Farm across some ten acres but on a larger scale by renowned producer A E Brown Farms, based at the farming hamlet of Hale Common near Arreton. It is, however, quality more than quantity that is the hallmark of the Brown family's enterprise, their superior spears having graced the tables of more than one royal banquet, together with early- and late-season availability. In his quest for perfection, Ben Brown believes in leaving his crop exposed to the elements for a fuller flavour and lusher colour, and in picking and packing within 24 hours.

Following hot on the heels of the asparagus season is sweetcorn, again a crop in which the Island excels and Brown Farms specialize, harvested by hand from the last week of July until the beginning of October and celebrated at the annual Sweetcorn Fayre held at Arreton Barns (see page 159). And it is on the site of this working craft village that you will find Farmer Jack's Farm Shop, a partnership

between the Browns and another family with a long Island farming pedigree the Pierces, designed to showcase and sell their seasonal specials – including the latter's superb cherries and apricots and related products (see page 81) – as fresh from the field as they can be. The shop also offers the chance to survey and sample fresh produce from other local farmers and many locally produced food and drink items. With the onset of autumn, you can enjoy a stunning offering of pumpkins and winter squash, and from then on into the winter months, an exotic selection of brassicas such as purple and yellow cauliflower and white and red kale, all also grown by Ben Brown. Quarr Abbey also grows excellent asparagus and sweetcorn, along with various heirloom varieties of veg and fruit (see page 130).

Ben Brown's corn, tender and sweet enough to eat raw.

The Isle of Wight is now renowned the length and breadth of the country by the discerning shopper and chef alike for a more everyday crop, tomatoes, but elevated to a whole new level of ripeness, sweetness and flavour thanks to The Tomato Stall and their dedication to the finer details of cultivation, earning *Good Housekeeping*'s Food Hero crown in 2016. The same sun-soaked, fertile valley of Arreton that serves the Browns so well is home to Wight Salads' more than 60 acres of glasshouses. The Tomato Stall's Managing Director Paul Thomas and his team grow over

40 different varieties and trial up to 200 including speciality and heritage tomatoes in all shapes, sizes and colours, both organically and conventionally, and using a completely biodegradable system. They also process their premium crop to make tomato juices and passata, a pressed tomato and cucumber cordial, roasted and oak-smoked tomatoes, condiments and preserves.

One sure way of buying into the pick of the Island's crops is to check out Living Larder and their veg box scheme. Based at Apse Heath, widely respected and passionate producer Will Steward with his wife Aimee, another Island family with a rich horticultural background, grow a wonderful array of veg and fruit, heritage varieties as well as modern hybrids, outdoors in the traditional non-intensive way using organic practices as far as possible, and harvesting by hand at the optimum point of maturity and condition. Besides supplying the top Island dining establishments including Thompson's of Michelin-starred chef Robert Thompson fame in Newport and the farm shops such as in Bembridge, their freshly picked weekly seasonal selections can be delivered to your door across the Island (see the inviting example pictured on page 111) complete with a sheet of storing and cooking tips and recipes. And you can order a jar of raw unprocessed honey collected from their own bees by expert local beekeeper Dave Cassell at the same time.

Horringford Gardens, another family business in the horticultural hub of the Arreton Valley, also supplies veg boxes of fresh locally grown seasonal produce direct to members who sign up to its scheme across the Island, plus free-range eggs and owner Erica's distinguished range of homemade preserves and chutneys using her own home-grown and other local ingredients.

On the wholesale side of the fruit and veg scene, the longstanding family firm of Hunt's is committed to supporting local growers, producing a monthly newsletter detailing local produce currently available. And similarly, Medina Foodservice, another old family business, sources direct from local growers and producers as much as possible (they have been awarded Gold membership for supplying at least ten Wight Marque-approved products), and compile a seasonal crop report as a guide to availability. Delivering to businesses and markets both around the Island and in Hampshire and the New Forest, they are sole wholesale distributors of The Isle of Wight Ice Cream Company's range of luxury dairy ice creams and sorbets.

Artisanal Alcohol

Brewing in Britain and no doubt the Isle of Wight predated the Roman invasions, ale being a favourite tipple of the Celts, but in the past it was generally brewed on the premises where it was consumed from Roman villas to medieval ale houses. On the Island this was the case with the 11 breweries in Ryde and 40 in Ventnor alone in the 1850s, many linked to a single pub; there were something like 140 brewing enterprises overall at that time. Beer was drunk with every meal and supplemented by *swizzle* or *rot gut* (in the Wight dialect), the 'small beer' provided to farmworkers at *lebb'n o'clock* in the morning not to be confused with the stronger *nammet* beer taken with a snack mid-afternoon.

Gradually the small breweries closed or were absorbed by the dominant Mew Langtons of Newport, whose bonded warehouse survives today as the Quay Arts building by the harbour. Mew was the first UK brewer to introduce canned beers in the early 20th century, initially for IPA (India Pale Ale) exported for the British troops in India. By the 1930s only two other breweries survived, the Shanklin Brewery, founded in 1864 but going out of business in 1953, and Burts of Ventnor, founded in 1844 and benefitting, like the other Ventnor breweries, from the quality of the water purified by the chalk of St Boniface Down, but sadly also closing in 1992. Its name reappeared on bottles only to disappear again in 2009 with the closure of the Ventnor Brewery. Meanwhile, Mew Langtons had also succumbed, ending up as part of Whitbread in 1968 and subsequently closed down.

Fortunately today there are once more three breweries producing a total of nearly 30 craft beers, widely available in both cask and bottle from the Island's c. 170 pubs as well as supermarkets, farm shops and other retail outlets. Goddards of Ryde, founded in 1993, brews the famous Fuggle-Dee-Dum, along with specials like Mocha Stout using Island Roasted's coffee beans and locally grown barley and the festival favourite BestivAle, and also produces ales for third parties such as Quarr Abbey. In a partnership between its master brewer Xavier Baker and Conrad Gauntlett, owner of Rosemary Vineyard, the Island's first and only distillery has been established, producing Great Taste-awarded Mermaids Gin and Rock Sea Vodka, as well as Apple Pie Moonshine and a special-edition HMS Victory Navy Strength Gin, aged in barrels that incorporate pieces of oak from Nelson's flagship itself. Isle of Wight Distillery's first Island whisky, a single malt using Island barley, is steadily maturing in oak casks ready for release in two or three years' time.

Award-winning ales made by Yates' Brewery, founded in 2000 and based at Newchurch, are now widely distributed to Wadsworth pubs on the mainland, its Yule Be Sorry (7.6% ABV) being a notable seasonal hit. It also brews Black Garlic Beer for The Garlic Farm. The Island Brewery,

Adgestone Vineyard with the view down to Brading Roman Villa where Island wines may have begun.

founded at Shalfleet in 2010, won a bronze medal for its Yachtsman's Ale at the 2016 World Beer Awards, following on from its gold medal success for Wight Christmas in the flavoured beer category the year before. It also brews special ales such as The Islander, produced exclusively for the Island Yacht Club but available to the public at Cowes Week every August.

Apart from the Island's pure water and high-quality barley, hops continue to flourish in the wild and Ventnor Botanic Garden has revived the historic local tradition of hop-growing in establishing a productive hop yard, the crop being community harvested and celebrated at its annual Hop Festival in early autumn (you can visit the restored hop kilns at Briddlesford Lodge Farm, built in the latter part of the 19th century for providing beer for the whole Briddlesford estate). The handpicked and dried hops go to make VBG's Original Botanic Ale (and other Island ales such as Goddards' Wight Squirrel, as well as Mermaids Gin), brewed by Yates, whereas its green Sovereign hops are combined with other dried hops to create a limited-edition strong (weighing in at a hefty 7.5% ABV) pale ale brewed by Goddards. VBG also hand-makes, to order, a cordial concentrate from its own harvested eucalyptus leaves blended with sugar and citrus.

Other spirit-related Island initiatives include the Tipsy Wight range of flavoured vodka liqueurs and vodkas, made using the profusion of wild fruits and berries that grow on the family business's Medham Farm near Cowes by the River Medina, or infused with honey collected from their own hives. A short distance away at Michelin-awarded The Little Gloster Restaurant and Bar in Gurnard, they are busy creating various special libations including aquavit infusions using herbs from their own garden. Similarly, The Taverners Pub in Godshill makes its own seasonal tipples, such as vin d'orange, limoncello and muld wine, as well as its own ale.

Wight Wine
Although the Celts liked beer, the Belgae, who arrived on the Island from France in 85BC a century before the Roman settlement, naturally preferred wine but probably imported it rather than engaged in viticulture. The Romans, who were even more committed to wine drinking, certainly brought in vines and they would have come to the Island after its conquest by the future Emperor Vespasian in 43AD. The climate was benign at that time, and given its southern-facing well-drained chalky slopes just a few hundred yards from the great Roman villa at Brading, it is reasonable to suppose that the Romans grew grapes on the site of what is now Adgestone Vineyard. In the

so-called Dark Ages after the withdrawal of the Romans, winemaking probably died out, but was revived when King Alfred re-established the monasteries in southern England and given a further boost following the Norman invasion in 1066. Of the 42 vineyards recorded in the Domesday Book, none were in Hampshire or the Isle of Wight, though that evidence is not necessarily conclusive. Thereafter vineyards flourished or declined with climatic changes and the impact of outside events such as the English crown's control for some centuries of Aquitaine with its wonderful Bordeaux wines and the Loire Valley. Henry VIII's dissolution of the monasteries was a heavy blow to wine production, which gradually became more an aristocratic hobby, finally dying out by the end of the First World War. There followed a complete halt in commercial wine-growing until the 1950s when a gradual rebirth began, which makes Adgestone Vineyard with its remarkable system of six purpose-built subterranean cellars, established in 1968, one of the oldest vineyards in England, followed by Rosemary Vineyard near Ryde in 1986.

Aromatic Phoenix grapes, a new-generation hybrid variety.

Generally the conditions in the UK favour white wines and especially sparkling whites. Half the grape varieties grown in the UK are Chardonnay, Pinot Noir or Pinot Meunier, but the virtually frost-free, south-facing, well-drained locations of the Island's vineyards allow a wider range of varieties to be used, including Bacchus, Schönberger, Orion, Seyval Blanc and Rondo. Adgestone produces a popular blush (a pale pink white wine) and Rosemary a rosé, and in addition to still white wine, both vineyards produce sparkling whites (Rosemary a Rosé Brut, too) and passable reds, plus a variety of other country wines and cordials. Adgestone is probably unique in the UK for cultivating its own root ginger outdoors, a plant more at home on the Indian subcontinent, for ginger wine.

Orchard Enterprise

With its remarkable heritage of apple growing (see page 129), it is unsurprising that the Island is strong on cider-making and apple-pressing, although somewhat less so with the prospective retirement from the scene of Sharon Orchard near Ryde, although their range of quality ciders and single-variety pressed apple and other fruit juices (plus fruit-flavoured spirits and liqueurs) will happily still be available for some time to come. The Godshill Cider Company grows a carefully selected mix of cider apple varieties mainly in its Watergate Farm orchard near Newport, namely Yarlington Mill, Pig's Snout, Porter's Perfection, Somerset Redstreak, Sweet Cleave, Tan Harvey, Taunton Fair Maid, Town Farm No. 59, Tremlett's Bitter and White Alphington, which it supplements with a few additional varieties from local growers, including the legendary Kingston Black. Harvested over the course of the autumn according to when the different apples are ready to pick, they are then pressed, fermented and matured in the traditional way before being blended to create a range of ciders, from the heavy-duty Gait Crasher and traditional Draught Scrumpy to the dry Lazy Lob and medium sweet Passion Juice. The family-run business also sells a lightly carbonated pear cider, plus mead, traditional ginger beer and various fruit-flavoured country wines and liqueurs, available at their own shops in the villages of Godshill and Old Shanklin.

Rosemary Vineyard also produces cider, as well as apple juice, from their own Cox and Bramley apples including the sweet Rosemary Rambler, and Smallbrook Steamer, both in still and sparkling forms. Rosemary also processes the many fine apples from the orchards of Quarr Abbey to make the Abbey's own-brand pressed apple juice and still and sparkling dry ciders.

The Full Wight

We were only just into May, but that didn't stop us staging our breakfast-into-brunch outdoors. Which is the beauty of the Wight with its mild temperatures and enviable sunshine record, especially tucked out of the wind and down by the sea as we were fortunate to be at our peeling, creaking but beloved old beach hut overlooking Forelands Beach in Bembridge on the eastern extremity of the Island (i.e. the right-hand point of the diamond). And what better context than *al fresco* (*al mare* indeed) can you get for enjoying the first of the local new-season produce – luscious asparagus, succulent mushrooms, fragrant tomatoes, sweet new spuds, vibrant greens, tender rhubarb.

Whatever the season and personal taste, it's a remarkable fact that every breakfast item you can possible think of can be sourced here on the Island. If cereals are your preferred nosebag, porridge oats and muesli are produced by Calbourne Water Mill the traditional water-powered stoneground way. This naturally leads us on to items dairy where you can choose from fresh goats' milk or seriously creamy cows' milk, both unpasteurized and pasteurized, also made into premium yogurt and butter. Meat enthusiasts can feast on dry-cured and smoked bacon, black pudding, sausages and chipolatas from local free-range pork, plus an array of other handmade meat (and vegetarian) sausages, while fishy folk can savour Island-smoked kippers, pollack and haddock. Local bakeries and farm shops offer freshly baked breads for toasting and artisanal loaves and rolls for lathering with the many sweet preserves available, made using locally grown or gathered fruits and berries, or topping with the Island's pure gold – raw honey, whether clear, naturally crystallized, soft set, set or honeycomb. And back on the savoury side, those same fragrant fresh tomatoes go to make quality ketchup, or try tickling up your bangers with the Island Mustard Company's gourmet selection including Wight Wine, Ginger & Orange and Three Spice Hot.

In a positive twist on the old adage that you are never more than 20 feet from a rat, I swear that you are never more than half a mile from a freshly laid free-range egg on the Island – just look out for hand-painted signs advertising eggs for sale on the roadsides and you will soon see what I mean. In fact, you could compose yourself a box of eggs of varying hues from the speciality breeds of chicken along with ducks, geese and bantams that you are sure to discover.

And to drink? The Wight can even boast its own Carisbrooke Blend of tea produced by Betapak in Rookley with the local hard water in mind or that blended by neighbouring Southsea tea merchants All About Tea, or choose from a range of craft-roasted single-origin and espresso coffees from Island Roasted or Jasper's (see page 97). And for a cool beverage in every sense, The Tomato Stall's Sunshine Juice made from its vine-ripened golden tomatoes hits the spot, with or without a slug of the Isle of Wight Distillery's Rock Sea Vodka.

Seasonal scrambled eggs

These are not just scrambled eggs, these are fresh-as-a-spring-daisy eggs from happy hens, cooked until creamy and combined with either Island-cultivated exotic mushrooms including yellow, pink and grey oysters or asparagus, or locally caught crab or maybe prawns. Delysia Farm shop near St Helens sells freshly cooked large prawns caught deep in the Channel off Ventnor, while in late summer you could be lucky enough to sample a singularly local delicacy, the Bembridge prawn nabbed off the Bembridge Ledge, better described as a shrimp in size. These critters are gorgeously tasty, so keep an eye out at Captain Stan's or The Best Dressed Crab in Town for their fleeting guest appearance, or you may be able to get some frozen ones.

3–4 large locally produced free-range eggs
a little milk or soya or another plant-based milk
knob of butter or glug of olive oil
100g The Mushroom Farmer Gourmet Mix mushrooms or other
*   wild mushrooms, brushed clean, large ones torn into*
*   small pieces; OR locally grown asparagus spears,*
*   woody ends snapped off, well washed, blanched in*
*   lightly salted boiling water for 3 minutes, drained and*
*   cut into 4cm lengths; OR cooked peeled locally caught prawns;*
*   OR Island mixed brown and white crabmeat*
sea salt and freshly ground black pepper
2 wild garlic leaves, when available (see page 24), washed and
*   patted dry, then stacked, rolled and sliced, or a few*
*   chives, snipped, plus wild garlic flowers and/or scapes or extra*
*   chives, to garnish*
slices of Smoked Tomato Soda Bread, lightly toasted and spread
*   with butter or dairy-free spread, to serve (see right)*

Beat the eggs with the milk and some salt and pepper in a bowl. Heat the butter or oil in a non-stick or heavy-based frying pan. If using mushrooms, fry them for about 5 minutes over a medium heat, stirring, until they have released their liquid, then continue frying until the liquid evaporates but without browning them. If using asparagus, fry for about 5 minutes until just tender and lightly coloured. If using prawns, fry for 2 minutes over a medium heat just to heat through. Add the wild garlic, if using, and cook, stirring, for about 30 seconds or so until just wilted, or simply stir in the chives (if using crabmeat, this will be your next step after beating the egg mixture and heating the butter or oil).

Pour in the egg mixture, stir to mix with a wooden spoon and leave for about 10 seconds undisturbed. If using crabmeat, add it now, stir and leave to sit again for a few seconds. Repeat until the eggs are softly set but still runny in places, then turn off the heat, add more salt if needed and leave to stand until the eggs are firm enough to your liking.

Pile onto the toast, add a final grinding of pepper and serve, garnished with wild garlic flowers and/or scapes if available or extra chives.

{ *Instead of wild garlic or chives, look out for feathery, slightly aniseed-flavoured chervil, at its perkiest in May but still good onwards through the summer.* }

Smoked tomato soda bread

The idea of making your own bread can be compelling, like answering a primal call, but limitations of time and space can all too often intervene. Soda bread is the unbelievably quick and simple solution. I've replaced the traditional buttermilk with the Island's own yogurt produced by family-run business Calbourne Classics near Shalfleet, a luxuriously creamy product made with the premium fresh local milk. Experiment with other flavourings such as chopped fresh herbs, olives or The Garlic Farm's smoked garlic, or other spices like black onion (nigella) or cardamom seeds.

INGREDIENTS | MAKES I SMALL LOAF (SERVES 4)

1 tsp each fennel seeds and cumin seeds, or 2 tsp of either
175g Calbourne Water Mill Fine Wholemeal Flour or other
*   wholemeal strong bread flour (or use half wholemeal and half*
*   white strong bread flour), plus extra for dusting*
1 tbsp brown sugar, any kind
¾ tsp bicarbonate of soda
½ tsp sea salt
about 40g drained The Tomato Stall Oak Smoked Vine Ripened
*   Tomatoes, roughly chopped, oil reserved for oiling*
about 165–170g Calbourne Classics Whole Milk Yogurt

Preheat the oven to 200°C/Gas Mark 6. Brush a baking sheet with a little of the tomato oil. Toast the seeds in a dry frying pan over a medium-high heat for a few minutes until lightly browned and smelling toasty – fennel seeds need a fair bit of toasting so that they are easier to crush. Tip onto a cool plate and leave to cool slightly before crushing lightly using a pestle and mortar, or enclose in a resealable plastic bag and roll over with a glass bottle or rolling pin.

Mix all the dry ingredients together in a bowl, then stir in the tomatoes. Make a well in the middle, add the yogurt and quickly mix together with your hands to a soft, slightly sticky dough, adding a little extra yogurt if necessary. Form into a round on the oiled sheet, cut a deep cross in the top, then dust with flour. Bake for 25–30 minutes until risen and nicely browned. Transfer to a wire rack to cool.

Variations: For a gluten-free alternative, instead of the wholemeal flour use half gluten-free buckwheat flour and half potato starch, mixing in 1 tsp xanthan gum before using. For a dairy-free option, use about 160ml soya or another plant-based milk in place of the yogurt, adding ½ tsp freshly squeezed lemon juice.

Smoked pollack kedgeree with asparagus

If you go down to the woods today, instead of teddy bears picnicking you are much more likely to find wild garlic, traditionally called ransoms and sometimes in Island dialect 'gipsy onions', its oniony, garlicky aroma advertising its presence (a failsafe way of establishing its identity is to crush the leaves and give them a sniff). I say 'woods' but you'll find it along wooded waysides to avoid risk of trespassing, although choose carefully to avoid dog contamination and wash thoroughly before use. It's not only the leaves that can be used to permeate a dish with a subtle garlic flavour but also the flower stems with the unopened flower bud atop, known as scapes, plus the dainty heads of star-like flowers once they have opened. The wild garlic season happily coincides with that of asparagus, which traditionally runs from St George's Day, 23 April, to the summer solstice, around 20–22 June, though the Island's master asparagus grower Ben Brown has succeeded in exploiting our ideal growing conditions of sandy soil, salty air and sunshine to stretch the season so that it extends from mid-April to early July as well as to produce a superior-tasting and -textured crop.

These seasonal specials bring a boost of fresh flavour and colour to this fragrant brunch favourite, made with locally caught pollack available smoked from Phillips Seafood & Smokehouse in Cowes or J & B Fisheries in Freshwater, or ask John Day of Delysia Farm shop near St Helens to smoke some for you. Otherwise, use some decent smoked haddock, also available from the same sources.

INGREDIENTS | SERVES 2

250g locally smoked pollack or undyed haddock fillet
1 chicken stock cube or 1 tsp vegetable bouillon powder
30g sultanas or raisins
15g butter or 1 tbsp vegetable oil
1 small onion or 2 shallots, finely chopped
about 150g locally grown asparagus spears, when in season,
*   woody ends snapped off, well washed and cut into short lengths*
2–4 cardamom pods (depending on whether you're a big fan or
*   less so), roughly crushed*
½ cinnamon stick
1 green chilli, deseeded and cut into rings
1 bay leaf, preferably fresh, torn
2 tsp Madras curry powder
½ tsp ground turmeric
125g basmati rice, rinsed in cold water until the water runs clear
1 tbsp The Garlic Farm Peach and Mango Chutney, PINK'S
*   Commonwealth Mango Chutney or The Borneo Pantry Spicy*
*   Mango Chutney*
4 foraged wild garlic leaves, if available, stacked, rolled and sliced
2 large locally produced free-range eggs
squeeze of lemon juice, to taste, plus lemon wedges to garnish
sea salt and freshly ground black pepper
flat-leaf parsley or coriander leaves, to garnish

Put the fish into a shallow pan, cover with boiling water from the kettle and leave to poach, off the heat, for 10 minutes. Then drain off the water into a measuring jug – you will need 250ml, in which you need to dissolve the stock cube or bouillon powder and to which you need to add the dried fruit to plump up. Once cool enough to handle, remove the skin from the fish and wrap it in foil to keep warmish.

While the fish is poaching, heat the butter or oil in a heavy-based saucepan, add the onion or shallots and sauté over a gentle heat, stirring, for about 5 minutes until softened. Add the asparagus, if available, and cook for another few minutes until just softened. Gently stir in the cardamom, cinnamon, chilli and bay and cook for another couple of minutes. Then stir in the curry powder and turmeric and cook, stirring, for a minute or two.

Tip in the drained rice and stir gently for a minute, then stir in the stock and plumped dried fruit and the mango chutney. Bring to the boil and stir well, then line the lid of the pan with a clean tea towel so that it fits the pan super snugly, reduce the heat to low and cook for no more than 10 minutes, then turn off the heat and leave to stand, covered, for no less than 10 minutes. Then stir in the fish, gently breaking into large chunks, and wild garlic, if available, and re-cover until ready to serve.

While the rice is standing, place the eggs in a small saucepan of cold water, bring to the boil and then gently simmer for 6 minutes until soft boiled. Drain and briefly run under cold water to cool enough to peel, then halve.

To serve, season the kedgeree with lemon juice and salt and pepper to taste, then divide between 2 plates (fishing out the cinnamon and bay), add the egg halves and garnish with the lemon wedges and herb leaves.

Sausage, potato and nettle fry-up

If you're never more than a half mile or so from a freshly laid free-range egg on the Island, the similar yardstick could be applied to a handmade sausage, available not only from the good distribution of proper butchers' shops but from the many decent farm shops and farmers' markets, plus Southern Co-operative stores and other outlets stock Hamiltons Fine Foods' (which also has its own butchers' shops) traditionally made bangers. And you really will be spoilt for choice, ranging from both traditional pork sausage styles and exciting flavour combinations, through every other sort of meat including high-welfare veal, venison and chicken to gluten free and vegetarian.

To balance the nutritional scales here, I went for a favourite foraged green that's at its perkiest in the spring and something that you hardly need to hunt for given its rampant nature, namely the nettle, bristling with beneficial vitamins (C in particular) and minerals. But also, and less fortunately, bristling with stinging hairs, so don a pair of gloves to protect your hands while picking and prepping, plucking just the young, tender leaves from the plant tops (I confess I don't bother, as I actually find the tingling sensation invigorating; it is, after all, a traditional remedy for rheumatism). But be assured that once the nettles hit the heat, they will be rendered innocuous. If, however, this nettle lark doesn't appeal, use some in-season young spinach instead, or try another wild leafy green, sea spinach/beet – see page 40 for more on this.

INGREDIENTS | SERVES 2

1 tbsp Oil of Wight or Wild Island cold pressed rapeseed oil,
or olive oil
½ Spanish onion, thinly sliced
1 good-sized The Garlic Farm smoked garlic clove, finely chopped
300g new potatoes, preferably locally grown, well washed and
halved or thickly sliced, depending on their size
salt
3–4 locally produced butchers' meat, gluten-free or vegetarian
sausages of your choice
a few fleshy rosemary sprigs, chopped, plus extra (including
flowers if available) for garnishing (optional)
1 tsp sweet paprika
2 large handfuls of foraged fresh young nettle leaves, or spinach
leaves or sea spinach/beet (see page 40), well washed
sea salt and freshly ground black pepper

To serve (optional)
2 large locally produced free-range eggs
sunflower or vegetable oil, for frying

Heat the rapeseed or olive oil in a large, non-stick or heavy-based sauté or frying pan and fry the onion over a medium heat, stirring until the rings have separated and started to soften. Then stir in the garlic, cover with a lid smaller than the pan so that it fits closely over the onion and leave to sweat down over a gentle heat while you boil the spuds.

Cook the potatoes in a saucepan of salted boiling water for about 8 minutes until just tender, then drain and leave the steam to rise for a couple of minutes while you slit open the sausages and discard the skins.

Add the potatoes and rosemary to the onion and garlic, turn up the heat a bit and fry until the potatoes are starting to brown. Crumble in the sausage meat, keeping it in rough nuggets, add the paprika and a good grinding of pepper and fry until the sausage is well browned and cooked through. Stir in the nettles or spinach and cook for a few minutes until softened or wilted. Check the seasoning and add sea salt if the dish needs it.

If you fancy a fried egg to go with, while the pan-fry is cooking, fry your eggs in a little sunflower or vegetable oil in a separate non-stick frying pan to your liking, then serve the pan-fry topped with the eggs, garnished with extra rosemary if you like.

If you just can't make your mind up which
sausages to choose out of the many tempting
varieties, end the agony and opt for Hamiltons'
bumper multipack of gourmet sausages – a
lucky-dip mix of flavours from their handmade
range. For an autumn or winter treat, try Shanklin
master butcher Paul Murphy's game sausages.

Potato, purple sprouting broccoli and chive cakes

These potato cakes have a healthy twist, too, again with the addition of another seasonal veg sensation, purple sprouting broccoli, or spring greens if you prefer, both available freshly harvested on the Island. Chives are also at their most tender and vibrant-tasting and -looking in springtime. You can use all potato instead if you wish, but the parsnip gives the cakes a hint of sweetness and a slightly lighter texture.

Serve the potato cakes with one of the Wight's true wonders of fresh produce, The Tomato Stall's tomatoes, renowned throughout the foodie world as the sweetest in all the land, which you can buy by the variety, such as large beefsteak, Kumato or classic large vine for grilling or frying, or as a box of mixed speciality toms in different sizes and colours. And why not sauté up a few of the locally cultivated gourmet mushrooms (see page 22), or if you're a meat-lover, don't miss the opportunity to sample Brownrigg's dry-cured bacon from their free-range pigs, trotter deep in clover, or try Island Foods' or Hamiltons Fine Foods'/Hamiltons Butchers' house-cured or smoked options. Go for the full Wight works and top the cakes off with a soft poached or fried egg and release the yolk to run seductively down the sides.

INGREDIENTS | SERVES 2

*300g floury potatoes, preferably locally grown, peeled and cut
into small chunks*
*200g parsnips, preferably locally grown, peeled and cut into
small chunks*
salt
*100g locally grown purple sprouting broccoli, cut into small
sprigs, or spring greens, chopped*
knob of butter
a little milk
4 spring onions, finely chopped
a few chives, finely snipped, plus extra for garnishing
plain flour, for dusting
olive or sunflower oil, for shallow-frying
sea salt and freshly ground black pepper

Cook the roots in a large saucepan of lightly salted boiling
water for about 15 minutes until tender, adding the broccoli
or spring greens for the final 5 minutes. Drain thoroughly in
a colander and leave for the steam to rise. Return to the pan
and add the butter and milk. Season well with sea salt and
pepper and roughly mash, then stir in the spring onions and
chives. Leave until cool enough to handle.

Dust your hands with flour, then form the mixture into 4
cakes. At this stage, you can cover and refrigerate the cakes
until ready to fry, i.e. overnight for the next day – they will
helpfully firm up in the process. Remove from the fridge 30
minutes before frying. Otherwise, fry them straight away.

Pour some oil into a heavy-based or non-stick frying pan
so that it just covers the base and set over a medium heat.
Lightly dust the cakes with flour and fry for a good 10 minutes
until the underside is well browned and the cakes have heated
through, then carefully turn over and brown the other side.
Sprinkle with extra chives to garnish before serving.

Variations: For a dairy-free alternative, use Oil of Wight or
Wild Island cold pressed rapeseed oil or olive oil in place of
the butter and soya or other plant-based milk instead of cows'
milk. For a gluten-free option, use some buckwheat flour (see
overleaf) or other gluten-free flour for dusting.

LIFE'S A BEACH HUT

As we were pottering around fixing our fry-up down
at our rickety beach hut, named Ernie's Haven after
my dear old pater who narrowly missed the joys of a
sunny sojourn out on deck, such is the cruelty of fate,
I thought again of the profound insight I've had thanks
to living on the Island. Namely, that a beach hut isn't
just a beach hut. It's a state of mind, a way of casting
oneself adrift from all the minor worries that we
plague ourselves with, as well as the larger concerns
that we often can't resolve anyway, just for one or
two or hopefully a few hours. That's because the
whole point of a beach hut is its simplicity, offering the
bare necessities of shelter, a deckchair and a camping
stove, yet with the luxury of a front-row seat at a
never-ending screening of an ever-shifting seascape.
And although having access to a beach hut, however
humble, is an undoubted privilege, even without one,
hunkered down in a sunny spot in the lee of a cliff or
tucked in against the sea wall, anyone can attain the
state of Wight nirvana. So let's all sing, 'A-hutting we
will go, a-hutting we will go, ee-i-adio a-hutting we will
go' (to the tune of 'The Farmer's in His Den').

Rhubarb and orange muffins

Although we associate the arrival of rhubarb with the coming in of the warmer months, it's actually a handy locally grown choice for much of the year – the flamboyant-pink forced crop is available from end December to March, then the main crop takes over from April to September.

Buckwheat flour makes a particularly appropriate choice here, as it comes from a plant in the same family as rhubarb, and although traditionally used for making blinis and other such pancake-type items, its nutty flavour somehow suits breakfast-time, or probably more like elevenses if you're taking it leisurely. The added bonus is that it's naturally gluten free for those wishing or needing to avoid gluten, although make sure you choose a product that is guaranteed free of any traces of gluten.

INGREDIENTS | MAKES 10

280g (prepped weight) locally grown rhubarb, washed and
trimmed, cut into 2–2.5cm lengths
1½ tbsp Island clear honey
grated zest and juice of 1 organic (unwaxed) orange
200ml Calbourne Classics Whole Milk Yogurt
1 large locally produced free-range egg
50ml Oil of Wight or Wild Island cold pressed rapeseed oil (or
organic coconut oil, melted)
50g Calbourne Water Mill Porridge Oats or other traditional
porridge oats guaranteed gluten free if necessary, plus 2 tbsp
for the topping
200g buckwheat flour, guaranteed gluten free if necessary
100g light muscovado or soft light brown sugar, plus ½ tbsp for
the topping
1 tsp ground ginger
1½ tsp bicarbonate of soda
1½ tsp gluten-free baking powder
pinch of salt

Preheat the oven to 200°C/Gas Mark 6. Place the rhubarb in a shallow ovenproof dish or baking/roasting tray, drizzle with the honey and sprinkle with half the orange zest and all the juice. Roast for about 20 minutes until the rhubarb is just tender to the tip of a knife. Strain off the liquid into a small saucepan and bubble away until reduced and syrupy. Add to the rhubarb and leave to cool. You can do this stage in advance and keep, covered, in the fridge for up to 2–3 days.

Lower the oven temp to 190°C/Gas Mark 5, or preheat the oven if you roasted the rhubarb in advance. Line 10 cups of a muffin tin with paper muffin cases. Beat the yogurt, egg, oil and remaining orange zest together in a bowl, then gently stir in the rhubarb and its syrup. In a separate small bowl, mix together the 2 tbsp oats and ½ tbsp brown sugar for the topping and set aside.

Put the 50g oats into a bowl, then sift in the remaining dry ingredients and mix together. Make a well in the centre, pour in the wet ingredients and swiftly fold one into the other until only just combined – be careful not to overdo the mixing, otherwise you'll end up with leaden muffins.

Spoon the mixture evenly into the muffin cases, sprinkle with the oat topping and bake for about 20 minutes until risen, lightly browned and a skewer inserted into the centre of a muffin comes out clean. Leave to cool on a wire rack before serving. They will keep for 3–4 days in an airtight container, and actually improve in flavour the next day.

Variations: If gluten isn't an issue, try using half white plain flour and half wholemeal flour, such as Calbourne Water Mill Fine Wholemeal Flour. You can replace the yogurt with a dairy-free product – I made a batch with Alpro plain soya yogurt, which worked well.

Sun-up sippers

Wight virgin Mary

The Tomato Stall's Tomato and Cucumber Cordial brings a delicately fruity dimension to this cool, almost clear take on the classic Mary mocktail. To enhance its fresh appeal, I slid onto the rim a slice cut from a green tomato among a box of The Tomato Stall's mixed speciality tomatoes, then added some designer-looking scapes (unopened flower stems) from the clump of chives growing in my herb patch. You'll find this as refreshing as it looks, with a wake-up nudge provided by the perky salt mix.

INGREDIENTS | SERVES 1

2 tbsp The Tomato Stall Tomato and Cucumber Cordial
3 tbsp freshly squeezed lime juice
pinch of The Garlic Farm Sea Salt with Garlic & Black Pepper
1 fresh bay leaf, torn into small pieces
ice cubes
175ml chilled Wight Crystal Sparkling Spring Water
green tomato slice and chive scapes or chives, to garnish, if available

Shake the cordial, lime juice, salt mix and bay over ice in a cocktail shaker or stir together with ice in a mixing glass, then strain over some ice in a tall glass. Top up with the chilled sparkling water.

Garnish with a green tomato slice with a slit cut into it and carefully pushed onto the rim of the glass, and then add a few chive scapes or chives to the glass if you can lay your hands on some.

WIGHT CRYSTAL – DRINKING FOR A CAUSE

In buying Wight Crystal's Sparkling and Still Spring Water, bottled from a natural source in Knighton, you will not only be tapping into an authentic Island product but contributing to the company's laudable charitable endeavour of giving 24/7 support to those living with mental health issues and disabilities, inspiringly named the Way Forward. They also make various other soft drinks including Traditional Ginger Beer and Traditional Lemonade, which I've featured in other recipes in the book and are both helpfully sugar free. These products are available from Southern Co-operative stores Islandwide and Tesco Extra in Ryde among many other retail outlets.

Wight sunrise Mary

This Mary may look the innocent but she's about as wicked as she can get, especially for a breakfast/brunch cocktail – a hell of a way to start your day. Although I plumped for The Garlic Farm's truly felling Vampire Slayer, you can have fun sampling other killer chilli condiments at House of Chilli at Branstone near Apse Heath, including the Bloody Hell Hot Sauce appropriately packaged in a skull-shaped bottle. You have been warned!

INGREDIENTS | SERVES 1

ice cubes
3 tbsp Isle of Wight Distillery Rock Sea Vodka
½ x 200ml bottle The Tomato Stall Sunshine Juice
5 tbsp freshly squeezed orange juice
2 tbsp freshly squeezed lemon juice, plus extra for rimming the glass
1 tsp Wild Island Cherry Vinegar
1–2 dashes of The Garlic Farm Vampire Slayer Seriously Hot Sauce or other chilli sauce, to taste
2 dashes of Worcestershire Sauce
pinch of The Garlic Farm Sea Salt with Garlic & Black Pepper, plus extra for rimming the glass
2 tsp chilled reduced lobster stock (see page 93; optional)
1 locally grown asparagus spear, well washed, to garnish

First prepare the glass. Squeeze some lemon juice onto a saucer or small plate and grind the salt mix onto a second saucer or small plate to create a layer. Roll the rim of your chosen, large glass first in the juice and then in the salt mix to coat. Carefully add some ice to the glass.

Shake the remaining ingredients over ice in a cocktail shaker or stir together with ice in a mixing glass, then carefully strain into the prepped glass and add the asparagus spear.

Dinner for the Crew

I t took until the 19th century for sailing to take off as a recreational and competitive pastime, and the Isle of Wight was at the forefront from the outset. The Yacht Club was first set up in 1815 at a meeting in London, and then two years later, Lord Yarborough, whose memorial pillar stands atop Culver Down, introduced the Prince Regent as a member. When 'Prinny' ascended the throne in 1820, it became the Royal Yacht Club, staging its first races at Cowes in 1826, and subsequently renamed the Royal Yacht Squadron in 1833 under the patronage of the 'Sailor King' William IV when its permanent base was established on the Island.

Today the Island remains one of the most important sailing venues in the UK, having more than a dozen yacht or sailing clubs, in greatest concentration around Cowes, where Cowes Week continues to be the oldest annual regatta in the world with over 1,000 vessels competing in 50 classes. Additionally, Cowes is the starting point for the sometimes perilous biennial Fastnet Race and the spectacular annual Round the Island Race.

The second focus for sailing on the Island is in the east between Ryde, Seaview and Bembridge, with Bembridge Harbour alone boasting two clubs, the Bembridge Sailing Club, founded in 1886, and the Brading Haven Yacht Club, in 1950. The harbour has also long been notable for a very different boating feature – a row of houseboats, the first to moor being *The Ark* in 1902 (the decommissioned and renamed Bembridge lifeboat *Queen Victoria*), where it survived until 1989. This was joined by only a handful of other boats until after the Second World War, when a number of mainly old naval vessels and landing craft without even basic facilities tied up alongside. An exception was the *Xoron*, Motor Gunboat 320, which, after extensive active service, was converted into a well-appointed and still flourishing B&B.

Over the last couple of decades or so, the faded charms of the more ramshackle boats have quietly faded away altogether, and a gradual process of renewal and renovation has begun, culminating more recently in some cleverly designed conversions among the more than two dozen mostly shipshape moored craft. We were fortunate to be invited aboard one such example, The Harbour Houseboat *Sturdy*, as guest hosts of our dinner for 'the crew' (friends and family), where we took full advantage of its panoramic views across the harbour and beyond into the Solent to a fascinating flow of shipping, from cruise ships out of Southampton to cross-Channel ferries; naval vessels out of Pompey to fishing and pleasure boats. Used as a second home by its owners but also available to rent, it is hard to believe that the capacious accommodation inside is all mounted onto the humble hull of a 72-foot Thames lighter. We kicked off with the warm-up act up on the sundeck, then descended to the open-plan kitchen-cum-dining area where we all got stuck into the main event. But from time to time we found ourselves drawn out onto the main deck to gaze over the rippling incoming tide, birds flapping homewards over Brading Marshes backing the harbour as the dregs of sunlight drained away.

Seasonal spiced tempura

In an echo of the slogan for The Codfather chippie on Ryde Esplanade, feel free to batter anything you like here or what you can source on the day. As June progresses, watch out for The Garlic Farm's garlic scapes, i.e. the in-bud flowering stems that hardneck varieties of growing garlic (see page 39) throw up, which are snipped off to save the plants diverting their energies away from the bulb, and taste a bit like garlic-flavoured asparagus. To prep, trim the tough base and tips of the stems, wash well and pat dry, then cut into manageable lengths, dip in the batter and deep-fry as above. Around the same time, you may also spot courgette flowers attached to mini courgettes (from Living Larder, for instance), which can be given the same tempura treatment. To prep, use a small knife to gently remove the stamen inside each flower and trim the courgette end, then gently wash and pat dry.

Do look out for fresh turmeric (I bagged mine from The Farm Shop, Bembridge), as it has such an intriguing fragrant flavour, in addition to its many well-publicized health benefits including acting as an anti-inflammatory, improving kidney and digestive function and balancing blood sugar. A word of caution, though – the fresh stuff stains even more seriously than the dried, so protect your work surface with clingfilm or foil, although you obviously can't do the same with the grater. But rest easy – a squeeze of lemon juice should budge any neon-orange traces.

INGREDIENTS | SERVES 6 AS A STARTER OR SNACK WITH THE 2 DIPS OR A DOUBLE QUANTITY OF 1 DIP

600g skinless firm white fish fillets, such as pollack, whiting or cod; OR 2 bunches of fine asparagus spears (about 500g in total); OR similar quantity of baby leeks; OR a mixture
sunflower oil, for deep-frying
150g plain flour or a gluten-free plain flour mix such as Doves Farm
70g cornflour
¾ tsp baking powder or gluten-free baking powder
½ tsp salt
a finger of fresh turmeric, peeled and finely grated, if available (or used dried – see below)
about 240ml chilled Wight Crystal Sparkling Spring Water, with a couple of ice cubes

For the spice mix
½ tsp cumin seeds
½ tsp coriander seeds
seeds from 4 cardamom pods
small piece of cinnamon stick
½ tsp ground turmeric, if not using fresh

Depending on which ingredients you are using, cut the fish into strips about 2cm wide by 5cm long. Snap off any woody ends from the asparagus, wash thoroughly to remove any residual sandy soil and pat dry. Trim and well wash the baby leeks, then pat dry.

Toast the whole spices in a dry frying pan for a few minutes until fragrant. Finely grind using an electric spice or coffee grinder or a pestle and mortar, or enclose in a resealable plastic bag and finely crush with a glass bottle or rolling pin. Mix in the ground turmeric if not using the fresh stuff.

Pour oil into a large, deep saucepan to a depth of about 10cm and heat over a medium-high heat. Meanwhile, sift the dry ingredients into a bowl. Stir the fresh turmeric, if using, into the water and quickly beat enough of the liquid into the dry mixture to make a batter the consistency of single cream. Avoid overbeating, so don't worry about a few lumps. Test the oil temperature – a cube of bread should brown in about 40 seconds. Dip your ingredients, one by one, into the batter to coat, then drop into the oil, a few at a time, and fry for up to 5 minutes until crisp and a nice golden colour all over. Remove with a slotted spoon or tongs, drain on kitchen paper and serve hot with the dips or dip.

Fresh veg dip duo

Should your crew be famished after a day messing about on boats, these dips will help slake their hunger the healthy but not the worthy way, as they pack a hefty flavour punch. In early summer, fresh young peas and carrots are as sweet as they are colourful, to which I've added seasonal watercress and foraged dandelion leaves respectively to give a contrasting peppery bite. Serve with crudités or some good bread such as The Island Bakers', toasted if you like, or with the tempura.

INGREDIENTS | SERVES 6

150g locally grown carrots, new-season where available, scrubbed and roughly chopped
150g fresh podded peas, preferably locally grown (or use frozen)
salt
50g pine nuts
1½ tsp cumin seeds
1 The Garlic Farm fat green garlic clove (see page 38), roughly chopped
handful of mint sprigs, chopped
4 tbsp freshly squeezed lemon juice
5–6 tbsp Oil of Wight or Wild Island cold pressed rapeseed oil
12g Hampshire watercress, well washed and patted dry, then chopped
12g foraged young dandelion leaves (or use rocket), well washed and patted dry, then chopped
splash of Wild Island Bay & Juniper Balsamic Dressing and Dip or balsamic vinegar, to taste (optional)
sea salt and freshly ground black pepper

Blanch the carrots and peas separately in a saucepan of lightly salted boiling water for about 3–8 minutes or until just tender. Meanwhile, toast the pine nuts in a dry frying pan over a medium heat for a few minutes until lightly browned. Tip out and then toast the cumin seeds in the same pan for a few minutes until fragrant.

Drain the veg separately and refresh under cold running water. Tip the drained peas into a food processor (or use a Pyrex measuring jug and a stick blender) with half of the following: the toasted pine nuts and cumin, garlic, mint, lemon juice and oil. Add all the watercress, then blitz until fairly smooth and season to taste. Remove and repeat with the carrots, the remaining half quantity of ingredients, the dandelion and balsamic, if using.

Lamb cobbler with orange and garlic gremolata

Lamb and garlic is a classic, well-loved pairing but raised to a higher level using locally reared lamb fed on grassland continually exposed to salty sea breezes, which enhances both the taste and texture of the meat, and the newly harvested green garlic from The Garlic Farm.

This juicy young garlic is mild enough to use raw, as here in a gremolata to give the dish a finishing pop of bright, zingy flavour. As you're cooking for a whole crew, neck is a mercifully inexpensive cut of lamb, and don't be put off by its less than good looks because it will cook down with this long and slow treatment to a rich, melting result. The cobbler topping is an easy-to-make crew-pleaser, hearty but lighter on fat compared to a pastry lid.

INGREDIENTS | SERVES 6

*Oil of Wight or Wild Island cold pressed rapeseed oil or olive oil,
    for sautéeing and browning*
1 large onion, halved and thinly sliced
1½ tsp cumin seeds
1½ tsp coriander seeds
*6 medium locally grown carrots, scrubbed and cut into
    chunky rounds*
2 The Garlic Farm green garlic cloves, finely chopped
2 bay leaves, preferably fresh
several fleshy thyme sprigs
2 heaped tbsp plain flour
*1kg locally produced lamb neck fillet, trimmed of any major bits
    of fat and gristle and cut into 4cm chunks*
100ml red wine
550ml lamb stock
dash of Worcestershire sauce
180g locally grown podded broad beans
sea salt and freshly ground black pepper

For the herby cobbler topping
230g self-raising flour
40g butter, diced
handful of flat-leaf parsley, finely chopped
2 large locally produced free-range eggs, beaten
a little milk

For the orange and garlic gremolata
1 The Garlic Farm fat green garlic clove, peeled
*15g mixed flat-leaf parsley leaves and coriander leaves
    and stems*
grated zest of 1 organic (unwaxed) orange

Heat 1 tbsp of oil in a large, heavy-based saucepan and gently sauté the onion for a few minutes until softened. Meanwhile, toast the spice seeds in a dry frying pan for a few minutes until fragrant, then crush lightly using a pestle and mortar, or enclose in a resealable plastic bag and roll over with a glass bottle or rolling pin. Set aside about 1 tsp for the gremolata and add the rest to the sautéed onion along with the carrots. Cook for a few minutes until the carrots have slightly softened, stirring frequently. Stir in the chopped garlic, bay leaves and thyme and cook briefly, stirring. Tip everything out of the pan into a bowl.

Heat a drizzle of oil in the same pan over a medium-high heat. Season the flour well, then toss in the lamb to coat, add a batch to the pan and brown all over. Remove and repeat with the remaining lamb. Return all the lamb to the pan with the sautéed onion and carrot mixture, then add the wine and stock and bring to the boil, stirring to deglaze the pan. Add the Worcestershire sauce, cover and simmer gently for 1¼–1½ hours until the lamb is tender. Towards the end of the cooking time, preheat the oven to 200°C/Gas Mark 6. Blanch the broad beans in a saucepan of boiling water for 2 minutes, then drain, cool under cold running water and peel off the skins if you like (or peel a proportion until you get bored, as I did). Stir into the stew, then tip the whole lot into a large baking dish.

For the cobbler topping, combine the flour and a good grinding of sea salt in a bowl, then rub in the butter with your fingertips until you have a fine breadcrumb-like texture. Stir in the parsley. Mix in the eggs lightly along with enough milk to make a dropping consistency, then spoon large dollops of the mixture on top of the stew around the outside of the dish. Bake in the oven for about 25 minutes until well browned.

Prepare the gremolata while the cobbler is baking by roughly chopping the garlic and herbs, then finely chopping together, incorporating the orange zest and reserved crushed spices. Tip into a small serving bowl.

Serve the cobbler in the dish, scattering some of the gremolata onto the stew, with the rest served separately for folk to add to taste.

Variations: For a gluten-free alternative, use gluten-free plain and self-raising flour mixes such as Doves Farm instead and omit the Worcestershire sauce. For a dairy-free option, use dairy-free spread and soya or other plant-based milk for the cobbler topping.

{ *I served this with some lightly cooked spring greens and roasted sweet potatoes. For the latter, scrub and halve, then score the flesh diamond style. Arrange cut side up in a roasting tray, drizzle with oil and season well. Place on the top oven shelf after you have turned it on while you fiddle with the topping, then move below the cobbler once you have put that in to bake. They should be done by the time the cobbler is ready.* }

KNOW YOUR NECKS
All varieties of garlic can be divided into two basic types:

Hardnecks, which have a firm flowering stalk, as the term indicates, including Chesnok Wight, Lautrec Wight, Purple Moldovan, Red Czech, Red Donetsk and Red Duke Wight, and elephant garlic (see page 77)

Softnecks, which have a softer stem and usually no flowering stalk, including Albigensian Wight, Early and Extra Early Purple Wight, Iberian Wight, Picardy Wight, Provence Wight, Solent Wight and Tuscany Wight

New-season vegetable curry Goan style

This is a veritable veg fest, featuring the Island's superlative asparagus still cropping well into the summer, along with tender new potatoes – look out for the first early variety Lady Christi with its firm, creamy flesh or Living Larder's exclusive 'family secret' spuds available from late May through the summer – and sweet young carrots. And a dark green leafy veg goes in for the final flourish, spinach being the obvious choice, but why not sample a seaside special, sea spinach or sea beet, to be found growing along the foreshore in profusion (see the photo opposite to aid identification). Even the small young leaves, the ones you want, are relatively thick and glossy yet are surprisingly tender and truly delicious after just a few minutes' cooking. However, bear in mind that the plants are often ideally sited for our canine companions, famously legion on the Wight, so select and prepare with care, or safer still, buy a plant from The Coastal Gardener at Fakenham Farm near St Helens to give you a near-constant home supply.

The Kashmiri chillies are smoked after being dried, so they deliver a rich, mellow note with a medium heat (remove their seeds and innards if you want a milder result). Check out the House of Chilli at Branstone near Apse Heath for its range of whole dried chillies; Mulato have a similar level of heat to Kashmiri, while Guajillo are a bit hotter and New Mexico a tad milder.

INGREDIENTS | SERVES 6

500g locally grown new potatoes, scrubbed and thickly sliced
450g locally grown new-season carrots, scrubbed and thickly
   sliced on the diagonal
salt
1 tbsp organic coconut oil
1 bunch of spring onions, white and green parts separated,
   chopped
250g locally grown asparagus spears, well washed, trimmed and
   cut into short lengths
400ml vegetable stock
400ml can full-fat coconut milk (shake the can well
   before opening)
125g foraged small young sea spinach/beet leaves or ordinary
   spinach leaves, preferably locally grown, well washed
handful of coriander, stems and leaves separated, stems chopped
1–2 tbsp PINK'S Red Chilli Jelly or Erica's Homemade Chilli Jam,
   or about ½ tbsp palm or other dark brown sugar, to taste
sea salt and freshly ground black pepper

For the spice paste
1 tbsp coriander seeds
1½ tsp cumin seeds
1 tsp cloves
½ tsp black peppercorns
3 dried Kashmiri chillies
4 The Garlic Farm garlic cloves, crushed
5cm piece of fresh turmeric (or add 1 tsp dried turmeric to the
   dry spices), peeled and finely grated
5cm piece of fresh root ginger, peeled and finely grated
1 tbsp tamarind paste
1 tsp crushed sea salt

boiled or steamed basmati rice, to serve

Parboil the spuds and carrots together in a large saucepan
of lightly salted boiling water for about 5 minutes until slightly
softened, then drain (reserve the cooking water for making
stock if using bouillon powder).

Meanwhile, make the spice paste. Toast the whole spices
in a dry frying pan for a few minutes until fragrant. Finely grind
using an electric spice or coffee grinder or a pestle and mortar,
or enclose in a resealable plastic bag and finely crush with a
glass bottle or rolling pin. Mix with the remaining ingredients
to make a paste, adding a little water if necessary.

Heat the coconut oil in a large, heavy-based saucepan and
gently sauté the white spring onion parts for a few minutes
until softened but not coloured. Add all the other veg and
gently sauté for 5 minutes. Add the spice paste and cook,
stirring, for a couple of minutes or so. Stir in the stock and
coconut milk, season to taste with salt and pepper and bring
to the boil, then cover and simmer gently for about 20 minutes
until all the veg are just tender.

Stir in the spinach with the chopped coriander stems, add
the chilli jelly/jam or sugar to taste and cook for a few minutes
until the spinach has just wilted. Check for seasoning, then
serve scattered with the coriander leaves with basmati rice,
into which you can stir the chopped green spring onion parts.

{ *Once the asparagus season comes to a close,
you can use locally grown French beans or runner
beans instead through the rest of the summer,
with later-cropping varieties of firm potatoes such
as Maris Peer or Harlequin and bunched
rainbow carrots.* }

Chocolate, strawberry and gorse blossom flan

This is very definitely not health food but certainly a restorative treat, not least for the galley crew! It's also a way of celebrating the first of the summer strawbs – the early crop is usually from Hampshire but that still counts as local – with the crisp choc-chip biscuit case and classic vanilla- (and gorse, if you're up for it) flavoured crème pâtissière or pastry cream coming together to provide them with a platform they deserve. Admittedly, the gorse petals are a little painstaking to crystallize for the optional decoration, but the younger crew members could be roped into the activity for a spot of indoor entertainment as a respite from wrestling with the elements.

INGREDIENTS | SERVES 8

2 x 150g packs Isle of Wight Biscuit Company Chocolate
  Chip Cookies
grated zest of 1 organic (unwaxed) lime (reserve the lime for
  juicing for your cocktail – see overleaf)
100g butter, melted, plus extra for greasing
300ml locally produced whole milk
½ vanilla pod, split lengthways and seeds scraped out
handful of foraged gorse flowers, plucked from their green bases
  and shaken to remove any wildlife but not washed, plus petals
  for decorating (optional)
4 large locally produced free-range egg yolks (reserve 1 egg
  white for crystallizing the gorse petals, if using, or use a 4.5g
  sachet egg white powder)
55g golden caster sugar, plus extra (optional) for crystallizing the
  gorse petals
15g plain flour
20g cornflour
150ml locally produced whipping or double cream
400g locally grown strawberries, hulled and halved
2 tbsp Gorse Blossom Syrup (see overleaf) or 1 tbsp Island clear
  honey, for glazing

Put the biscuits into a resealable plastic bag and bash to
crumbs with a rolling pin or glass bottle, or pulse in a food
processor to crumbs. Tip into a bowl, add the lime zest and stir
in the melted butter. Tip into a greased 24cm loose-bottomed
flan tin and press firmly to line the base and sides of the tin in
an even layer. Chill in the fridge for a few hours or overnight
until firm.

Pour the milk into a saucepan and add the scraped-out vanilla
pod, reserving the seeds, and the gorse flowers, if using. Heat
slowly until just below boiling point, remove from the heat and
leave to infuse for a few minutes while you beat the egg yolks
and sugar together in a large bowl until thick and pale (use a
balloon whisk and elbow grease, or a hand-held electric whisk
if available). Then beat in the flours until well mixed.

Gradually strain the hot milk through a sieve onto the egg
mixture while whisking constantly. Return to the pan, add the
vanilla seeds and heat over a medium heat, stirring vigorously
with a wooden spoon, until thickened. The mixture will turn
alarmingly lumpy, but hold your nerve and simmer for a few
minutes until very thick and smooth, without overdoing the
heat. Leave to cool a little, then pour into a bowl and cover
the surface with clingfilm to prevent a skin forming. Once fully
cooled, chill in the fridge.

To crystallize the gorse petals, if you want to, beat the egg
white lightly with a fork, or reconstitute the egg white powder
according to the sachet instructions. Using a fine paintbrush,
paint the gorse petals, a few at a time, on both sides with

the egg white, then toss gently in a bowl of caster sugar until
well coated, carefully remove and lay on a sheet of baking
parchment. Leave to air-dry for a few hours or overnight.

Whizz the chilled crème pâtissière in a food processor or
blender, or with a stick blender or hand-held electric whisk,
until smooth. Whip the cream into soft peaks, then fold into
the pastry cream. Release the tin side from the biscuit case and
set on a serving platter. Spoon the pastry cream into the case
and arrange the strawberry halves on top. Boil up the gorse
syrup, or the honey with a little water, in a small saucepan until
thick and syrupy, then brush over the strawberries to glaze
and leave to set. Decorate with the crystallized gorse petals, if
you've made them, before serving.

Variations: For a dairy-free version, replace the chocolate
cookies with Isle of Wight Biscuit Company Walnut Cookies
or other dairy-free cookies; the 100g butter with 80g organic
coconut oil, melted, plus a little sunflower oil for greasing the
tin; the cows' milk with coconut milk; and the dairy cream
with a coconut- or soya milk-based whipping cream such as
Soyatoo, or simply omit as I did. For a gluten-free version, use
gluten-free cookies and replace the ordinary plain flour with a
gluten-free plain flour mix such as Doves Farm.

{ *For a quick-fix alternative, simply serve some
luscious strawberries with the Island's own
luxurious Dark Belgium Chocolate Chip
Shortbread handmade by CFO Foods, also
available in a gluten-free version, adding a drizzle
of the gorse syrup or Island honey, if you like. You
can gently warm the strawberries, drizzled with
the syrup or honey, in a baking dish in the oven
with the shortbread, quartered, on top so that the
chocolate starts to ooze.* }

Pitcher perfect

Gorse blossom syrup

Strongly associated with heathland, the dazzling yellow pea-like flowers of the gorse bush are also a familiar, cheery sight on dry, sandy soils in coastal areas and therefore widespread on the Island. It has long been a habit of mine to stand and admire those little bursts of sunshine before breathing in their delicate coconutty/almondy scent, especially on a warm day, but it's only recently that I realized you could preserve something of their unique properties for culinary use. And it gives you just one more reason for a stroll along an Island footpath (with over 500 miles of them to choose from), preferably in spring into early summer for the best blooms, being mindful just to pick a few flowers here and there, and wearing gloves to protect you from the prickles.

INGREDIENTS | MAKES ABOUT 300ML

3 handfuls of foraged gorse flowers, plucked from their green
  bases and shaken to remove any wildlife but not washed
grated zest of ½ organic (unwaxed) orange
juice of 1 lime
500ml water
200g golden caster sugar

Put the gorse flowers into a bowl with the orange zest and lime juice. Gently heat the water and sugar in a saucepan, stirring, until the sugar dissolves, bring to the boil and boil for 10 minutes. Pour over the flowers and citrus and stir well. Cover the bowl with a clean tea towel and leave to cool. Pour back into the pan, bring to the boil and simmer briskly for 10 minutes. Leave to cool.

Scald out a 330ml screw-top glass drinks bottle with boiling water from the kettle. Strain the syrup through a fine-mesh sieve lined with muslin (or improvise with a large clean cotton hanky) into a jug, then pour into the sterilized bottle and seal. Store in the fridge for up to a couple of months. If you want to keep it for longer, pour into ice-cube trays and freeze.

Solent breeze

A Wight take on the favourite summer pitcher, Sea Breeze, which comprises vodka and cranberry juice with a touch of grapefruit juice. Here I've gone for locally grown early summer rhubarb to make an alternative tart-tasting and colourful juice to cranberry, mixed with apple juice, its sweetness balanced with lime juice. The vodka produced from column-distilled grain comes from the Island's only distillery and is aptly supplemented with sea salt for a silky smooth finish and blended with locally sourced spring water. The sun being well over the yardarm, let's get mixing.

INGREDIENTS | MAKES 1.5 LITRES

350ml Isle of Wight Distillery Rock Sea Vodka
950ml chilled Rhubarb Juice (see below)
250ml locally produced pressed apple juice, such as
  Quarr Abbey or Rosemary Vineyard
juice of 3 limes, plus lime slices (optional) to garnish
ice cubes

For the rhubarb juice (makes just under 2 litres)
1kg trimmed locally grown rhubarb, cut into 2.5cm pieces
1.4 litres water
70g golden caster sugar

To make the rhubarb juice, put the rhubarb, water and sugar into a stainless-steel saucepan and heat gently, stirring, until the sugar has dissolved. Bring to the boil, then simmer for about 15 minutes. Cover and leave to cool.

Strain through a fine-mesh sieve (or use a muslin or a well-rinsed new J-cloth), then pour into a well-washed 2-litre plastic drinks bottles, or divide between two 1-litre bottles, and refrigerate. It will keep for up to a week. If wanting to store longer term (up to 6 months), decant into freezer bags and freeze.

To serve, stir all the cocktail ingredients together in a glass pitcher with ice, adding lime slices to garnish if you like, then pour into tall glasses over ice.

Heathland breeze

Use the rhubarb juice to make a sophisticated alcohol-free long drink to quench the crew's raging thirst after a battering on the high seas, or at least after tacking across Bembridge Harbour. The signature addition here, though, is the syrup made from foraged gorse flowers of heathland fame, which acts as a superior sweetener and colourant.

INGREDIENTS | MAKES 1.5 LITRES

950ml Rhubarb Juice (see above)
500ml Wight Crystal Traditional Ginger Beer
juice of 3 limes
3 tbsp Gorse Blossom Syrup (see above left)
ice cubes
foraged gorse flowers, plucked from their green bases and
  shaken to remove any wildlife but not washed, to garnish
  (optional)

Stir all the ingredients together in a glass pitcher with ice, then pour into tall glasses over ice and garnish with gorse flowers if you like.

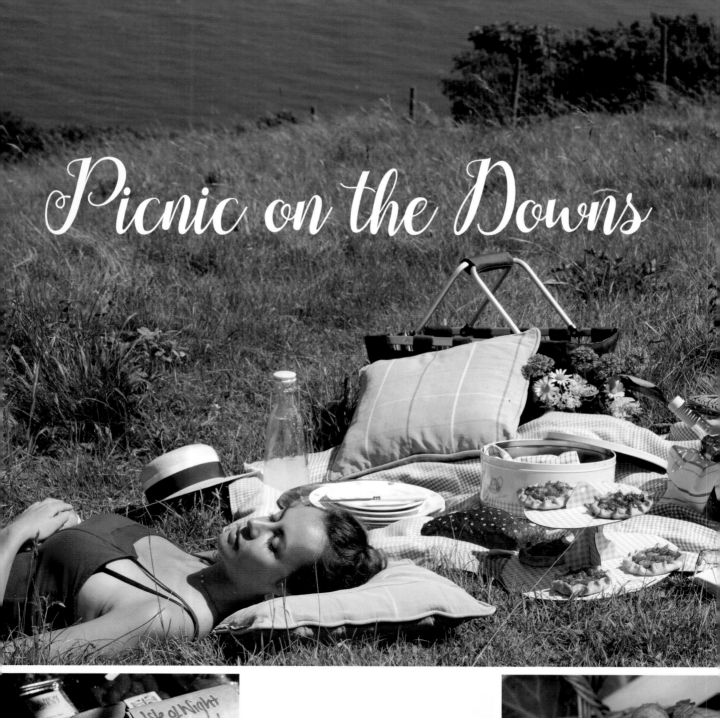

Picnic on the Downs

Extraordinarily complex and diverse geologically, comprised of a wide variety of sedimentary rocks laid down by the sea, the Isle of Wight's dominant feature today is the great chalk backbone that runs from The Needles and Tennyson Down in the west to Culver Down in the east, with southern outriders in the form of St Boniface Down and St Catherine's Down in the south, the two highest points.

This ridge is just one part of a much larger geological structure – the Southern England Chalk Formation, which runs from Dorset and Wiltshire in the west to Sussex and Kent, including Salisbury Plain and the North and South Downs. It was formed 145–66 million years ago by deposits of microscopic sea creatures as well as, famously, dinosaur remains and, less well known, prehistoric crocodile and turtle remains. The Needles, the signature geological feature of the Island, once joined up with Old Harry Rocks on the Isle of Purbeck in Dorset, and the chalk ridge in the east is replicated in the chalk cliffs of Normandy. The three Needles themselves are a fascinating example of tectonic change, the chalk having been forced up at a vertical 90 degrees to form stacks rather than needles as such, though the missing fourth needle was thinner and more column-like, but that meant it was washed away in a great storm in 1764.

These days the Wight's downlands constitute an amazing leisure resource. Almost totally accessible for walking on a network of public footpaths, the Island's spine accounts for the main part of the Walk the Wight charity event, the largest of its kind in Europe. The main walk is just shy of 27 miles, but there are variations to suit all ages and levels of fitness. Outside of that mega one-day event, the Downs offer all manner of uncrowded walking experiences as well as adventurous cycling routes.

On the other hand, for those wishing to abandon themselves to total peace, relaxation and reflection – and a damned good lunch – the Downs also offer many scenic picnic sites, some conveniently accessible by car. Mottistone Down in west Wight, for instance, has a car park at the top of the road leading up from Brighstone, while there are several parking spots on Culver Down to the east of Sandown from which you can enjoy stunning panoramic views out over the Channel, westwards and across the Solent, with both a charming roadside café and a welcoming pub nearby if you are in need of top-up sustenance.

For our picnic outing, however, we chose a walk on the wild Wight side and ventured up the precipitous St Boniface Down, which provides such a dramatic backdrop to Ventnor and where you are more likely to encounter the resident herd of wild goats than any other folk. And there we spent a gloriously sunny afternoon, lounging about in a wildflower-strewn upland meadow perched high above the expanse of glittery sea, with the chalk cliffs of Culver Down hazy in the distance, the scent of elderflower on the air.

Tomato and green garlic pesto tartlets

The Tomato Stall's tomatoes, grown in the rich, fertile soil of the Arreton Valley and left to ripen fully on the vine under all those Island rays to maximize their flavour, deserve to be the star of the show, wowing in looks just as much as in taste. So here they are playing solo, gently roasted with fragrant thyme and cupped in pastry spread with a punchy pesto made with The Garlic Farm's fresh young garlic, topped off with a slick of sticky sweet-sour glaze for good measure.

The pastry is made like a rough-puff but without the traditional higher fat content to give a lighter result. It also makes for a relatively robust pastry case so that it won't easily shatter or crumble en route to the picnic site.

INGREDIENTS | MAKES 8

glug of olive oil
1 tbsp thyme leaves
500g or 2 x 250g boxes The Tomato Stall mixed yellow and red
    baby plum tomatoes or other locally grown ripe baby toms,
    halved around their bellies
2 tbsp Wild Island Raspberry Vinegar or Cherry Vinegar
½ tbsp brown sugar, any kind
sea salt and freshly ground black pepper

For the pastry

220g plain flour, plus extra for dusting
½ tsp salt
115g unsalted butter, frozen for about 45 minutes, plus extra
    for greasing
about 5–6 tbsp ice-cold water

For the green garlic pesto

1 The Garlic Farm plump green garlic clove, crushed
handful of mixed basil and mint leaves, chopped, plus extra torn
    basil leaves to garnish
2 tbsp toasted and chopped blanched almonds (see page 65)
2 tbsp finely grated Isle of Wight Cheese Co. Gallybagger or
    Parmesan cheese (optional)
2 tbsp extra virgin olive oil
grated zest and juice of ½ organic (unwaxed) lemon, or latter
    to taste

First make the pastry. Sift the flour and salt into a bowl. Swiftly grate in the frozen butter using the large holes of a grater and stir in evenly with a table knife. Gradually mix in enough ice-cold water until the mixture starts to clump together, then gather into a ball, wrap in foil and chill in the fridge for 15 minutes.

Roll out the pastry on a well-floured work surface into a thick rectangle, portrait-wise. Fold the top third down over the middle third, and the bottom third up over the top. Turn the pastry a quarter turn, then press the open edges with the rolling pin to seal and across the pastry slab at regular intervals for a ribbed effect. Repeat the folding process 4 more times, dusting with flour to prevent sticking but without overdoing it and handling quickly and lightly. Re-wrap and chill while you prepare the filling or until you are ready to use it.

Heat the oil in a large, heavy-based frying pan and scatter with the thyme. Season the cut sides of the tomatoes with salt and pepper, then arrange cut side down in the pan in a single layer, cramming them in to fit. Cook over a low heat for about 15 minutes or until they soften and release their juices.

Meanwhile, for the pesto, put all the ingredients into a Pyrex measuring jug and blitz with a stick blender to a paste,

adding enough lemon juice to taste and salt and pepper, or pound together using a pestle and mortar.

Preheat the oven to 200°C/Gas Mark 6. Lightly grease a large baking sheet. Divide the pastry into 8 pieces and shape each into a ball. On a lightly floured work surface, flatten each ball, then roll out into a 10–12cm round. Place 4 rounds spaced slightly apart on the baking sheet. Spread the pastry rounds with half the pesto, leaving about a 3cm margin around the edge. Using a fish slice, carefully transfer half the tomatoes to the pastry rounds, arranging them cut side up and alternating in colour on the pesto areas. Gently lift up the pastry margin around the edge of each round and pinch at even intervals, then ease the pastry wall slightly inwards around the tomatoes to help avoid the pastry flopping backwards while baking.

Add the vinegar and sugar to the tomato juices in the pan and cook gently, stirring, until the sugar has dissolved, then cook over a medium-high heat until syrupy to make a glaze (add a little boiling water if it becomes too stiff). Drizzle half over the tomatoes.

Bake the tarts for about 10–12 minutes until the pastry is cooked and lightly browned around the edges. Remove from the oven and leave to cool on the sheet for a few minutes, then transfer to a wire rack to finish cooling. Repeat with the remaining ingredients. Once cooled, pack the tartlets between layers of baking parchment in a lidded container for transporting, and serve scattered with torn basil.

Variations: For a gluten-free version, replace the ordinary flour with a gluten-free plain flour mix such as Doves Farm, mixing in a scant ½ tsp xanthan gum, and keep the chilling of the pastry to a minimum before using. For a dairy-free alternative, use chilled dairy-free spread, finely diced, in place of the grated butter, and give the pastry a couple of extra foldings (you can also do this with the butter pastry if you have forgotten to freeze the butter first). Alternatively, use Twins Gluten Free ready-to-roll Gluten, Dairy and Soya Free Pastry.

Ham, chicken and tarragon plait pie

Picnic = pie as far as I'm concerned, and tradition would indicate a raised pie as in a pork pie. But I had in mind something more summery for our frolic on the Downs, and one that would provide a vehicle for more of the astonishingly good Island free-range pork in another guise – seven-day dry-cured and cooked ham, as produced by Brownrigg's at Sheepwash Farm near Godshill for their Isle of Wight Bacon Company enterprise (or buy one of their gammon joints for cooking up yourself). In this instance, I bagged my cooked ham from my outstanding local butcher, Woodford's in Bembridge, and fortunately more than I needed, as its deep flavour and crumbly texture drove me to scoff great chunks before it had the chance to be used as intended.

Tarragon is such a distinctive summer herb, its aniseedy notes working well with both ham and chicken (Brownrigg's are also free-range poultry specialists), its aromatic intensity counterbalancing the creamy sauce and (relatively) rich pastry.

INGREDIENTS | SERVES 6

*250g locally produced cooked ham, cut into generous
    bite-sized pieces*
*150g cooked boneless, skinless chicken, preferably locally
    produced, cut up to match the ham*
beaten egg, for glazing
sea salt and freshly ground black pepper

For the lemon and thyme pastry
250g plain flour, plus extra for dusting
½ tsp salt
grated zest of 1 organic (unwaxed) lemon
1 tbsp thyme leaves
80g lard, frozen for about 45 minutes
50g butter, frozen for about 45 minutes, plus extra for greasing
about 6–7 tbsp ice-cold water

For the tarragon white sauce
500ml locally produced semi-skimmed milk
4 tarragon sprigs
2 fresh bay leaves, torn
1 tsp mixed peppercorns
a few outer layers or other scraps of onion
30g unsalted butter
30g plain flour
*1 tsp The Island Mustard Company Thyme and Tarragon
    Mustard or other herby locally produced mustard*

First prepare the pastry. Sift the flour and salt into a bowl, then stir in the zest and thyme. Swiftly grate in the frozen lard and butter using the large holes of a grater and stir in evenly with a table knife. Gradually mix in enough ice-cold water until the mixture starts to clump together, then gather into a ball, wrap in foil and chill in the fridge for 15 minutes. Roll out the pastry as instructed for the tarts on the previous page, then re-wrap and chill while you prepare the filling or until you are ready to use it.

Make the sauce. Pour the milk into a saucepan and add 3 of the tarragon sprigs (keep the 4th one for later), roughly torn, the bay, peppercorns and onion scraps. Slowly bring to simmering point, then turn off the heat and leave to infuse for about 10 minutes before straining out the flavourings. Melt the butter in the cleaned saucepan, stir in the flour and cook over a medium heat, stirring constantly, for a minute. Remove the pan from the heat and gradually stir in the infused milk.

Heat, stirring constantly, until boiling, then simmer for a couple of minutes or so, stirring frequently, until thick, smooth and no trace of flour remains in the taste. Beat the mustard into the sauce, then season to taste with salt and pepper. Cover the surface with clingfilm to stop a skin forming and leave until fully cooled.

Preheat the oven to 200°C/Gas Mark 6. Lightly grease a large baking sheet. Roll out the pastry on a lightly floured work surface to about 29cm square, then lift it onto the baking sheet. Fold the ham and chicken into the cooled sauce with the leaves picked from the remaining tarragon sprig, finely chopped, and check/adjust the seasoning. Spoon the mixture down the centre of the pastry square into a roughly flattened log 9–10cm wide, leaving a 2.5cm margin of pastry top and bottom. Starting from the top corner of the filling on either long side, make 8 gently downward-sloping cuts, about 3cm apart, running from the filling to the outside edge of the pastry (it's reassuring to make a paper template first, which you can use as a guide to cutting, but you can just wing it by eye). Dampen the edges of the pastry and first fold the top and bottom margins in over either end of the filling, then fold the pastry strips, one at a time, alternating from one side to the other, over the filling, overlapping the ends to create a plaited effect. Brush with beaten egg to glaze.

Bake the plait for about 35 minutes or until the pastry is nicely browned and the filling is piping hot. Leave to cool for a few minutes on the baking sheet, then carefully transfer to a wire rack to finish cooling before wrapping in foil for transporting. It's best served at an ambient temperature on the day, cut into slices, but otherwise store in the fridge if making in advance.

Variation: For a gluten-free alternative, replace the ordinary flour for the pastry with a gluten-free plain flour mix such as Doves Farm, mixing in ½ tsp xanthan gum, and keep the chilling of the pastry to a minimum before using. Also use the gluten-free flour, or cornflour, for the sauce.

{
*You could serve the plait instead as a main course
for dinner, hot from the oven with some boiled
new potatoes tossed in a little melted butter and
snipped chives, along with lightly cooked local
tender runner beans and/or pearly florets of
summer cauli.*
}

Fregola summer salad

This is an update on the picnic staple of old, the pasta salad, using fregola – tiny nuggets of durum wheat that are also misleadingly called giant couscous, the latter being of Middle Eastern origin rather than Sardinian but otherwise very similar. If you avoid stirring them while cooking lest you release their starch, the mini pasta balls will remain pleasingly firm in texture and will separate once cooled. Some brands come ready-toasted *(tostata)*, which are especially nutty-tasting and al dente as a result.

Small, cute and sweet yellow courgettes will look the part here, and I couldn't resist running them through my spiralizer – a faddy item of kit maybe but nevertheless great for adding texture and drama. I had to settle for imported grapes on the day instead of the intended local goosegogs, sadly slightly late in ripening due to the unusually wet spring, but do grab some if you can for a tarter result, although the grapes worked well.

INGREDIENTS | SERVES 4

drizzle of olive oil
a few thyme sprigs, leaves picked
150g fregola (see recipe intro)
300ml hot vegetable stock
120g locally grown French beans
salt
handful of flat-leaf parsley or lovage, leaves picked and most
*   chopped, reserving the rest for garnish*
2 spring onions, thinly sliced
2 locally grown small yellow courgettes or 1 medium green
*   courgette, trimmed and thinly shaved with a vegetable*
*   peeler (or spiralized)*
100g Isle of Wight Cheese Co. Gallybagger, crumbled
100g red grapes, halved and deseeded if necessary, or ripe
*   gooseberries, sliced*
40g walnut halves, toasted (see page 57), cooled and then
*   broken into chunky pieces*
sea salt and freshly ground black pepper

For the caramelized elephant garlic slices (optional)
2 The Garlic Farm elephant garlic cloves (see page 77)
glug of olive oil
1 generous tsp Island clear honey
1 tsp dried oregano

For the dressing
6 tbsp extra virgin olive oil
2 tbsp Wild Island Raspberry Vinegar
squeeze of lemon juice, to taste
a little Island clear honey, if needed (if using tarter gooseberries)

Heat the olive oil with the thyme leaves in a saucepan over a medium heat, add the fregola and toast for a couple of minutes or so. Pour in the hot stock and stir once, then cover the pan and cook over a very low heat for about 12 minutes. Turn off the heat and leave to stand, covered, for a few minutes.

Meanwhile, top the beans, cut into thirds and cook in a saucepan of lightly salted boiling water for 4 minutes. Drain, then refresh under cold running water, drain well and pat dry.

For the caramelized elephant garlic, if you want to go for this, preheat the oven to 180°C/Gas Mark 4. Peel the cloves and slice thinly, about 1mm thick if you can. Lay the slices out between 2 pieces of kitchen paper and press down to blot the excess moisture. Whisk the oil, honey, oregano and a good grinding of salt and pepper together in a bowl. Add the garlic slices and toss to coat, then spread out on a baking sheet and place on a low shelf in the oven for about 15 minutes, flipping over halfway through, until well browned and caramelized but definitely not burnt, otherwise it will turn bitter, so check how it's doing after a few minutes and lower the heat if necessary. Leave to cool.

Put the dressing ingredients into a clean screw-top jar with some salt and pepper, screw on the lid and shake well. Drain off any remaining liquid from the fregola and tip into a bowl. Pour over a little of the dressing and some of the chopped herbs, gently fold through and leave to cool completely. Replace the dressing jar lid ready to transport, together with the herb leaves reserved for garnishing and the caramelized garlic slices if you've prepared them.

While the pasta is cooling, prepare the remaining ingredients, then toss gently with the fregola, seasoning with more salt if needed and plenty of pepper. Cover and keep cool until ready to serve, then add the remaining dressing, toss gently to coat and scatter with the caramelized garlic, if using, and the reserved herbs.

{ Feel free to use runner beans, trimmed and sliced diagonally, instead of green beans. If you can't find gooseberries for the locally grown option, look for early-season cherries. Later in the summer there should be some sweeter red or yellow gooseberries to bag, and try young raw kohlrabi, peeled and cut into matchsticks, in place of the courgettes. Use any other summer herbs, such as summer savory, marjoram or chervil. }

Potato salad with fresh peas and radish

This is another picnic perennial and for good reason, as it never fails to please. It's also something that can be dressed up for an occasion with some seasonal additions, as I've done here with minted fresh peas and peppery crisp radish – look out for locally grown bunched beauties including showstopping rainbow radish.

Freshly dug new potatoes are incomparable in flavour, so source the real deal from one of the Island's farm shops or order up a veg box from Living Larder for delivery direct to your door, securing your peas along with a selection of other freshly harvested goodies at the same time. Lovely waxy varieties to look out for include Maris Peer and the curvaceous Belle de Fontenay, as well as Living Larder's closely guarded 'family secret' spuds and, later in the summer, Harlequin, a cross between Charlotte and Pink Fir Apple.

You may want to make this a garlic-free zone, but the toasted garlic mayo from The Garlic Farm is ideally laid-back and mellow in flavour for this particular purpose.

INGREDIENTS | SERVES 4

500g locally grown waxy new potatoes, well washed and halved, or quartered if large
salt
2 mint sprigs, plus a small handful of leaves
about 90g podded locally grown peas (about 400g in the pod)
2 tbsp Wild Island or Oil of Wight cold pressed rapeseed oil or extra virgin olive oil
2 tsp Wild Island Raspberry Balsamic Dressing and Dip or balsamic vinegar
1 tsp The Island Mustard Company Wholegrain Mustard or other locally produced mild mustard
squeeze of lemon juice, to taste
4 spring onions, thinly sliced
a few chives, snipped, plus chive flowers to garnish if available
6 locally grown radishes, trimmed and thinly sliced
4 generous tbsp The Garlic Farm Toasted Garlic Mayonnaise
sea salt and freshly ground black pepper

Cook the potatoes in a saucepan of salted boiling water with the mint sprigs added for about 15 minutes until tender, adding the peas for the last 4 minutes.

Meanwhile, whisk together the oil, balsamic and mustard, adding the lemon juice and salt and pepper to taste.

Drain the spuds and peas, discarding the mint, tip into a serving bowl and leave to cool a little before adding the spring onions and half both of the mint leaves, roughly torn, and the snipped chives, drizzling over the dressing and tossing to mix. Leave to cool completely.

Add the radishes and most of the remaining herbs to the potatoes and toss to mix, then add the mayo and turn to coat lightly. Cover the bowl with clingfilm ready to transport (along with the rest of the herbs) and keep cool until ready to serve, scattered with the reserved herbs and chive flowers should you be able to source some.

{ *To make this into a main course salad, add some locally produced hot-smoked trout or mackerel fillets, skinned and flaked into large chunks. Places to source Island-smoked fish include the Island Fish Farm near Brighstone (trout), Phillips Seafood & Smokehouse in Cowes, J & B Fisheries in Freshwater and Delysia Farm near St Helens.* }

WILD ABOUT THE OIL OF WIGHT

Say 'Oil of Wight' and it sounds uncannily like 'Isle of Wight' in the Island's own regional accent without you even trying, so for an instant you can pretend you're a native, although to be entitled to the epithet 'Caulkhead' your family has to extend back at least three generations on the Island. Fortunately, anyone can enjoy this essence of the Wight countryside in sunny yellow bloom captured in a bottle, produced from a gentle cold pressing of locally grown rapeseed by Caroline Knox at her family farm in Merstone, a far cry from the heat- and chemical-processed industrial stuff. With its light, nutty taste and nutritional benefits of substantial omega-3 and -6 fatty acids and vitamin E content, yet half the saturated fat of olive oil, plus a high smoke point making it ideal for cooking at high temperatures, it's no wonder that the locally produced premium rapeseed oil has become such a sought-after product.

Wild Island has capitalized on Oil of Wight's qualities to create a range of handmade infused oils and flavoured dressings, along with other locally sourced ingredients such as honey, herbs and cider vinegar (from Godshill Cider Company), the latter also being used to make fruit vinegars like their award-winning Cherry Vinegar.

Carrot, apricot and elderflower loaf

Super-sweet new-season carrots are equally good in a cake context as they are in their traditional savoury role, as in this light, fragrant, summery version of the classic bake with not a whiff of cream cheese frosting in sight.

Elderflowers are one of the quintessential sights and scents of summer, together with roses of course (more on those anon), to be found in hedgerows or along roadsides practically everywhere, not just on the Island, and they have a relatively long flowering season, from mid-spring (round here at least) to high summer. And even if you don't go the whole hog in making the cordial, just a few of their lovely lacy heads will go a long way in flavouring and decorating a cake, as here, or in perfuming a glass of lemonade or other cooling drink, or a refreshing green tea infusion.

INGREDIENTS | MAKES I LARGE LOAF (SERVES 6–8)

50g soft pitted prunes and about 4 tbsp hot apple or orange juice (or enough to make a purée – see method);
OR 85g butter
100g walnut halves
2 fresh apricots, halved, stoned and chopped
125g scrubbed locally grown carrots, grated
2 elderflower heads, shaken free of any bugs but not washed and flowers roughly plucked, plus extra to decorate
100g soft light or muscovado sugar, if using prune purée, or 110g if using butter
2 large locally produced free-range eggs, beaten
225g plain flour
1 tbsp baking powder
¼ tsp bicarbonate of soda
¼ tsp salt
pinch of cream of tartar (if using dried fruit purée instead of butter or spread)
1 tsp ground cinnamon
2 tbsp elderflower cordial, preferably homemade (see page 59)
squeeze of lemon juice

Preheat the oven to 190°C/Gas Mark 5. Line a large loaf tin (about 21.5cm × 11cm, 6.5cm deep) with baking parchment. If using prunes, cut them up with kitchen scissors into a Pyrex measuring jug, pour over the hot juice and leave to soak for a few minutes, then blitz to a purée with a stick blender, adding a little extra water if necessary. If using butter, melt it in a small saucepan and leave to cool for a while before using.

Meanwhile, spread the walnuts out on a baking sheet and toast in the oven for 10 minutes. Leave to cool, then break into chunky pieces.

Put the apricots, grated carrots, prune purée or melted butter, elderflowers, sugar and eggs into a large bowl and beat together with a fork to combine. Sift the flour, baking powder, bicarb, salt, cream of tartar, if using, and cinnamon together into a separate bowl, then sift again into the cake mixture and fold in. Fold in the walnuts. Pour the mixture into the lined tin and smooth the top with a round-bladed knife. Bake for 45 minutes–1 hour or until a skewer inserted into the centre comes out clean. Check after 30 minutes or so for overbrowning and cover with a sheet of baking parchment.

Remove from the oven and leave to cool for a few minutes in the tin on a wire rack, then lift the loaf out of the tin onto the rack. Boil up the elderflower cordial and lemon juice in a small saucepan for a few minutes until syrupy, then brush over the top of the loaf and sprinkle with a few individual elderflowers. Leave to cool completely, then transfer to an airtight container for transporting.

Variations: For a gluten-free alternative, use a gluten-free plain flour mix such as Doves Farm in place of the ordinary plain flour and gluten-free baking powder. For a dairy-free version, either choose the prune purée option or use dairy-free spread instead of butter.

{ *Further on into the summer, from around mid-July, look out for the Island's own apricots to use (see page 81), and you should still be able to find a few good elderflowers well into the month, although they are in their prime earlier in the summer.* }

Berry balsamic
and citrus
semi-freddo

The idea here is for a fuss-free and fat-, dairy- and egg-free dessert assembled in individual jars for no-mess transporting and serving, where the sorbet inevitably melts en route into a *semi-freddo* state ready to be spooned from the jar with the marinated berries. Balsamic vinegar is known to enhance the flavour of strawberries, so I used one produced by Wild Island with the addition of raspberries for an extra fruity dimension. A dash of elderflower cordial contributes a floral perfumed note, with the basil providing a lively contrasting aromatic hit as well as an injection of fresh green colour.

INGREDIENTS | SERVES 4

300g locally grown strawberries
grated zest and juice of 1 organic (unwaxed) orange
1 tbsp elderflower cordial, preferably homemade (see right)
2 tsp Wild Island Raspberry Balsamic Dressing and Dip or
   balsamic vinegar, or to taste
550g tub of Minghella Sicilian Lemon Sorbet, well frozen
a few basil leaves, roughly torn

Hull the strawberries and then slice them into a bowl. Add the orange zest and juice, elderflower cordial and balsamic and toss to mix. Cover the bowl with clingfilm and chill in the fridge for an hour.

When ready to depart on your picnic, divide the sorbet between 4 well-washed screw-top jars (each about 300ml in capacity), spoon over the marinated strawberries and their juice and scatter over the basil. Seal the jars, pack into chilled wine cooler bags or wraps and keep in your cool bag until ready to serve in the jars.

{ *You can use a mixture of strawberries and raspberries if you like. And if you prefer, use Minghella Sicilian Lemon Ice Cream in place of the sorbet, or mint instead of the basil.* }

Homemade elderflower cordial

Foraging doesn't get any more rewarding than for elderflowers, as their heady, sweet scent is perfectly preserved, if not enhanced, when made into a cordial, producing a distinctive Muscat-tasting syrup. Having first ensured that you have correctly identified the elder tree or bush (see page 126 for a sourcing suggestion) – the elderflowers' unique perfume will guide you – the standard advice is to pick the blooms on a dry day first thing in the morning, but you can't really go wrong, although make sure you avoid ageing, browning blooms.

INGREDIENTS | MAKES ABOUT 1 LITRE

20 foraged elderflower heads
grated zest and juice of 2 organic (unwaxed) lemons and
   ½ organic (unwaxed) orange
1 tbsp Godshill Cider Company cider vinegar
750ml water
500g golden caster sugar

To make the cordial, shake the elderflower heads to remove any insects but don't wash them, then put them into a large bowl with the citrus zest and juice and vinegar. Gently heat the water with the sugar in a saucepan, stirring until the sugar has dissolved, then pour over the flowers in the bowl and stir well. Cover with a clean tea towel and leave overnight.

Strain the mixture through a sieve lined with muslin (or improvise with a large clean cotton hanky) into a saucepan and heat to simmering point. Leave to cool, then pour into a well-washed empty plastic drinks bottle and screw on the lid tightly. Store in the fridge, where it will keep for a couple of months or so. If you wish to keep it for longer, decant into ice-cube trays and freeze.

{ *There are so many uses for elderflower cordial beyond making drinks with it. I use a dash of it in place of boring old sugar for gently poaching summer fruits like apricots, redcurrants and/or blackcurrants and blackberries, and it's a classic flavouring for gooseberries, whether for a dessert as in a fool or to make a sauce for smoked fish, as I've done on page 89.* }

Elderflower, strawberry and rose cup

Make a toast with family and friends to many more sunny days to come with this cup of summer cheer. For preparing the rose petal syrup, you will need to source roses free from pesticide sprays and with a good strong scent. Look out for the deep pink-coloured *rosa rugosa*, which has naturalized along waysides and the foreshore in many places on the Island and has a wonderfully powerful perfume as well as colour, or use the more delicately fragranced and formed blooms of wild dog roses to be found in many a hedgerow. Alternatively, Bartletts Farm Flowers just outside Ryde near the Tesco Extra store will be happy to help you (they also grow borage if you want the flowers for adding to the Wight's No. 1 Elderflower and Fruit Cup opposite). I used Adgestone Vineyard's Sweet Elderflower Wine, but there are other locally produced ones you can try from Rosemary Vineyard and Godshill Cider Company.

INGREDIENTS | SERVES 1

100ml puréed locally grown strawberries (blitzed with a stick blender in a Pyrex measuring jug or simply mashed with a fork if very ripe)
100ml locally produced elderflower wine
1 tbsp Rose Petal Syrup (see below)

For the rose petal syrup (makes about 100ml)
handful of scented rose petals (see recipe intro), trimmed of their bitter white bases
150g golden caster sugar
about 5 tbsp water
good squeeze of lemon juice

To serve
a few ice cubes
a few scented rose petals and/or individual elderflowers

To make the syrup, whizz the rose petals and sugar together in a food processor, or pulse with a stick blender or mash together with a fork in a bowl, then cover and leave in a cool place overnight. Tip the mixture into a saucepan with the water and lemon juice and heat gently, stirring, until the sugar has dissolved, then bring to the boil and simmer for a few minutes until you have a clear syrup. Leave to cool.

Scald out a small screw-top glass drinks bottle. Strain the syrup through a fine-mesh sieve lined with muslin (or improvise with a large clean cotton hanky) into a jug, then pour into the bottle and seal. Store in the fridge for up to 2 months. If storing for longer, pour into an ice-cube tray and freeze.

Add all the drink ingredients to a well-washed screw-top jar (at least 250ml in capacity), screw on the lid and shake well. Pack in your cool bag ready to transport.

To serve, add the ice, petals and/or elderflowers and a straw.

Wight's no. 1 elderflower and fruit cup

I've drawn inspiration from the classic long summer cocktail Pimm's to create this non-alcoholic alternative based on that other summer drink favourite, elderflower cordial – so easy and so gratifying to make yourself. The traditional garnish for Pimm's includes the pretty bright blue, star-shaped flowers of the borage herb, which taste faintly of cucumber, and sometimes the young leaves as well. The most practical way of using them here is to add a flower to each compartment of an ice-cube tray before filling up with water and freezing, something you can do with other edible flowers (see the photo on page 24 where I used primrose ice cubes).

INGREDIENTS | SERVES 1

50ml elderflower cordial, preferably homemade (see page 59)
1 organic (unwaxed) orange slice
1 locally grown strawberry, hulled and halved
1 mint sprig (optional)

To serve
150ml Wight Crystal Traditional Lemonade
borage flowers frozen in a few ice cubes or flowers only, or a few plain ice cubes

Pour the elderflower cordial into a well-washed screw-top jar (at least 250ml in capacity), add the fruit, and mint if using, and screw on the lid. Pack in your cool bag ready to transport.

To serve, top up with the lemonade, add the ice cubes or borage flowers to the jar and drop in a straw.

Festival Nammet

THE GARLIC FARM

GARLIC MUSHROOMS

CHEESY GARLIC BREAD

BEEF CHILLI

Nammet, an old Island dialect word still in use, originally referred to a substantial mid-afternoon snack, usually *bren cheese* (bread and cheese) and a pint of strong *nammet* beer. In today's context, it applies to a packed lunch or meal on the go. So in summary, it means food and drink that is portable, sustaining and easy to prepare and consume – just the job if you are among the multitude of festival-goers attending the Island's many music events.

The most famous of these is the Isle of Wight Festival, an event with a history in two parts. The first festival was staged on August Bank Holiday 1968 on a field near Godshill with The Jefferson Airplane and Arthur Brown headlining, and also featuring The Move (of Roy Wood fame), Fairport Convention and Marc Bolan's Tyrannosaurus Rex, which drew just 10,000 people. The next year attendance mushroomed to c. 150,000, thanks in part to the organizers luring Bob Dylan to headline at Wootton rather than Woodstock, along with The Who, Moody Blues and Joe Cocker. That success was to be completely overshadowed in 1970 when an allegedly world record audience of up to 600,000 (four times the Island's resident population) assembled on Afton Down to hear a galaxy of 50 performers including Jimi Hendrix, Miles Davis, The Who, The Doors, Joni Mitchell, Joan Baez and Leonard Cohen. Although the event was an undoubted musical triumph, it was at times overwhelmed by the huge logistical challenges. It literally proved to be the festival to end all festivals on the Island, as the next year Parliament passed the Isle of Wight Act banning any gathering of more than 5,000 without a licence. It took until 2002 for the Festival to be re-established on the outskirts of Newport and has since seen attendance grow from 8,000 to just under its upper limit of 60,000. It has also continued to draw legends of the music scene, from The Rolling Stones, David Bowie, Bruce Springsteen and Paul Weller to Amy Winehouse, Coldplay, Kings of Leon, The Prodigy, Stereophonics, Pharrel Williams and, yet again, The Who.

Bestival, held at Robin Hill Country Park 2004–16, grew to rival the Festival in popularity with its 'boutique' feel, emphasis on indie bands, fancy-dress theme and The Feast Collective offering world street food highlights alongside the Best of British WI Tea Tent. Having since united Bestival with its little sister Camp Bestival at Lulworth Castle in Dorset, curator DJ Rob da Bank and his wife Josie plan to host an all-new smaller event on the Island, with Vectis Ventures staging the boutique-style Eklectica at Robin Hill from September 2017.

Other, niche music festivals have been launched in recent times, including Acoustic Isle, Ventnor Fringe, Newport Jazz Weekend, Wolverton Folk and Blues Fair, V-Dub Island, Rhythmtree Festival, Island Highland, Harp on Wight, Jack up the 80s and Classic Isle.

Whether you are preparing to head Island-wards for your festival of choice, or just fancy recreating the vibe watching or listening to the highlights back at base, knock up these nifty energy-boosters for stashing in your *nammet* bag and you are ready to rock.

Overnight brekkie
booster

This is a take on the traditional Bircher muesli, so named after its late-19th-century creator Swiss physician and nutritionist Maximilian Bircher-Benner, where a mix of raw oats, fruit and nuts is soaked overnight in apple juice or water, which plumps the dried fruit and turns the oats satisfyingly creamy and also easily digestible.

I've cranked up the nutritional tally still further here in the interests of fuelling the festival fun with the addition of chia seeds, a rich source of omega-3 fatty acids as well as B vitamins, plus a host of dietary minerals. They also contribute to the gratifyingly gungy texture, as they turn into a gel when mixed with liquid.

INGREDIENTS | SERVES 1

handful of raw hazelnuts or almonds in their skins
1 generous tbsp sunflower seeds
50g Calbourne Water Mill Porridge Oats or other traditional
  porridge oats, guaranteed gluten free if necessary
4 unsulphured dried apricots, cut into small pieces
1 tbsp goji berries or dried cranberries
1 tbsp chia seeds
¼ tsp ground mixed spice
about 150ml locally produced or other pressed apple juice or
  Wight Crystal Still Spring Water or other bottled water

Preheat the oven to 180°C/Gas Mark 4. Spread out the nuts on a baking sheet and lightly toast in the oven for about 10 minutes, then remove. If using hazelnuts, tip into a clean tea towel, wrap up and leave to steam for a minute or so, then rub with the cloth until most of the skins come off. Toast the sunflower seeds in the same way but for only about 7–8 minutes (be careful not to burn). Leave to cool.

Put the nuts and seeds into a small airtight container with the rest of the dry ingredients and mix well, then add the lid. Pack up with the rest of your festival kit.

Before (if?) you crash out for the night, stir in the juice or water, replace the lid and leave until ready to eat, adding a little more liquid if it's a bit too gungy. Otherwise, add the liquid an hour before eating.

In keeping with Bircher-Benner's original approach, you could chop up an apple and add to your brekkie booster before eating, although you needn't be slavish to the good doctor's prescription and include core, pips and all.

Miso pot noodle

Fast food doesn't come more healthy than this, featuring super-nourishing, high-energy Japanese miso – i.e. fermented soya beans and grains – with added seaweed and/or dried, fermented and smoked tuna, plus high-protein, nutrient-rich cashew nuts. That's all in addition to a fat-free carb, the rice noodles – energy-providing but without the ballast to slow you down. They are also gluten free, as is the Clearspring Miso Soup option, largely (the box says it may contain traces), which is also vegan.

INGREDIENTS | SERVES 1

handful of raw cashew nuts
bundle of dried rice vermicelli noodles (about 50g)
1 sachet of Clearspring Organic Miso Soup with Sea Vegetables
  (dried) or Yukata Yellow Miso Soup (paste), Awase Flavour
½ tsp Thai seven-spice or Chinese five-spice powder
sprinkling of dried coriander
The Garlic Farm Sea Salt with Garlic & Chilli, to taste

Preheat the oven to 180°C/Gas Mark 4. Spread out the cashew nuts on a baking sheet and lightly toast in the oven for about 10 minutes. Alternatively, toast in a dry frying pan over a medium heat for about 5 minutes, turning frequently, until lightly browned. Leave to cool and then roughly chop.

Put the bundle of rice noodles into a small airtight container – they will be easier to eat if you break them up a bit. If using dried instant miso soup, scatter the contents of the sachet into the pot together with the rest of the ingredients, then add the lid. If using the paste, pop the unopened sachet into the pot after adding all the other ingredients. Pack up with the rest of your festival kit and keep as dry and cool as is practical.

When ready to eat, boil up a kettle of water on a camping stove and pour over just enough to cover the noodles (a generous two-thirds of a mug should do it). Stir well and then leave to stand for about 3 minutes until the noodles have softened. Now get slurping.

Biltong pot couscous

INGREDIENTS | SERVES I

60g wholewheat couscous
heaped ½ tsp vegetable bouillon powder
¼ tsp toasted and coarsely ground cumin seeds (see page 41)
large pinch of smoked paprika
large pinch of piri piri seasoning
sprinkling of dried coriander
½ sachet of Greeff's Beef Biltong, preferable Oak Smoked or
    Sweet Chilli flavour
small handful of raisins
small handful of toasted flaked almonds

Put the couscous into a small airtight container. Sprinkle over the vegetable bouillon powder, then scatter over all the spices and dried coriander.

Chop the biltong into small pieces and scatter over the couscous with the raisins and flaked almonds, then add the lid. Pack up with the rest of your festival kit and keep dry and cool as much as is practical.

When ready to eat, boil up a kettle of water on a camping stove and pour over enough to cover the couscous by about 3mm. Stir well, replace the lid and then leave to stand for about 10 minutes until the couscous has absorbed all the water. Fluff up the grains with a fork and dive in.

Another near-instant, energizing hot pot, this time based on the high-protein, low-fat carb durum wheat in the form of couscous – the wholewheat variety for extra dietary fibre. But the star act here is the award-winning, air-cured British beef biltong produced on the Island by Nick Greeff with his (vegetarian!) wife Sarah, using a recipe passed down to him from his *oupa* (grandfather) as prepared on his family's cattle ranch in Zimbabwe. Besides being delicious and a heavy protein hitter, it makes ideal festival fodder, since biltong originally came about as a method of preserving meat without the benefit of refrigeration, so there is no worry about food safety here.

{ *Light and compact, a pack of Greeff's Beef Biltong, available in a range of flavours, makes the perfect high-protein snack to slip into your back(nammet)pack should you be Walking the Wight, cycling the Isle of Wight Randonnee or engaged in one of the Island's walking or cycling festivals, or tackling something a little less physically challenging.* }

Supercharged energy bars

I've maxed out here on nutritional highs to help power you through the proceedings. The ultra-crunchy, nutty-tasting seeds of the hemp plant (yes, the same species as cannabis, but a different strain and with only minute traces of the psychoactive component THC) deliver top-quality protein with the full complement of amino acids, a hefty dose of essential fatty acids including omega-3, -6 and gamma linolenic acid (GLA) and a rich source of vitamin E. Pumpkin seeds are also a good source of protein and a variety of beneficial minerals such as magnesium, zinc and iron and antioxidant phytonutrients, while walnuts are packed with omega-3s and a very good source of manganese and other minerals, plus they contain various antioxidant and anti-inflammatory compounds.

Prunes are rich in fibre, potassium and beta-carotene; dates also in potassium as well as iron and bags of antioxidants. And the cool-tasting (literally), mineral-rich, vegan cacao nibs contribute the mild yet long-lasting stimulant theobromine. The coconut flakes just taste great, although their high saturated fat content is arguably of the healthier sort.

INGREDIENTS | MAKES ABOUT 12

120g walnut halves
90g pumpkin seeds
70g whole (unhulled) hemp seeds
100g coconut flakes
140g soft pitted dried or semi-dried dates
90g soft pitted prunes
1 tsp ground allspice or ginger
1 tbsp Bear Preserves Lemon & Lime Marmalade or similar
2 tbsp raw cacao nibs

Preheat the oven to 180°C/Gas Mark 4. Line a shallow baking tin about 20cm square or equivalent rectangular tin (mine was 25cm × 16cm) with clingfilm, with enough overhanging the sides to fold over and cover the mixture later.

Spread out the nuts, seeds and coconut flakes, each in turn, on a large baking sheet and lightly toast in the oven – about 15 minutes each for the nuts and the 2 seeds (the pumpkin seeds will start popping, so don't be alarmed), and about 7–8 minutes for the coconut flakes, turning over halfway through and being careful not to burn. Remove and leave to cool.

Meanwhile, snip the fruit into small pieces with kitchen scissors into a bowl, then pour over just enough boiling water from the kettle to cover and leave to plump up for at least 20 minutes.

Tip the toasted ingredients into a food processor and pulse until coarsely chopped but not too finely. Add the plumped fruit with its soaking liquid, spice and marmalade and process until the mixture begins to clump together. Add the cacao nibs and process briefly to combine. Turn the mixture into the lined tin, spread out evenly and press down thoroughly. Cover the top with the overhanging clingfilm and press down again. Chill in the fridge for an hour or so until firm.

Unwrap the clingfilm and cut the block into bars, then lift the whole caboodle out of the tin by grasping the excess clingfilm. Pack the bars into an airtight food container and keep as dry and cool as is practical. They should keep for up to 5 days.

Best festival flapjacks

While I wouldn't claim these to be health food, they are likely to have greater nutritional value and be less fat- and sugar-laden than most of the flapjacks you can buy, and they are so easy to make. The flaxseeds provide extra protein, fibre and omega-3 fat in the form of alpha-linolenic acid (ALA), and are an excellent source of magnesium, manganese and thiamine, plus health-promoting antioxidant lignans. These beneficial properties are best absorbed when the flaxseeds are ground, so it's worth going to the extra trouble. Chock-full of polyunsaturated oil, sunflower seeds are also rich in vitamin E, pretty rich in vitamin B1 and copper and also good for various other minerals.

INGREDIENTS | MAKES ABOUT 12

40g flaxseeds
40g sunflower seeds
400g Calbourne Water Mill Millers Mix Muesli or other good-quality muesli
1 tsp ground cinnamon
100g PINK'S Chocolate Peanut Butter (or Nutella)
100g organic coconut oil
65g Island honey
grated zest of 1 organic (unwaxed) orange
1 large locally produced free-range egg white, lightly beaten

Preheat the oven to 160°C/Gas Mark 3. Line a shallow baking tin about 20cm square or equivalent rectangular baking tin (mine was 25cm x 16cm) with baking parchment.

Spread the flaxseeds out on a large baking sheet and lightly toast in the oven for about 7–8 minutes. Remove from the oven and tip the seeds onto a plate to cool, then repeat the toasting procedure with the sunflower seeds. Once the flaxseeds have cooled, grind coarsely using an electric spice or coffee grinder or a pestle and mortar, or enclose in a resealable plastic bag and crush with a glass bottle or rolling pin. Tip into a bowl with the sunflower seeds and add the muesli and cinnamon.

Gently heat all the remaining ingredients except the egg white in a large saucepan until the oil and peanut butter are molten, then stir together well to mix. Tip in the seed and muesli mixture and stir to mix, then add the beaten egg white (which helps to bind the mixture) and stir thoroughly. Tip into the lined tin, spread out evenly and pack down well.

Bake in the oven for about 30 minutes until nicely browned. Remove from the oven and mark into bars or squares, then leave to cool in the tin on a wire rack. Carefully lift the bars out, then pack them into in an airtight food container and keep as dry and cool as is practical. They should keep for a week or more.

Variation: For a vegan alternative, use a vegan peanut butter instead and stir 1 tbsp vegan cocoa powder or raw cacao powder into the peanut butter mixture once molten, then replace the egg white with 1 tbsp chia seeds, soaked in 3 tbsp water for 15 minutes or until a gel.

WIGHT SUMMER SUPPERS

The beers below are those available in bottles (but bear in mind that you can't take these into a festival, with the exception of White Gold – see below); more are available in cask.

Ale of Wight 4.0% ABV – a blonde ale with delicate citrus notes and fragrant hoppiness on the nose, and a long lemongrass, grapefruit, scented hop palate from the infusion of Cascade, First Gold and Challenger hops; available all year round (Goddards)

Blonde Ale 4.5% ABV – golden beer with a malty aroma; tastes hoppy and bitter, with smooth malt support and subtle lemon notes, and has a dry hoppy aftertaste (Yates)

Inspiration 5.2% ABV – pale, refreshing, zingy ale, with lots of hoppy aromas and flavours; available through the summer (Goddards)

Isle of Wight Lager 4.2% ABV – pale golden lager; crisp and light refreshing finish (Yates)

Undercliff Experience 4.1% ABV – an amber ale with a bittersweet, malt and hop taste, with a dry, lemon edge that dominates the bitter finish (Yates)

White Gold 4.0% ABV – a golden brown ale, with rounded malt and hops throughout, plus the characteristic afterbite of a true craft beer; also available in small cans, so ideal for taking to a festival (Island Brewery)

Wight Knight 4.5% ABV – a yellow-coloured, strong, refreshing traditional English ale full of body (Island Brewery)

Yachtsman's Ale 4.2% ABV – a chestnut-coloured ale with a rich, malty taste, counterbalanced by 'sufficient hops to rise to the nose and to refresh the throat of the most parched of sailors'; awarded the bronze medal in the World Beer Awards 2016 (Island Brewery)

Red rave juice

Goji berries, long valued in Traditional Chinese Medicine, have now been hailed by the West as a superfood. Among their many alleged attributes is the ability to increase vitality, energy levels and stamina, as well as to promote an upbeat frame of mind (it's known as the 'happy berry'). What is indisputable is that goji delivers a good dose of protein, fibre and vitamins A–C, plus bags of iron and beta-carotene. So combined with the omega-3-rich chia seeds (see page 65) and the fresh seasonal fruit and raw beet, you've got a nutritional powerhouse in a bottle.

While a juicer is the quickest and easiest way to make both this and the Wight Popeye, if you don't have access to one, no worries – just use a blender or food processor and a sieve, following the instructions given below, or use a Nutribullet if you have one, in which case there is no need for straining.

INGREDIENTS | SERVES 1

1 tbsp chia seeds
3 tbsp water
170g strawberries, preferably locally grown, hulled
1 smallish (about 100g) locally grown raw beetroot, peeled and quartered
1 tbsp goji berries
4 medium locally grown super-ripe red tomatoes
juice of ½ orange or about 75ml water, or more if you want to thin down, if using a blender or food processor

If you have the wherewithal, serve in a plastic goblet dressed up with a big fresh strawberry slit and slid onto the rim.

Soak the chia seeds in the water while you prep the other ingredients so that they form a gel. This will ensure that the seeds are incorporated into the mixture rather than getting caught up in the machinery.

If using a juicer, feed the ingredients through in the order listed, adding the chia seeds with the tomatoes.

If using a blender or food processor, halve the strawberries, coarsely grate the beetroot or chop into small pieces and chop the tomatoes. Add all the ingredients plus the juice or water to the jug/bowl/cup. Pulse in bursts until broken down, then blend until smooth. Pass through a fine-mesh sieve (unnecessary if you've used a Nutribullet) and discard the remaining seeds/pulp, adding a bit more liquid if you want to thin it down.

Decant into a well-washed plastic drinks bottle, screw on the cap and pack in a cool bag. Give the drink a good shake before swigging it back.

Wight Popeye

Spinach's reputation for building biceps as showcased by the US cartoon character Popeye was apparently founded on a misplaced decimal point in a 19th-century medical journal, thus mistakenly increasing its iron content tenfold. Nevertheless, it's still a very good source of iron and other essential minerals, plus protein, dietary fibre and vitamins including A, C and E. Its wild counterpart, sea spinach or sea beet, is similarly rich in minerals and vitamins, and regarded by many as superior in flavour (I'm with them!), so if you can get some of the Wight's best (see page 40 for foraging/sourcing details), do give it a try. And carrots are bursting with beneficial beta-carotene and vitamin A, celery is rich in a variety of phytonutrients and orange is an excellent source of vitamin C. But if this all sounds a bit too virtuous, have no fear, as its spiked with a serious slug of gin, although admittedly a superior gin in the form of the Island's own small-batch Wight Mermaids Gin.

INGREDIENTS | SERVES 1

2 oranges, peeled and white pith removed, then halved, or 2½ oranges, squeezed, if using a blender or food processor

100g foraged small young sea spinach/beet leaves (see recipe intro) or ordinary spinach leaves, preferably locally grown, well washed

100g locally grown carrots, scrubbed and halved

1 celery stick, trimmed and strings removed, then halved

2½–3 tbsp Isle of Wight Distillery Wight Mermaids Gin or other gin of choice

If using a juicer, first feed through one of the oranges, then some of the spinach, followed by half the carrots. Next add the rest of the spinach, alternating with the other orange, then the rest of the carrots, alternating with the celery.

If using a blender or food processor, shred the spinach leaves, grate the carrot and chop the celery. Add to the jug/bowl/cup with the orange juice and pulse in bursts until broken down, then whizz until smooth. Press through a fine-mesh sieve and discard the pulp (unnecessary if you've used a Nutribullet).

Pour the juice into a well-washed plastic drinks bottle, add the gin and screw on the cap, then shake well before packing into a cool bag. Give it another good shake just before drinking.

{ *To serve in style, pour into a plastic goblet and add an extra celery stick complete with its frilly leafy top to the drink as a swizzle stick.* }

A Victorian Tea Party

Although the Chinese have been infusing tea leaves for at least 7,000 years, and drinking tea caught on in England at the court of Charles II back in the 1660s, it took until 1840 for the tea party to come into its own, allegedly instigated by Anna, Duchess of Bedford. At that time breakfast was a blowout, but 'luncheon' was often a light affair and dinner moved to later in the evening following the advent of gas lighting. Consequently, the duchess began to get 'that sinking feeling' in the afternoon and was served bread and butter and tea in her boudoir at Woburn Abbey. Friends were invited to join her, and when she returned to her Mayfair townhouse, the tea party was elevated to the drawing room with ladies dressed in their tea gowns. The Duchess was a lady-in-waiting to Queen Victoria and so introduced the tea party to the Royal Court in the 1850s.

The meal itself developed to include delicate sandwiches — much refined from the hunks of bread and meat served to the Earl of Sandwich in the 1780s at the card table so that he could carry on gambling — as well as cakes and, later, savouries. Tea was the beverage of choice and only come the 1920s was the decorous event rounded off with cocktails.

Converse to their respective positions in society, the upper classes had their tea at around 4pm on what we would now call coffee tables or trolleys, i.e. 'low tea', while the lower and middle classes favoured 'high tea', a more substantial meal served at a dining table at 5–6pm.

We were no doubt following in the footsteps of residents from the 1880s when we served our afternoon tea in the gardens of Seaview House, living up to its name in its glorious outlook over the Solent and with cool, lush bowers provided by its exotic planting. Seaview was a mere hamlet in the 1840s with a few fishermen's cottages and the saltpans on the Salterns below the much older neighbouring village of Nettlestone, but thereafter adopted by discerning developers of the day. By the 1850s the centre of the village including the High Street and Circular Road had been completed, and in 1870 Lord Calthorpe built a mansion in Woodlands Vale, after which, between 1877 and 1881, a magnificent suspension pier was erected (destroyed in a great storm in 1951). Further mansions such as Seaview House were soon added to accommodate the increasing influx of summer visitors, with daily ferry services operating from the pier to Portsmouth, Bembridge and Ryde, and in 1893 Seaview's status as a fashionable resort was confirmed with the establishment of the sailing club.

Today, the lavish Victorian and Edwardian mansions of Seaview have mostly been divided into more manageable yet still spacious family homes and apartments, many of which are holiday rentals (as with our chosen location), so opportunities for staging your own elegant tea party in a sun-dappled garden running down to the sea are there for the booking.

Pinwheel and finger sandwiches

These summery savouries are dainty enough to be held with the requisite three fingers in accordance with high tea etiquette, pinkie and fourth fingers crooked, and ideally sized for our vintage guest Ted E Bear, who breezed by for a bite. Convention ends there, though; flouting it with the fillings, I've gone for a mashup of classic cucumber with peanut butter and jelly, as in chilli with lime and lemongrass not trad fruit; a dashing red and white duo of sweet Romano/Romero red pepper (look out for locally grown) and the Island's deliciously mild soft goats' cheese, tickled up with mellow roasted elephant garlic; and creamy avocado and local crabmeat flavoured with aromatic, feathery fennel or dill.

Two or all three of these will make enough sandwiches for 4–6 as part of a tea party.

INGREDIENTS

*medium slices of soft white and wholemeal bread from a tin/
   sandwich loaf, crusts trimmed; for pinwheels, roll over with a
   rolling pin until evenly flattened*
sea salt and freshly ground black pepper

For cucumber, peanut butter and chilli jelly sandwiches
½ cucumber, peeled and thinly sliced lengthways into strips
salt
PINK'S Smooth Peanut Butter, for spreading
PINK'S Green Chilli Jelly, for spreading
finely chopped coriander, for sprinkling

Put the cucumber strips in a colander, sprinkle lightly with salt and leave for about 20 minutes to drain. Pat dry with kitchen paper.

For pinwheels, lay a slice of the flattened bread on a sheet of clingfilm with one shorter side nearest to you. Spread generously with the peanut butter, then with a little of the chilli jelly. Top with the cucumber strips, cutting them to length if necessary, then sprinkle with the coriander. Roll up from the side nearest to you tightly, and use the clingfilm to wrap around and secure the roll, twisting it at either end to seal. Chill in the fridge for 30 minutes, then use a very sharp knife to slice across into dainty pinwheels.

For finger sandwiches, top an unflattened slice of wholemeal bread with the filling ingredients, cover with an unflattened slice of white bread matching in size and press firmly together, then cut across into cute fingers.

For goat's cheese and roasted red pepper sandwiches
*1 Romano/Romero red pepper, preferably locally grown, halved,
   cored and deseeded*
a few lemon thyme sprigs, plus extra, chopped, for sprinkling
olive oil, for drizzling
2 The Garlic Farm elephant garlic cloves, unpeeled (see panel)
80g pot The Green Barn Soft Goats' Cheese with Chives
squeeze of lemon juice, to taste

Preheat the oven to 200°C/Gas Mark 6. Place the pepper halves skin side up on a baking sheet lined with foil. Scatter with the thyme sprigs, drizzle with oil and season. Place the unpeeled elephant garlic cloves on a separate square of foil and drizzle with oil, then wrap up in the foil.

Place the baking sheet in the oven with the garlic parcel alongside on the shelf and roast the pepper for about 20 minutes until soft and the skin is blackened in places. Remove,

enclose the pepper in the foil (use an oven glove) and leave for a few minutes, then peel off the skin and cut the flesh lengthways into thin strips. Add any collected juices in the foil to the goats' cheese in a bowl. Leave the garlic in the oven for another 15 minutes or so until very soft, then remove and allow to cool enough before squeezing the flesh out of the skins into the cheese. Beat together, adding lemon juice to taste and adjusting the seasoning.

Spread the cheese mixture over the bread, top with the pepper slices and sprinkle with extra chopped lemon thyme. Roll up into pinwheels or make finger sandwiches as before.

For crabmeat and avocado sandwiches
1 small ripe avocado, halved and stoned
1 lemon, halved, for squeezing
100g Island mixed brown and white crabmeat
chopped fennel or dill sprigs, for sprinkling

Peel the avo, immediately squeezing over some of the juice from the lemon to prevent discolouration, then add to a bowl. Mash and then whip with a fork until smooth and creamy.

Add the crabmeat and season well, adding more lemon juice to taste. Use to make pinwheel or finger sandwiches as before, sprinkling with the fresh herb. Don't leave longer than 30 minutes to chill before cutting into pinwheels and serve ASAP, otherwise the filling will turn unappealingly muddy coloured.

Variation: Use gluten-free bread if you prefer or need to.

THE ELEPHANT IN THE GARDEN

Elephant garlic is something of a misnomer, since although it's certainly jumbo-sized (a single bulb can weigh up to 1kg), it isn't strictly speaking garlic at all but a member of the leek family. Then again, it tastes much more like mild garlic than leek. Look out for its oversized bulb in its green form complete with chunky stalk attached in June and later on in the year dried, also available as a few separate monster cloves in a net bag. If you prefer to use a whole bulb here, slice it in half around its middle and lay on a larger square of foil, then drizzle the cut sides with olive oil and season with salt, bundle up in the foil and roast for about 45 minutes–1 hour, depending on the bulb size, or until the flesh is very soft. The extra roasted garlic can be spread onto hot, lightly toasted bread or stirred into soups, stews or sauces as a flavouring.

Rose and lavender queen cakes

Flowers were something of an obsession in the Victorian age, when a whole language was devised around them and posies or tussie-mussies were composed to convey discreet declarations of affection or adoration, regret or disappointment. Lavender was a particular favourite of Queen Victoria's, her passion for its fresh scent throughout the royal households leading to a rash of commercial lavender products, such as soaps, perfumes, pomades and waxes. The Victorians were also dead keen on using edible flowers and fragrant herbs both to flavour and ornament dishes.

Here I've echoed the classic planting partnership of roses and lavender in these dainty cakes for a celebration of sensuous summer scents, made using a light whisked Genoise sponge-type batter rather than the usual creamed mixture. I have previously given suggestions on sourcing scented roses and you will also be able to get cut lavender from Bartletts Farm Flowers (see page 60). But if you're as crazy for it as the Victorians, get along to Isle of Wight Lavender near Newport for the total lavender immersion experience.

INGREDIENTS | MAKES 8

handful of scented rose petals (see page 60), trimmed of their
bitter white bases, then roughly torn
75g golden caster sugar
75g unsalted butter
2 medium locally produced free-range eggs, at room
temperature
100g plain flour
½ tsp bicarbonate of soda

For the icing
3 tbsp locally produced milk
4–5 fresh lavender flowers (see recipe intro), plus a couple of
scented rose petals trimmed of their bitter white bases
100g icing sugar

For the decoration (optional)
8 fresh lavender flowers or a few rose petals for each cake
1 large locally produced free-range egg white, lightly beaten, or
4.5g sachet egg white powder, reconstituted according to
the sachet instructions
a bowl of white caster sugar

For the icing, put the milk in a bowl and add the lavender flowers and rose petals (the latter should take away any grey tinge to the icing from the lavender). Cover with clingfilm and leave to infuse in the fridge for a few hours or overnight.

For the cake mixture, at the same time, add the rose petals to the golden caster sugar in a bowl and muddle together with the end of a rolling pin. Cover with clingfilm and leave to infuse at cool room temperature.

Meanwhile, for the decoration, if you are up for it, use a fine paintbrush to paint the flowers and petals lightly all over with the egg white, a few at a time, then toss gently in the bowl of white caster sugar until well coated. Carefully remove, lay on a sheet of baking parchment and leave to air-dry for a few hours or overnight.

Preheat the oven to 220°C/Gas Mark 7. Line 8 cups of a muffin tray with paper cases. Melt the butter gently, then leave to cool. Work the rose petal sugar through a sieve to remove the bits of petal. Warm your mixing bowl, break in the eggs and add the rose-flavoured sugar. Beat with an electric whisk until thick, pale and doubled in volume. (You can use a stand mixer fitted with the whisk attachment instead.)

Sift the flour and bicarb together, then sift into the whisked mixture and fold through very gently in a figure-of-eight motion using a large metal spoon. Drizzle the cooled melted butter in around the edge of the bowl and gently fold in. Divide the mixture between your paper cases (they should be no more than about two-thirds full), then tap once on the work surface to release any large air bubbles. Bake for about 10 minutes until well risen and lightly browned. Leave to cool on a wire rack.

Strain the icing milk. Sift the icing sugar into a bowl, then slowly beat in 1 tbsp of the milk with a balloon whisk until smooth. Add a bit more of the milk until you have a runny but still thick icing. Spoon over the tops of the cupcakes, decorate with the crystallized lavender or rose petals, if you've made them, and leave to set.

Variations: For a gluten-free alternative, replace the plain flour with 50g gluten-free plain flour mix such as Doves Farm and 6 × 8g sachets arrowroot combined. For a dairy-free alternative, use dairy-free spread instead of butter for the cake mixture and coconut milk in place of cows' milk for the icing.

Instead of preparing the crystallized flowers, you can simply use the extra lavender flowers or rose petals as they come to decorate the cakes before leaving the icing to set.

Cherry and almond scones

Cakes are never going to be health food, but I have long been looking for ways to enjoy a sweet bake without taking the attendant hit of refined sugars, 'bad' fats and countless calories, and to create a vehicle for fresh seasonal fruit flavours. Enter the afternoon tea standard the scone, which, with the customary lathering of jam and cream being ditched in favour of naturally sweet ripe summer fruit, ticks all my boxes.

Cherries have a natural affinity with almonds – they are, after all, from the same plant genus, *Prunus* – so here I've used ground almonds in place of the usual butter, which you simply mix in rather than having to rub in, and complementary-tasting coconut milk instead of cows', making it a useful dairy-free option for those needing or wanting to avoid it.

INGREDIENTS | MAKES 12

sunflower oil, for oiling
115ml coconut milk, light or full fat
2 tsp freshly squeezed lemon juice
2 large locally produced free-range eggs, beaten, about 1²/₃
*   for mixing, the rest for glazing*
a few drops of almond extract
340g self-raising flour
1½ tsp baking powder
¾ tsp cream of tartar
pinch of salt
50g ground almonds
40g golden caster sugar
200g cherries, preferably locally grown (see panel), stalks and
*   stones removed, roughly chopped*
flaked almonds, for sprinkling

Preheat the oven to 200°C/Gas Mark 6. Lightly oil a baking sheet. Measure the coconut milk into a measuring jug. Add the lemon juice and then the 1²/₃ of the beaten eggs and almond extract and beat together well.

Sift the flour, baking powder, cream of tartar and salt into a large bowl, then stir in the rest of the ingredients except the flaked almonds. Make a well in the centre and gradually pour in the liquid mixture while mixing in lightly and swiftly with a fork, then gently draw the mixture together with your hands, adding just enough to make a soft but not too sticky dough.

Remove the dough from the bowl and gently pat into a round about 2–2.5cm thick. Working quickly and with a light touch, use a 6cm round fluted cutter to cut out the scones, gathering together the trimmings until you've used up all the dough – it should make 12. Lay on the baking sheet, brush the tops with the remaining beaten egg and sprinkle with flaked almonds. Bake for about 12–15 minutes until golden brown. Transfer the scones to a wire rack to cool. These are best served freshly baked but will keep in an airtight container in a cool place for a day or so.

Variations: For a gluten-free version, use a gluten-free self-raising flour mix such as Doves Farm and a gluten-free baking powder. You may need to add a little more of the liquid mixture when mixing the dough, as it tends to be on the dry side. These really won't keep, so eat on the day of baking.

{ *To create a tea-table centrepiece, arrange 9 of the cut-out rounds on the baking sheet to form a ring and bake as above. Once cool, carefully transfer the ring to a pretty plate and fill the centre with more fresh cherries. For a special treat, serve with a pot of Briddlesford's clotted cream.* }

GODSHILL ORCHARDS – A FRUITFUL ENTERPRISE

Among the many superlative crops that the Island produces are cherries, grown by Godshill Orchards formed from a partnership between two Wight families, the Medways and the Pierces (the latter of Farmer Jack's Farm Shop fame). This luscious summer fruit is as rewarding to the eye as it is to the taste buds, as delicious lightly cooked to release its sweet juices as it is simply popped into the mouth. So come the cherry season, I still can never resist dangling a joined pair of glossy orbs over my ears to make 'earrings' as I did as a girl after my dad had yet again braved the towering wooden ladder required to reach the fruit atop our old giant of a tree.

Picking cherries has since become a whole lot easier thanks to the introduction of dwarfing Gisela root stock, and that, together with the establishment of newer, larger and fleshier varieties and improved cultivation systems, has revitalized commercial cherry growing in recent times. The Island's kind climate is once again the icing on the cake, and in the judicious mixing of 12 varieties among their c. 5,000 trees, Godshill Orchards aims to maximize the season, from the heavy cropping dark red Merchant, through mid-season red/yellow Merton Glory and deep red/black Sasha, to the mid- to late-season very sweet Sunburst and the late-ripening, firm, dark red and superb-tasting Hertford, and finally the very large, true black Colney. Picked in the cool of the evening and stored overnight in a cold room, they're on sale the next day ready to be enjoyed within 24 hours of harvesting.

But Godshill Orchards' bounty doesn't end there – in addition to growing plums and greengages, they are also now the largest producer of apricots in the UK, helped by the fact that the precious blossom, which appears particularly early in the year in March, is more likely to remain safe from frost tucked up on the Island than anywhere else in the country. Six different varieties are grown over 22 acres, with the pink-blushed fruits being harvested from around the middle of July until the end of August. Used as we are to buying apricots imported from southern Europe, these locally grown fruits are gloriously sweet and intensely flavoured, so they are definitely not to be missed.

Victoria sandwich with blackcurrant filling

By all accounts, Queen Victoria was a committed cake lover, her sweet preference first enscribed in the recipe for 'Victoria Sandwiches' in *Mrs Beeton's Book of Household Management* of 1861, which has endured to this day as the quintessential teatime confection. The traditional method was to match the total weight of four eggs in their shells with that of butter, sugar and flour, then beat the mixture, by hand of course, for an agonizing ten minutes to achieve the necessary degree of aeration in the absence of any raising agent, despite a modern form of baking powder having been discovered and manufactured back in 1843.

I have taken serious liberties with that approach here and used a fatless whisked sponge instead, the fat quota being reserved for the cream filling; the original was simply spread with a fruit preserve. I used Briddlesford's Guernsey double cream and it was a revelation, its consistency and taste a world away from the insipid supermarket stuff, its golden hue due to its high beta-carotene content. Then there is the citrus-oil sugar used for the batter where orange peel is muddled with sugar and then left for the latter to draw out the fragrant citrus oils, a crossover technique from punch-making that was actually being used at the same time as the advent of the Victoria Sandwich by bartending legend Jerry Thomas on the other side of the pond. (I have Lottie Muir and her fabulous book *Wild Cocktails from the Midnight Apothecary* to thank for this *oleo saccharum* idea, who in turn credits cocktail historian David Wondrich for its discovery and development.) And the crystallized decorations? They were very much a Victorian craze.

INGREDIENTS | SERVES 6–8

sunflower oil, for oiling
4 large locally produced free-range eggs
100g self-raising flour

For the citrus-oil sugar
175g golden caster sugar
3 organic (unwaxed) oranges, finely pared (minus the white
 pith) in small strips with a sharp knife or vegetable peeler
a few lemon thyme sprigs

For the filling
150g locally grown blackcurrants, stalks removed
2 tbsp golden caster sugar, or to taste
150ml locally produced double cream
2 tbsp icing sugar, sifted, plus extra for decorating
½ tsp vanilla extract

crystallized blackcurrants and leaves, to decorate (follow the
 instructions on page 79; optional)

For the citrus-oil sugar, put all the ingredients in a bowl and
bash together with the end of a rolling pin. Cover tightly with
clingfilm and leave at room temperature for at least 4 hours,
preferably overnight, muddling occasionally. Pass the sugar
through a sieve, pressing on the zest and then discarding, and
measure out 100g for the cake (reserve the rest for making
the drinks overleaf). Tip into a large bowl.

For the sponge, preheat the oven to 180°C/Gas Mark 4.
Grease two 20cm round sandwich tins and line the bases
with baking parchment. Add the eggs to the sugar and whisk
together with a hand-held electric whisk until pale, voluminous
and thick enough for the beaters to leave a trail on the surface.
(You can use a stand mixer fitted with the whisk attachment
instead.) Sift over the flour and gently fold in with a large metal
spoon, being careful not to knock the air out. Divide the batter
between the sandwich tins, tilting them to make sure that the
mixture is level. Bake for 20–25 minutes until well risen and
golden, and the sponge is springy to the touch. Leave to cool in
the tins for a couple of minutes, then turn out onto a wire rack,
carefully peel off the lining paper and leave to cool completely.

For the filling, gently heat the blackcurrants and caster sugar
together gently in a saucepan for a few minutes just until the
currants have oozed their juices and the sugar has dissolved.
Leave to cool. Whip the cream with the icing sugar and vanilla
until almost forming stiff peaks. Cover and chill both in the
fridge until ready to assemble.

To assemble, spread the blackcurrant mixture over the
bottom sponge, then top with the vanilla cream and cover
with the other sponge. Lay a doily on top, sift icing sugar over
the holes and then carefully remove to leave a stencilled lacy
design. Decorate with crystallized blackcurrants and leaves, if
you like.

Variation: For a gluten-free option, replace the plain flour
with 50g gluten-free plain flour mix such as Doves Farm and
6 × 8g sachets arrowroot plus 1½ heaped tsp gluten-free
baking powder combined.

{ *Vary the fruit for the filling according to what's
in season and available, adjusting the amount
of sugar according to its sweetness, such as
redcurrants or a combination of currants,
cherries, raspberries, gooseberries flavoured with
elderflower cordial (see page 59), blackberries or
loganberries, or a mix of berries.* }

Iced Wight chai

Since the adoption and reinvention of chai, the centuries-old Indian spiced milky tea, by the West, it has become wildly popular for its fragrant, soothing and reviving qualities, and I thought a chilled version would make a suitably sophisticated, refreshing beverage for our summer tea party. And it's an opportunity to sample and enjoy the Island's amazingly rich, creamy milk, in its natural, unpasteurized state or pasteurized if you prefer. Moreover, its Indian origins are particularly appropriate in relation to Queen Victoria, given her many links to the country.

Having assumed the title Empress of India in 1877, an 'Indian wing' was added to Osborne House 1890–91, designed by Lockwood Kipling (Rudyard's dad), on the ground floor of which is the now magnificently refurbished Durbar Room. In the adjacent corridor hangs a collection of portraits of Indian dignitaries as well as some of the monarch's servants by the Orientalist painter Rudolf Swoboda. One such is of Mohammed Abdul Karim, latterly the Queen's Indian Secretary, her special relationship with whom being the subject of the stellar-cast movie *Victoria and Abdul*, with Dame Judi Dench reprising her role as Queen Victoria, filmed on location at Osborne.

INGREDIENTS | SERVES 1

8 cardamom pods, bruised
6 cloves
1 cinnamon stick, broken in half
¼ tsp black peppercorns, cracked
½ tsp coriander seeds, cracked
6 tsp Assam loose-leaf tea
2 slices of fresh root ginger about 3mm thick, peeled
1½ tbsp brown sugar, any kind
500ml water
1 tbsp reserved Citrus-oil Sugar (see page 83) or Island clear honey
ice cubes
locally produced whole milk or full-fat coconut milk, to top up

Toast the spices in a saucepan over a medium heat for a few minutes until smelling fragrant. Stir in the tea, ginger, sugar and water and slowly bring to the boil. Turn off the heat and leave until cooled. Strain the tea through a tea strainer into a jug and stir in the citrus-oil sugar or honey to taste.

To serve, add some ice cubes to 4 glasses, pour over the tea and top up with the milk, then stir well and serve.

Flat Wight *martini*

If you're in the mood for something a little stronger drinkwise, and in keeping with the best tea party traditions of the roaring twenties, shake up the polite proceedings with this elegant, silky coffee concoction. For this aristocrat of a cocktail, source some of the locally craft-roasted coffee beans by Jasper's or Island Roasted (see page 97) – I chose the latter's Mocha Espresso Blend, but use whichever style of coffee takes your fancy – and match it for quality with some seriously creamy cream from Briddlesford Farm Dairy, Queen Bower Dairy or Coppid Hall Farm Wight Milk. And be sure to choose the Island's own extra-smooth Rock Sea Vodka to ensure that it slips down super-easy.

INGREDIENTS | SERVES 1

ice cubes
2 tbsp locally produced double cream
2 tbsp Kahlúa or other coffee-flavoured liqueur
2 tbsp Isle of Wight Distillery Rock Sea Vodka
1 tbsp Citrus-oil Sugar, reserved from the Victoria Sandwich (see page 83), or Island clear honey
3 tbsp strongly brewed locally small-batch roasted coffee (see recipe intro), cooled, plus whole beans to garnish

Add some ice cubes to a cocktail shaker, then follow up with the rest of the ingredients except the coffee beans.

Shake really well, then strain over 2 or 3 ice cubes in a chilled cocktail glass. Garnish with coffee beans and serve straight away.

Fishermen's Feast

The Island is a fisherperson's paradise whatever their persuasion. For freshwater fans, there are well-stocked lakes aplenty such as those at Arreton, Brighstone, Rookley and Whitwell. But it is the saltwater fishing from around the Island's c. 64 miles of coastline in waters heaving with a diversity of fish and crustaceans that remains the major draw for amateurs and professionals alike. There are charter boats available at Bembridge and Ventnor, as well as Yarmouth where the British Cod Championships are held every November. And there is good sea fishing to be had off the piers and jetties, and also rocky shelves like the Bembridge Ledge, where low tide gives access to deep water.

While for some fishing is for fun, sport or trade, for others fishing is for life, or rather several lives going back generations. Blake family members have been longshoremen at Ventnor since the 1830s, running a hire service in bathing machines (still for hire as stationary beach huts) and deckchairs in the early days besides fishing. Today they are the very face of Ventnor's fishing scene with their own New England-styled Ventnor Haven Fishery pier and shop, where you can not only buy 'wet' seafood but the Island's signature takeaway, crab on chips.

Continue westwards around the coast – on foot (or by water), as that is the only way to reach it – and you will come to Steephill Cove, a ridiculously picturesque cluster of cottages around a sandy beach and rocky shore, and the private sanctuary of another longstanding fishing family, 'Wheeler and Sons; Fishermen since the 1500s', as a sign proclaims. Landing the catch daily, especially crab and lobster and mackerel, to supply their own Boathouse Restaurant and Crab Shed eateries, the Wheelers also run luxury holiday lets at the Cove and maintain the beach, seafront and a tiny treasure of a public loo in immaculate condition.

From being an isolated haunt for fishermen, smugglers and maybe even wreckers, Steephill gained respectability when the Island's Governor built The Cottage there. The great chronicler of the Wight George Brannon bemoaned the fact that by 1840 access was largely blocked by a huge Neo-Gothic edifice, Steephill Castle. Much visited by Queen Victoria and Prince Albert, the castle with its tumbling terraced gardens was a grand sight in its time, but like several of the Island's great houses, it fell into disrepair and was demolished in 1963. Yet all is not lost on the great garden front, as the subtropical marvel of Ventnor Botanic Garden burgeoning in the microclimate of The Undercliff is ten minutes' walk away.

With all its fishy heritage, nowhere could have been more fitting for our fish feast than one of Steephill's traditional fisherman's dwellings, Beachside Cottage, sensitively modernized to create a stylish holiday home while retaining its original character, and with direct access to a café/bar no less. And there we sat on the decking under a fluttering palm, sipping a chilled glass of Adgestone Vineyard's Blush, anticipating the sumptuous harvest from the crystal waters below.

Hot-smoked trout with gooseberry sauce

Getting hold of fresh gooseberries can be a hit and miss affair, with different varieties ripening potentially from the end of May to August but the exact timing depending on how sunny the weather is. So when you do spot them, it's worth grabbing a double dose and freezing the extra for use in either classic dessert dishes or in a savoury context as here. But if all else fails, canned British goosegogs are an acceptable alternative for this purpose.

Native wild yarrow (*Achillea millefolium*) is to be found on most grass- or meadowland verges throughout the Island. Widely used in herbal medicine, yarrow's feathery leaves are aromatic, aniseedy and slightly bitter, and therefore work well as an alternative to fennel, while its frothy flat-topped flower heads, like the cultivated garden forms but more modest in size and always white, make a nice garnish.

Whether fly fishing for rainbow trout on the Island Fish Farm's lakes near Brighstone is your thing or nay, you can still pre-order or drop into their shop and pick up whole or filleted smoked trout that have been lightly brined and then smoked over cherry wood for a subtle, sweet result.

INGREDIENTS | SERVES 4 AS A STARTER OR LIGHT MEAL

2 x about 165g Island Fish Farm Cherry-smoked Trout Fillets or other locally hot-smoked trout (or hot- or cold-smoked salmon) fillets, halved lengthways
sea salt and freshly ground black pepper

For the gooseberry sauce

200g locally grown gooseberries (or 290g can)
1 tbsp water
1 tbsp elderflower cordial (see page 59 for homemade)
1 ½ tbsp The Garlic Farm Creamy Horseradish with Garlic
2cm piece of fresh root ginger, peeled and finely grated
a few foraged wild yarrow leaves or fennel fronds, washed and finely chopped, plus extra to garnish along with (optional) yarrow and/or fennel flower heads

For the blue cheese and apricot scones (makes about 15)

4 tbsp locally produced semi-skimmed milk, plus extra for brushing if needed
1 tbsp freshly squeezed lemon juice
1 large locally produced free-range egg
40g Isle of Wight Cheese Co. Blue cheese (minus rind)
225g self-raising flour or a gluten-free self-raising flour mix such as Doves Farm
1 tsp baking powder or gluten-free baking powder
½ tsp cream of tartar
½ tsp salt
30g butter, diced, plus extra for greasing
2 ripe apricots, locally grown if you can get them (see page 81), stoned and chopped
a few lemon thyme (or fleshy ordinary thyme) sprigs, finely chopped

mixed salad leaves, dressed with a little vinaigrette if you like (try Wild Island Isle of Wight Salad Dressing), to serve

For the sauce, if using fresh goosegogs, add to a saucepan with the water and cordial and cook for a few minutes until they start to release their juices, then leave to cool. Transfer to a bowl and mash with a fork, then beat in the horseradish sauce, ginger and chopped herb until fairly smooth and creamy. If using canned gooseberries, drain well, add to a bowl and mash with a fork, then beat in the other ingredients as before. Season to taste with salt and pepper, then cover and refrigerate until ready to serve.

For the scones, preheat the oven to 200°C/Gas Mark 6. Lightly grease a baking sheet. Measure the milk into a measuring jug, add the lemon juice and then the egg and (very soft) cheese, and beat together well. Sift the dry ingredients into a bowl, then rub in the butter until you have a fine breadcrumb texture. Stir in the apricots and thyme. Make a

well in the centre and gradually pour in the liquid mixture while mixing in lightly and swiftly, then gently draw the mixture together with your hands, adding just enough to make a soft but not too sticky dough. Transfer to a work surface and pat gently into a round about 2–2.5cm thick. Working quickly and with a light touch, use a 4.5–5cm round fluted cutter to cut out the scones, gathering together the trimmings until you've used up all the dough. Lay on the baking sheet, brush the tops with any remaining liquid, or a little extra milk if needed, and add a good grinding of sea salt. Bake for about 12–15 minutes until golden brown.

To serve, divide the trout between serving plates and add some mixed salad leaves. Spoon on the sauce and scatter over a little extra chopped herb, then grind plenty of pepper over the fish. Add a warm scone, or 2–3 if serving as a light meal, and garnish the plates with the herb flowers if you have them. Any leftover scones will keep in an airtight container in a cool place for a day or so. Reheat in a medium oven before serving.

Try Phillips Seafood & Smokehouse's (Cowes) delicate hot oak-smoked trout (or their cold-smoked salmon if you prefer) or Delysia Farm's (near St Helens) hot-smoked trout or salmon, or check out J & B Fisheries' (Freshwater) range of smoked fish. If making the sauce when elderflowers are still in flower, you can replace the cordial with a few flowers from a foraged flower head (see page 59). Serve the scones with the Island Fish Farm's smoked trout pâté instead.

Thai crab filo tartlets

Since the Island is blessed with an abundance of fresh crab, there is the opportunity to break out and use it in a variety of ways, particularly as its flavour is robust enough to hold its own against boasty, spicy ingredients. So here I've given it a fragrant Thai treatment, encased in a crisp, flamboyant filo nest, for a summery starter, or a light lunch with a more substantial salad accompaniment. Should you find orangey red chunks in your crab, lucky you – you have a hen crab with roe (coral), which is delicious. Simply mix it in with the brown meat, or enjoy it separately combined with a squeeze of lemon juice and/or mayo and seasoning, as it can be on the dry side.

Look out for locally grown sweet Romano/Romero red (and yellow or orange) peppers as well as chillies.

INGREDIENTS | MAKES 8

sunflower oil, for sautéeing and brushing
1 bunch of spring onions, finely chopped
1 small Romano/Romero red pepper, preferably locally grown,
  cored, deseeded and finely chopped
1 small red chilli, deseeded and chopped
2cm piece of fresh root ginger, peeled and finely grated
1 The Garlic Farm large garlic clove, crushed
grated zest of 1 organic (unwaxed) lime
handful of coriander, chopped
1 tsp toasted sesame oil
4 filo pastry sheets, each about 48cm x 25cm, defrosted
  if frozen
2 large locally produced free-range eggs
120ml coconut milk, light or full fat
about 170g Island mixed brown and white crabmeat
sea salt and freshly ground black pepper
a few seasonal leaves, such as frilly lettuce and watercress,
  to serve

Heat a splash of sunflower oil in a frying pan and sauté the spring onions, red pepper and chilli for about 5 minutes until starting to soften, then add the ginger and garlic and cook, stirring, for a couple more minutes. Finally, stir in the lime zest and coriander and then turn off the heat.

Preheat the oven to 180°C/Gas Mark 4. Whisk 1 tbsp sunflower oil with the toasted sesame oil and use to lightly brush 8 holes of a muffin tin.

Keeping the filo sheets you aren't working with covered in a damp tea towel, lay 2 sheets on top of each other and cut each sheet vertically in half with kitchen scissors. Stack the 4 long pieces and cut into 4 equal pieces, making 16 square-ish pieces, brushing each with the oil mixture as you lay them to one side. Repeat with the other 2 filo sheets. Layer 4 filo pieces into each muffin hole, offsetting each slightly.

Beat the eggs, coconut milk and some salt and pepper together in a jug. Divide the spring onion mixture between the pastry cups, then spoon in the crabmeat and pour in the egg and coconut milk mixture. Bake for about 20 minutes until the filling is just set and the pastry browned – check after 10 minutes to make sure that the pastry isn't catching, covering with a sheet of baking parchment to prevent overbrowning. Serve warm with the seasonal leaves.

HOW TO TACKLE A WHOLE COOKED CRAB

Don't be put off buying whole cooked crabs either by their scary looks or prep requirements, as they are the best value and deliver optimum flavour, and you can use the edible trimmings and any weedy legs to make stock (see page 121). It's actually a straightforward procedure and could provide a welcome diversion for the kids if the promised beach weather has failed to show.

1. Twist off the 2 big claws at the front, then twist off each leg and set aside.

2. Sit the crab on your work surface, top orangey brown shell facing downwards. Using your thumbs, push the middle body section upwards and away from the top shell. Pull off and discard the flabby, greyish 'dead men's fingers' from the body section and then set aside.

3. Slip the handle of a spoon under the pale pieces of shell either side of the main top shell and break off (reserve for stock, if making). Scoop out and discard the gooey stomach bit that lies just below the eyes and mouthparts, and any bony bits (jaw bones). Scoop all the brown meat from the top shell with a spoon. It may look rather gloopy and unappealing, but if you mash it up it becomes uniform and wonderfully creamy in texture. Keep the shell if you want it for scrubbing and using to present your crabmeat dressed in the traditional way.

4. Cut the body section in half and scrape away any brown meat, adding it to the rest. Then prise out all the flakes of white meat from the labyrinth of bony sections – a lobster pin is the pro tool for this job but you can easily improvise with a metal skewer. You will be amazed how much meat can be harvested from this unpromising section, but be careful to pick out any stray bits of cartilage.

5. Now for your reward. Twist and break the claws into their sections at the joints, then again prise out the white meat, first cracking the large sections open by wrapping in a tea towel and bashing with a meat mallet or a rolling pin. If the legs look sufficiently plump, twist and break into sections, then dig out the meat.

Lobster and vine-ripened tomato tagliatelle

While a cold lobster platter is an undeniably handsome, fine-tasting dish, the way to wring every ounce of flavour out of this prized beast is to cook down the shells to make a reduction with which to bathe the precious meat. What's more, with this approach you can make relatively little of this luxury ingredient go a long way. You will need some seriously ripe, gutsy tomatoes here, so be sure to go for the Island sun-blessed, vine-ripened options.

Marsh samphire makes the perfect partner in the veg department, which you can buy at the same time as your lobster if you're in the vicinity of Captain Stan's in Bembridge or Hancock's Fishmongers in Newport, but also now widely available from supermarkets. Approximating to a seawater-seasoned, firm, fine asparagus, it adds a pleasing contrast of both texture and colour.

INGREDIENTS | SERVES 4

1 large (or 2 small) freshly cooked locally caught lobster –
   ask for it to be split and claws cracked, or prepare it yourself
   (see panel)
good knob of butter
2 small onions, 1 chopped, 1 finely diced
1 carrot, scrubbed and chopped
1 celery stick, chopped
1 bunch of flat-leaf parsley
725ml boiling water
olive oil, for sautéeing
3 The Garlic Farm plump garlic cloves, crushed
grated zest of 1 organic (unwaxed) lemon
¼ tsp cayenne pepper
1 tbsp tomato purée
125ml dry white wine
250g The Tomato Stall strawberry vine or cocktail vine
   tomatoes, halved, or Piccolo cherry vine tomatoes, left whole,
   or other locally grown small ripe tomatoes
75ml locally produced double cream
500g dried tagliatelle or gluten-free tagliatelle
salt
100g marsh samphire, woody stems removed (prepped
   weight), well soaked in cold water to remove excess salt
   and drained
handful of chervil sprigs (optional)
sea salt and freshly ground black pepper

Remove all the lobster meat from the body shells and large claws (see panel) and refrigerate along with the unpicked legs. Break the shells into smaller pieces.

Heat the butter in a large saucepan until foaming and cook up the shell pieces for a couple of minutes, stirring. Add the chopped onion, carrot, celery and a few sprigs of the parsley and sauté for another couple of minutes. Pour in the water, return to the boil and leave it boiling away for 10 minutes or so until it's reduced by half while you prep the sauce base.

Heat a glug of oil in a separate large saucepan, add the finely diced onion and sauté gently with a grinding of salt for about 10 minutes until well softened but without colouring. Add the garlic, a handful of picked parsley leaves (reserve a few sprigs for later if you haven't sourced any chervil), roughly chopped, the lemon zest and cayenne and cook, stirring, for a couple of minutes. Stir in the tomato purée, then pour in the wine and boil until most of it has evaporated. Add the tomatoes and heat through gently.

Once the stock has reduced, strain it, discarding the shells and seasonings, return it to the pan and add the cream. Season well with black pepper and simmer briskly for 5 minutes or so until slightly thickened, then check for salt. Stir gently into the sauce base and keep warm, or leave to cool, cover and refrigerate until ready to use if preparing in advance.

Cook the pasta in a large saucepan of salted boiling water according to the packet instructions until only just al dente, adding the samphire to the pan for the last 2 minutes of cooking. At the same time, reheat your sauce, if necessary, then add your lobster meat to the sauce and warm through. Also, warm your serving platters or bowls.

Drain the pasta, reserving some of the cooking water to loosen your sauce if necessary, add to the sauce with a couple of chopped chervil sprigs if available, or use some of your reserved parsley, and toss to combine, then serve scattered with the rest of the chervil or parsley sprigs, garnished with the lobster legs.

Variation: For a dairy-free version, use organic coconut oil instead of the butter and replace the double cream with the cream scooped from the top of an unshaken can of full-fat coconut milk, but only gently simmer after adding to the reduced stock, stirring frequently, to avoid splitting.

HOW TO TACKLE A WHOLE COOKED LOBSTER

Lobster really is a doddle to prepare; quicker and easier than grappling with a crab.

1. Sit your lobster on a chopping board, flattening its tail out with the palm of your hand, with the head end pointing towards you. Using a large, heavy sharp knife, cut the head in half lengthways. Turn the board around and cut down the length of the lobster to divide it in half.

2. Remove and discard the bits of stomach sack below the eyes from each half and then, using the tip of the knife, winkle out the black intestinal vein running along the inside edge of the tail shell.

3. All the remaining meat in the body is edible, including the green bits (the tomalley or liver, but discard if you'd rather pass) and, sometimes in the case of a hen lobster, red bits (roe or coral), so lever it all out into a bowl.

4. Twist off the legs and claws. Break the former at the joints and wheedle out the meat with a pukka lobster pin or metal skewer, if you can be bothered, or reserve unpicked for making stock or for garnish.

5. Crack the claws with the knife, break off the small claw of each and remove all the meat, adding it to the bowl. Cover and refrigerate until needed.

Brill fillets with potato and kohlrabi boulangère

A large flatfish, brill is often compared to its close relative the turbot, but for my money brill is sweeter and, not least, better value; it's available through the summer months into early autumn depending on the daily catch (but feel free to use turbot, or sea bream). As the sun matures on the Island, so its peppers ripen, their sugars concentrating to make a sparky addition to salads. And when they are fiercely roasted, their sweet flesh takes on a slight smokiness and intensifies in flavour, the texture turning silken under the blistered skin. Which all goes to make a perky sauce to complement the fish.

If you are not yet acquainted with the alien-looking kohlrabi but a fan of broccoli or cauli stalks, do give it a go. In season from high summer into the autumn, this versatile brassica can be used raw, thinly sliced or julienned, in salads or to make slaws, or in a vegetable bake as here where it brings a turnipy twang to the familiar potato. Swiss chard is also at its best during the same period, which offers a two-for-one eating experience – its generous, ruffled leaves a gutsier-tasting spinach; its stems nutty and slightly sweet yet earthy, an echo of its cousin the beetroot. You can't miss rainbow chard in any sense, with its spectacular spectrum of ruby red, deep pink, bright orange and glowing yellow stems and veins.

INGREDIENTS | SERVES 4

2 large brill fillets (from 1 whole brill 1–1.5kg in weight),
   with skin, halved
sea salt and freshly ground black pepper

For the red pepper sauce
2 Romano/Romero red peppers, preferably locally
   grown, halved, cored and deseeded
½ tsp fennel seeds
2 tbsp olive oil, plus extra for drizzling
1 shallot, finely chopped
1 The Garlic Farm garlic clove, crushed
1 tsp smoked paprika
4 tbsp dry white wine
100ml vegetable or chicken stock
small handful of basil leaves, plus extra sprigs to garnish
squeeze of lemon juice, to taste
pinch of sugar, any kind, if needed

For the potato and kohlrabi boulangère
knob of butter and 1 tbsp olive oil
   (or use all olive oil, about 1½ tbsp), plus extra butter or oil
   for greasing, dotting or drizzling and frying
1 large onion, thinly sliced
500g locally grown Maris Piper potatoes
   (or Desiree or King Edward)
about 350g locally grown kohlrabi
1 tbsp thyme leaves
350ml hot vegetable or chicken stock

For the sauce, preheat the oven to 200°C/Gas Mark 6. Place the peppers cut side down on a small baking sheet lined with foil, season with salt and pepper and drizzle with oil. Roast on the top oven shelf for about 20 minutes or until soft and the skin is blackened and blistered in places. Remove, reducing the oven to 190°C/Gas Mark 5, and enclose in the foil (use an oven glove), then leave for a few minutes to steam. Peel off the skin and roughly chop the flesh.

For the boulangère, meanwhile, grease a large ovenproof dish. Heat the butter with the oil (or just oil) in a large frying pan, add the onion and cook over a medium heat for a few minutes, stirring, until beginning to soften. Cover with a lid smaller than the pan so that it fits closely over the onion, then cook gently for about 20 minutes until soft and golden.

Peel the potatoes and kohlrabi and very thinly slice – a mandolin is the ideal tool but otherwise use a veg peeler. Toss the onion with the potato and kohlrabi slices, thyme and plenty of seasoning in the baking dish, then pour over the hot stock. Dot the top with butter or drizzle with oil and bake in the oven for a good hour until the veg are entirely yielding to a knife tip and crisp and brown on top.

While the boulangère is baking, finish making the sauce. Toast the fennel seeds in a dry heavy-based saucepan over a medium-high heat for a few minutes until lightly browned and smelling toasty. Turn off the heat and leave to cool slightly, then crush lightly using a pestle and mortar, or enclose in a resealable plastic bag and roll over with a glass bottle or rolling pin. Return to the pan, add the 2 tbsp oil and the shallot with a grinding of salt and cook gently for about 7 minutes until soft but not coloured. Add the garlic and paprika and cook, stirring, for a minute. Stir in the wine and bubble over a high heat until mostly evaporated. Add the stock, red pepper and basil leaves and cook for a few minutes. Purée with a stick blender, then taste and adjust the seasoning with lemon juice, sugar, if needed, and salt and pepper. Keep the sauce warm.

When the boulangère is done, pat the fish dry with kitchen paper and season with salt on both sides. Lightly coat the base of a large, heavy-based (preferably cast-iron) or non-stick frying pan with oil and place over a medium-high heat. Once hot, add the fillets skin side down and cook, pressing down on them with a fish slice to prevent curling, for 3–4 minutes until the skin is browned and crisp. Turn over and cook for about a minute until the flesh is opaque. If not quite done, turn off the heat and leave to finish cooking in the residual heat. Serve the fish skin side up with the sauce and boulangère, garnished with basil sprigs, along with lightly cooked seasonal veg such as French beans and/or rainbow chard.

{ *To prepare chard, separate the stems from the leaves, slice and cook, covered, in a small quantity of water in a saucepan for about 5 minutes until just softened, then add the shredded leaves and cook briefly until just wilted.* }

Affogato with hazelnut and coffee bean biscotti

This is an easy dessert, as you can make the biscotti well in advance. It does, however, assume that your guests are coffee lovers, since it delivers a double whammy – chocolate-coated coffee beans added to the biscuits in addition to the *affogato* ritual itself, i.e. the 'drowning' of ice cream in hot, strongly brewed coffee. Although espresso is the traditional choice and excellent options are available freshly roasted from Island Roasted and Jasper's (see panel opposite), I used the latter's Congo CPCK Coop coffee beans, described on the packet as having 'a bright rounded acidity, floral aroma and sweet golden raisin with background citrus flavours'; characteristics that worked well here. There should, however, should be no break with tradition with the ice cream – only the best vanilla will do, and it doesn't come better than multi-award-winning Minghella, made with Briddlesford's premium Guernsey milk and cream.

INGREDIENTS | SERVES 4

For the chocolate-coated coffee beans
40g dark chocolate (70% cocoa solids)
15g locally small-batch roasted coffee beans or other freshly roasted coffee beans, plus extra beans ground and freshly brewed to serve

For the biscotti (makes about 16)
175g plain flour, plus extra for dusting
½ tsp bicarbonate of soda
pinch of salt
70g demerara sugar
70g hazelnuts in their skins, toasted and skins rubbed off (see page 65), then roughly chopped
¼ tsp vanilla extract
grated zest of 1 medium organic (unwaxed) orange
1 large locally produced free-range egg
1 large locally produced free-range egg white

550g tub Mr Minghella's Famous Vanilla Ice Cream, to serve

For the coffee beans, break the chocolate into a heatproof bowl set over a pan of barely simmering water (make sure the base doesn't touch the water) and leave until melted. Tip in the beans and stir to coat, then lift out individually with a fork and place separately on a sheet of baking parchment. Leave for a few hours to set.

For the biscotti, preheat the oven to 180°C/Gas Mark 4. Line a large baking sheet with baking parchment. Stir together the flour, bicarb, salt, sugar, nuts and most of the chocolate coffee beans (reserve a few for decoration) in a bowl. In a jug, beat together the remaining 4 ingredients with a fork. Pour the egg mixture into the flour mixture and stir together, then mix with your hands until the mixture clumps together into a soft dough. Turn out onto a well-floured work surface and knead lightly a few times. Shape with your hands into a flattened log about 2.5cm thick and transfer to the lined baking sheet. Bake for about 25 minutes until lightly browned and firm to the touch.

Remove from the oven, reducing the oven temperature to 160°C/Gas Mark 3, and sit the baking sheet on a wire rack for 10 minutes to cool, removing the lining paper once cool enough to handle. Transfer the log carefully to a bread board and, using a bread knife, cut on a slight diagonal into 1cm-thick slices. Lay the slices in a single layer on the baking sheet (dried off with kitchen paper) and bake for 10 minutes on each side. They may still be slightly soft in the middle but should harden when they cool. Transfer to a wire rack to cool completely,

then store in an airtight container in a cool, dry place – they will keep well for a few days.

To serve, brew a pot of strong coffee while you scoop the ice cream into serving dishes. Pour the hot coffee over the ice cream and serve with the biscotti, decorating the plates or dishes with the reserved chocolate-coated coffee beans.

Variation: For a gluten-free alternative, use a gluten-free plain flour mix such as Doves Farm in place of the ordinary flour and mix in ¾ tsp xanthan gum before using, adding a good squeeze of juice from the zested orange to help bind the mixture. Use a guaranteed gluten-free chocolate.

{ *To save time and effort, use ready-made chocolate-coated coffee beans, which gives you the perfect excuse to pay a visit to Mad Chocolate Cowes and at the same time bag your tub of Minghella ice cream from Bliss Ice Cream Parlour next door. Alternatively, replace them with 55g dark chocolate chips.* }

CHOOSING THE WIGHT COFFEE

Select from **Island Roasted's** range of sustainably sourced, small-batch, craft-roasted seasonal single-origin and espresso coffees; beans available from the company's own Caffe Isola in Newport (or online), which can be freshly ground on site to the required grind size. Or enjoy it the unique way – freshly ground by **The Break Lever**, Mat Tucker's low-carbon, pedal-powered coffee tricycle to be found in action at the Festival, Randonnee, Walk the Wight and other major Island events.

Alternatively, try **Jasper's Artisan Coffee**, ethically sourced green beans roasted at their base in Brading, such as Great Taste Award-winning Buxom Espresso Blend and 3-star winner Ethiopia Yirgacheffe Rocko Mountain Reserve from their range of seasonal single-origin speciality coffees, plus their Swiss Water Brazilian Decaffeinated; available as beans or ground from farm shops and other selected Island and mainland outlets, or from their Citroën H Van 'Josephine' at events.

Visiting Rookley Country Park? **Betapak's** trade counter nearby would be happy to supply you with Island Tea & Coffee products, including their hand-crafted range of ten filter coffee blends especially developed for the hard chalky Island water, from the smooth, rich Blue Mountain to the acidic, earthy Viennese, some roasted on site.

Beetroot and chilli brownies

Beetroot is another high summer into autumn/winter versatile veg, widely available bunched on the Island and, if you're lucky, with its leafy tops intact, which you can prepare and cook in the same way as chard (see page 95) for a bonus veg. Also look out for mixed bunches of heirloom varieties coloured orange and white, or with eye-catching candy-striped flesh within. But there is a case for not letting on to your guests that this salad staple features in these brownies until they have tucked in and given them the thumbs up, since rather than tasting of itself it contributes a slightly fruity, earthy sweetness. It also replaces the usual added fat, resulting in a lighter-weight yet satisfyingly squidgy brownie. Nor need you fess up in advance to the chilli, since the amount of the liqueur used should impart only a warming after-sensation, unless your hand slips with the bottle, which may literally end in tears, as it is flavoured with the Dorset Naga, one of the hottest chillies on the planet.

The fruit coulis gives a good contrast of tart flavour as well as colour, and it's worth trying to catch redcurrants, like delicately strung clusters of shiny red glass beads, in their all-too-short season around July–August time. I couldn't resist decorating the dish with two-tone petals plucked from the flowers of a potted dianthus courtesy of The Coastal Gardener (or source as a cut flower from Bartletts Farm Flowers), which are pleasantly clove-like in taste.

INGREDIENTS | MAKES 9

75g walnut halves
100g bar (dairy-free) dark chocolate (70% cocoa solids)
150g peeled and grated raw locally grown young beetroot
  (about 1 medium)
2 large locally produced free-range eggs, beaten
1½ tbsp Adgestone Vineyard Arson Fire Chilli Chocolate Liqueur
  (optional)
90g dark muscovado sugar
115g self-raising flour
1 tsp bicarbonate of soda

For the redcurrant and raspberry coulis (serves 4)
1 small punnet (about 180g) locally grown redcurrants, stalks
  removed (about 160g prepared weight)
50g raspberries, preferably locally grown
1 tbsp The Fruit Bowl Gooseberry and Redcurrant jam or other
  locally produced fruit jam, or to taste

a few dianthus (pinks) petals, trimmed of their bitter white
  bases, to decorate (optional)

Preheat the oven to 180°C/Gas Mark 4 and line a 23cm square baking tin with baking parchment. Spread the walnuts out on a baking sheet and toast in the oven for 10 minutes. Leave to cool, then break into chunky pieces.

Meanwhile, break the chocolate bar into a medium (not small, as you will be making the brownie mixture in this) heatproof bowl set over a pan of barely simmering water (make sure the base doesn't touch the water) and leave until melted. Take off the heat and leave to cool slightly.

Add the grated beetroot to the melted choc with the eggs and liqueur, if using, and beat well, then stir in the sugar. Sift the flour and bicarb together, then gently fold into the mixture with a large metal spoon, followed by the nuts.

Pour the mixture evenly into the lined tin and bake for 15 minutes until a skewer inserted into the centre comes out with moist crumbs attached. Sit the tin on a wire rack until cooled completely, then lift the brownie out using the lining paper, carefully peel the paper away and cut into 9 squares. They will keep for up to 3 days in an airtight container.

For the coulis, crush the fruit together in a bowl with a fork, then whisk in the jam to taste. Drizzle over the brownies to serve and decorate with the dianthus (pinks) petals if you can get them.

Variation: For a gluten-free version, use 100g gluten-free self-raising flour mix such as Doves Farm in place of the 115g ordinary self-raising flour, and source a dark chocolate that is guaranteed gluten free.

{ *You could use a pinch of dried chilli flakes instead of the chilli chocolate liqueur, or try replacing half the ordinary dark chocolate with House of Chilli Dark Chilli Chocolate, made by the Chocolate Apothecary, Ryde. If you can't get hold of redcurrants for the coulis, you can use all raspberries instead, adjusting the quantity of jam accordingly to taste.* }

Wight sling

This long, cool cocktail draws its inspiration from the classic Gin Sling but with a slant more Solent than Singapore, starting with the all-important spirit base. Isle of Wight Distillery uses an array of carefully selected botanicals for infusing their 2-star Great Taste Award-winning craft gin. Besides the essential juniper, these include Boadicea hops grown at Ventnor Botanic Garden and rock samphire (no relation to marsh samphire) handpicked from the Island's chalk cliffs. This once highly perilous practice has a long history, the Isle of Wight having historically been the main source of the sought-after crop in Britain, transported in casks of seawater to London and sold at street markets as 'crest marine'.

In place of the cherry brandy of the standard Singapore or indeed Sydney Sling, we have Island-produced cherry liqueur combined with another notable Island product, the apricot (see page 81). What is true to the original Sling is the lime (or lemon) juice and cold water, but even the latter is a uniquely Wight take.

INGREDIENTS | SERVES I

3½ tbsp Isle of Wight Distillery Wight Mermaids Gin
2 tbsp locally produced cherry liqueur, such as from Rosemary Vineyard or Godshill Cider Company
2 tbsp puréed ripe apricot flesh, preferably from a locally grown fruit
2 tbsp freshly squeezed lime juice
2 tbsp freshly squeezed orange juice
3½ tbsp chilled Wight Crystal Still Spring Water
ice cubes
orange slice segment and fresh cherry, to garnish

Stir all the ingredients together with ice cubes in a mixing glass or shake with ice in a cocktail shaker.

Strain over ice cubes in a highball glass. Cut a slit in the orange segment and cherry and perch on the rim to garnish before serving.

Wight virgin apricot Bellini

The Bellini, another legendary cocktail, is given the full Wight treatment here to make a classy non-alcoholic tipple. First invented by Giuseppe Cipriani back in 1948 at his own Harry's Bar in Venice, frequented by such luminaries as Ernest Hemingway, Truman Capote and Orson Welles, it was originally made with the region's Prosecco and white peaches and so only served during the latter's summer season. The addition of a little raspberry or cherry purée or juice gave rise to the Bellini's pink-tinged colour and thereby its name, as the cocktail's particular hue recalled that used in works by the Venetian Renaissance painter Giovanni Bellini.

In this reincarnation of the drink, more Ventnor than Venice, the Island's high summer fruit, the apricot, supplants the white peach, and is tinted with a shot of cherry juice or purée again from local produce, then topped up with the Wight's own sparkling spring water instead of Prosecco.

INGREDIENTS | SERVES 4

about 300ml chilled puréed ripe apricot flesh, preferably from locally grown fruit (about 7 apricots), plus 4 apricot wedges, each threaded onto a cocktail stick
4 tbsp freshly squeezed orange juice
2 tbsp Godshill Orchards Cherry Juice (see page 81), or purée a few stoned cherries
cracked or crushed ice
250ml chilled Wight Crystal Sparkling Spring Water, to top up

Stir the apricot purée, orange juice and cherry juice or purée together in a mixing glass.

Add some cracked or crushed ice to Champagne flutes, then divide the apricot mixture between them. Top up with the sparkling water, stirring well. Lay an apricot-threaded cocktail stick over the top of each glass and serve.

For an alcoholic version, in place of the sparkling water, top up the cocktail with some locally produced sparkling white wine from either Rosemary Vineyard or Adgestone Vineyard.

Barbie on the Beach

Wherever you may be on the Island, you are never further than a 20-minute drive away from a beach, and as there are many different types, you can head for whichever suits your preference on the day.

Long sweeps of sand make up the town beaches of Sandown and Shanklin with their traditional family attractions, but unrivalled is Ryde's spectacular swathe reaching way out into the Solent when the tide goes out. In between is Whitecliff Bay, sheltering beneath the stately chalk facade of Culver Down, and on the other side of the promontory, Yaverland strand backed by crumbling sandstone walls. For sun lovers, there is the southernmost beach of Ventnor, and just beyond lies the hidden gem of Steephill Cove (see page 87). Travel on and you hit the wild west with its uninterrupted run of untamed beaches from St Catherine's Point through to Brook and then Compton Bay, offering opportunities for surfing or searching for dinosaur teeth, or for letting the dog chase the waves. At the western extremity, what beaches are to be had are more difficult to access, such as Alum Bay renowned for its multi-shaded sands, which requires a long clamber down steps or a trip in a chairlift to reach, or the treacherous Scratchell's Bay just south of the Needles with its sheer chalk backdrop and cavernous caves.

Continuing round the Island and you are soon within spitting distance of the Hampshire coast and the site of the most challenging of beach cricket matches, held once a year on a sandbank in the middle of the Solent, which is exposed for just an hour and even then the 'pitch' is often waterlogged. Other unique treasures are to be found Solent-side, like Thorness Bay's Site of Special Scientific Interest with its fossilized plant and animal remains including crocodiles and turtles, and home to a host of unusual coastal plants. Further east you can visit Queen Victoria's exclusive beach at Osborne Bay where her children learned to swim and sit inside the bathing machine installed by Prince Albert to preserve the monarch's modesty.

But the Wight's beaches have a darker history. For centuries, the remote bays along the south and west coasts were favoured spots for smugglers, with their many secret caves providing perfect hiding places, and their chines – deep, often thickly wooded gullies cut by streams through the cliffs – handy escape routes.

So which beach to choose for our barbecue? Having been tempted by the dinosaur-trodden delights of Brook Bay and the silken sands of Appley watched over by its fairytale gothic tower, we decided upon the laid-back charms of St Helens beach. Enjoyed by watersport enthusiasts and dog-lovers, horse-riders and rock-poolers, it looks out to the closest and smallest of the Palmerston Solent forts, to which a happy holiday throng pick their way along a narrow spit on one late summer day only when the tide is at its lowest, and return safely, if a little soggy, to the beach for their own well-earned barbie.

Broad and butter bean kofta kebabs

Using summer seasonal broad beans combined with canned butter beans makes a change from the usual chickpeas here. The trick is getting the mixture firm enough to remain on the kebabs, so keep them chilled until ready to cook and then allow a crust to form on one side before attempting to turn when cooking.

I had a go at using bay as kebab sticks, which may strike some folk as extravagant, but bay trees grow like weeds on the Island and my garden and environs are overrun with them. (Just to make the point loud and clear, though, ransacking of any vegetation in the wild, however profuse, is a complete no-no.) Look for their glossy green leaves in hedgerows along footpaths and make doubly sure to correctly identify, passing if in doubt, although if you are familiar with their distinctive aroma, follow your nose by crushing one. Select the odd slender twig as you would for rosemary kebab sticks, stripping off most of the leaves but leaving a few attached to the end. The stripped leaves can be chucked on the coals for aromatic smoke and/or used in other dishes (see the barbecued fish on page 112 for example).

INGREDIENTS | SERVES 4

500g locally grown broad beans, podded (about 170g
   podded weight)
salt
100g wholemeal or gluten-free bread (without crusts)
400g can butter beans, drained and rinsed
1 onion, chopped
large handful of coriander, roughly chopped
2 The Garlic Farm smoked garlic cloves, roughly chopped
2 tsp cumin seeds, toasted and ground (see page 41)
1 tsp coriander seeds, toasted and ground (see page 41)
½ tsp ground ginger
½ tsp ground cinnamon
1 tsp harissa, or to taste
grated zest of 1 organic (unwaxed) lemon
1 large locally produced free-range egg, beaten
plain flour or any gluten-free flour, for dusting
1½ tbsp each Island clear honey and toasted sesame oil,
   mixed together
The Taverners Pub Dukkah, for sprinkling (crush up any larger
   pieces of nut)
sunflower oil, for oiling
sea salt and freshly ground black pepper

For the green yogurt and tahini sauce
180ml Calbourne Classics Greek-style Yogurt
2 tbsp tahini
handful of flat-leaf parsley, finely chopped
squeeze of lemon juice, to taste

Presoak some kebab sticks in water for about 30 minutes, 4
wooden ones about 30cm long, or 2 or 3 plus 1 or 2 slender
branches of bay, if you come across some, cut to a similar
length and mostly stripped of leaves (see recipe intro).

Cook the broad beans in a saucepan of lightly salted boiling
water for about 8 minutes until just tender, then drain, refresh
under cold running water and drain well again.

Whizz the bread in a food processor to crumbs. Add all
the beans, onion, fresh coriander, garlic, spices, harissa, zest and
¼ tsp sea salt and pepper to taste, and pulse until coarsely
chopped. Then add the egg and briefly pulse to combine. Dust
your hands with flour, then shape the mixture into fat sausage
shapes around the drained soaked kebab sticks, 2 koftas per
stick, pressing the mixture on firmly. Wrap the kebabs loosely
in foil and chill in the fridge for at least a couple of hours or
overnight. Transfer to a cool bag to transport.

Meanwhile, for the sauce, mix all the ingredients together in
a serving bowl, seasoning to taste with salt and pepper. Cover
and keep cool until ready to serve.

When ready to cook, i.e. when your barbecue coals have
burnt down enough to develop a grey ashy coating, brush the
koftas all over with the honey and oil mixture and sprinkle
with dukkah to coat. Brush the barbecue rack thoroughly with
oil, carefully place the kebabs on top and leave to cook for a
few minutes without disturbing until a crust has formed on
the underside, then carefully turn and continue cooking and
turning in the same way for about another 12 minutes or until
nicely charred all over. Serve with the sauce, sprinkled with a
little of the dukka, along with Spiced Flatbreads (see overleaf)
and a leafy salad.

Variation: The egg acts as a binding agent to hold the mixture
together, but for a vegan alternative, soak 1 tbsp chia seeds in
3 tbsp water for about 15 minutes until they form a gel and
use in place of the egg. In any case, you can form the mixture
into patties instead, which will be easier to handle and keep
in shape. You can substitute a dairy-free natural yogurt for the
Greek yogurt.

{ *Dukka is a fragrant, crunchy Egyptian mix of
hazelnuts, sesame seeds and spices, which you
can buy ready-made — I used one produced by
The Taverners Pub in Godshill — or knock
up yourself.* }

Persian beef skewers

In my humble opinion, barbecuing is the only way to enjoy prime beef steak if cooking it yourself, and it doesn't come primer than Mottistone Manor Farm's Aberdeen Angus, hung for a full 28 days and on sale at their own farm shop, the farmers' markets and other outlets, although there are other excellent Island beef producers besides (see page 13). Having said that, this recipe also works well with boneless lamb, especially since again the Wight boasts such cracking stuff, available from the various farm shop butcheries, the farmers' markets and quality butchers across the Island.

INGREDIENTS | SERVES 4

*600g (trimmed weight) locally produced rib-eye or sirloin
   steak trimmed of excess fat*
4 The Tomato Stall green tomatoes or other heirloom tomatoes

For the marinade

*large pinch of saffron threads, soaked in 1 tbsp hot water for
   20 minutes*
120ml Calbourne Classics Whole Milk Yogurt
1 onion, grated
1 tbsp olive oil, plus extra for oiling
2 The Garlic Farm garlic cloves, crushed
2 tsp sumac, plus extra for sprinkling over the sauce
handful of flat-leaf parsley, finely chopped
sea salt and freshly ground black pepper

For the lime yogurt sauce

200ml Calbourne Classics Whole Milk Yogurt
grated zest and juice of 1 organic (unwaxed) lime
handful of coriander sprigs, finely chopped

*marjoram sprigs, or extra flat-leaf parsley or coriander
   sprigs, to garnish*

Tenderize the meat by bashing with the end of a rolling pin, then cut into 3cm cubes. Mix all the marinade ingredients together in a large bowl, add the meat and toss to coat. Cover with clingfilm and leave to marinate in the fridge for at least a few hours, preferably overnight, or failing that, at room temperature for 30 minutes.

Meanwhile, mix all the sauce ingredients together in a serving bowl, seasoning to taste with salt and pepper. Cover with clingfilm and keep cool until ready to serve.

Thread the meat onto 4 metal skewers about 30cm long, adding a tomato to the end of each. Wrap loosely in foil and place in a cool bag to transport. Take the skewers out of the cool bag, but keep relatively cool while you prepare your barbecue for cooking.

When your coals have burnt down enough to develop a grey ashy coating, brush the barbecue rack thoroughly with oil, place the skewers on top and cook, turning frequently, for 10 minutes or until cooked to your liking. Serve with the sauce, sprinkled with a little sumac, garnished with herb sprigs, along with Spiced Flatbreads.

> *The fat trimmings from this premium beef are too good to waste: cut into chunks and render down in a roasting tray in a low oven for a couple of hours and you will have both toothsome beef scratchings and superior beef dripping for divinely delicious roasties.*

Spiced flatbreads

These are simple to make and especially good cooked on the barbecue, although a griddle plate, ridged griddle pan or heavy-based cast-iron frying pan on the hob, heated to medium-high and brushed with olive oil, would also work should you be forced indoors by the elements. In any event, make sure you have a clean tea towel on hand for blanketing the just-cooked bread, which is the best option for keeping them pliable as well as warm. I used za'atar – a herby mix of dried Lebanese or Syrian oregano, sesame, sumac, sea salt and olive oil – and cumin to flavour mine, but you can vary the spicing as you fancy, or according to what you have to hand, such as garam masala or ras el hanout spice mixes, or/and chuck in some sesame seeds.

INGREDIENTS | MAKES 8

250g plain flour, plus extra for dusting
1 tbsp baking powder
½ tsp sea salt
1 tsp za'atar
1 tsp toasted and ground cumin seeds (see page 41)
120ml water
4 tbsp locally produced semi-skimmed milk
2 tbsp olive oil, plus extra for oiling

Mix all the ingredients together in a bowl until they start to clump together, then use your hands to gather into a dough. Knead for a few minutes on a lightly floured surface until smooth, soft and pliable, adding a little more flour if sticky.

Divide the dough into 8 pieces, rolling each in turn into a ball, then flattening with a rolling pin into about a 13cm roughly shaped round. Tear off pieces of foil or baking parchment and brush with oil and dust with flour, then layer the flatbreads in between and wrap the stack loosely in foil. Keep cool.

Once ready to cook, brush the barbecue rack thoroughly with oil, then slap the flatbreads on and cook for 1–2 minutes until bubbles begin to form on top. Use tongs to flip them over and cook on the other side for a similar length of time. Wrap in your clean tea towel to keep them warm and pliable and serve ASAP with your skewers/kebabs and accompanying sauce, or just the latter such as the Green Yogurt and Tahini Sauce pictured opposite and the chargrilled veg on page 110.

Variations: For a gluten-free alternative, use a gluten-free plain flour mix such as Doves Farm or chickpea flour and gluten-free baking powder, plus 1 tsp xanthan gum or 1 tbsp chia seeds soaked in 3 tbsp water for about 15 minutes. Skip the pointless kneading in this instance and make them slightly smaller and thicker to save falling apart. To avoid dairy, use coconut milk in place of the cows' milk.

Teriyaki pork and plum kebabs

Pork shoulder is a good choice of cut to use here (especially in the case of the Island's sweet-tasting premium free-range pork – see page 14), which is relatively lean but with enough fat to ensure that the meat remains succulent and tender during the cooking process. And if you stick with the local quality pork, you won't be in danger of experiencing that unpalatable taint of hog otherwise often associated with cheaper cuts of pig. For a special treat, you could use Briddlesford Lodge Farm's rose veal in place of the pork.

Come late summer come the plum and greengage season, so look out for locally grown examples (from Godshill Orchards, for instance – see page 81). But if you can't source any, or if it's not the season for them, use wedges of fresh pineapple or chunks of green pepper instead.

INGREDIENTS | SERVES 4

*600g (trimmed weight) locally produced boneless pork
 shoulder trimmed of any excess fat, cut into 3cm chunks*
*about 6 locally grown ripe but firm plums (or greengages),
 halved and stoned*
groundnut oil, for brushing and oiling
sesame seeds, for sprinkling

For the marinade
4 tbsp The Garlic Farm Teriyaki Sauce with Black Garlic
5cm piece of fresh root ginger, peeled and finely grated
3 The Garlic Farm garlic cloves, crushed
grated zest of 1 organic (unwaxed) lime
4 tsp dark soy sauce
2 tsp Chinese five-spice powder
4 tsp Island clear honey
2 tsp Godshill Cider Company cider vinegar
4 tsp toasted sesame oil

For the peanut sauce
120g PINK'S Crunchy Peanut Butter
2 tbsp The Garlic Farm Hoisin Sauce with Garlic
1 tbsp dark soy sauce
*1 tbsp Godshill Cider Company cider vinegar or freshly
 squeezed lime juice*
1 The Garlic Farm garlic clove, crushed
1 tsp grated fresh root ginger
good pinch of dried chilli flakes, or to taste
dash of toasted sesame oil
about 4 tbsp water, plus extra if needed

For the marinade, mix all the marinade ingredients together in a glass or ceramic bowl, add the pork and toss to coat. Cover with clingfilm and leave to marinate in the fridge for as long as you can spare, preferably overnight.

Thread the pork onto 4 metal skewers about 30cm long, interspersing the plum (or greengage) halves at regular intervals. Wrap loosely in foil and place in a cool bag to transport. Take the kebabs out of the cool bag, but keep relatively cool while you prepare your barbecue.

Once your barbecue is nearly ready for cooking, i.e. when most of the coals have burnt down enough to develop a grey ashy coating, put all the sauce ingredients into an old saucepan and mix together well. Stand on the barbecue rack near the edge to warm up, stirring frequently and adding more water if necessary for the right consistency.

Brush the kebabs lightly all over with groundnut oil and sprinkle with sesame seeds to coat. Brush the barbecue rack thoroughly with oil, place the kebabs on top and cook, turning frequently, for about 15–20 minutes or until thoroughly cooked through. Serve with the warm peanut sauce, along with some chargrilled veg (see overleaf).

Look out for barbecue charcoal produced from locally sourced hardwood timber – I bagged my supply from Farmer Jack's Farm Shop at Arreton.

WHEN BLACK IS WIGHT

Even if you struggle a bit with standard garlic's pungency, both in terms of its taste and lingering odour, black garlic is sure to seduce you with its mild, sweet nature. But first you need to get over its unpromisingly shrivelled and overbaked looks, due to the long heat-ageing process that it has undergone but which produces a wonderfully deep, mellow caramelization and fudgy texture. Used in a similar way to smoked garlic, it adds a rich intensity of flavour to all manner of savoury dishes, as well as providing heath-promoting nutrients in the form of antioxidants (twice as many as raw garlic) and sulphur compounds, notably S-allylcysteine (SAC) reputed to help lower cholesterol. The Garlic Farm not only use it to enhance their condiments, such as the teriyaki sauce I added to the pork marinade, but have brought its unique qualities to bear in the creation of two beverage firsts – Black Garlic Beer and Black Garlic Vodka.

Chargrilled vegetable medley

The late summer season happily brings with it a rich harvest of Island-grown colourful veg that take on an added vibrancy when left to soak up some spicy seasonings, then whopped on the barbie and allowed to sizzle, smoke and char. This approach also means that your veg are conveniently portable and ready-prepped for the grill. Do look out for the Romanesco cauli, actually tasting somewhere between broccoli and cauliflower, a geometrical miracle of nature expertly cultivated by both Ben Brown and Will Steward (see pages 16–17) that's almost too beautiful to cut into, although still striking in cross section.

Serve a selection (any two sorts should be plenty to serve four) as an accompaniment to the pork or other kebabs (see previous pages), or with the barbecued fish overleaf. Alternatively, dish them all up as a veggie feast along with the Spiced Flatbreads (see page 107) and a choice of sauces from this chapter for dunking.

INGREDIENTS

olive oil, or oil from the oak-smoked tomatoes, for oiling

For the piri piri cauli steaks
1 small locally grown cauliflower
1 locally grown Romanesco cauliflower
Wild Island Piri Piri Dressing & Marinade, for marinating

For the lime butter coblets
2 locally grown sweetcorn cobs
50g butter (try the Island's – see overleaf) and a splash of
  olive oil (or use all olive oil, about 4 tbsp)
grated zest of 1 organic (unwaxed) lime
a good grinding of The Garlic Farm Sea Salt with Garlic &
  Black Pepper

For the oak-smoked tomato-stuffed peppers
4 locally grown Romano/Romero peppers, any colour or mixed
200g pack The Tomato Stall Oak Smoked Vine Ripened
  Tomatoes
oregano leaves, for scattering

For the cauli steaks, remove the leaves from each veg and then trim the stalk at the base so that it will sit upright on the chopping board (keep the trimmings along with any florets that fall off when slicing for making veg stock or adding to a stew or braise). Starting in the centre and working out, carefully cut vertically into slices about 2cm thick. Place in a large resealable plastic bag and pour in a good glug of the piri piri marinade. Seal the bag and gently massage to coat the veg thoroughly in the marinade. Leave to marinate in the fridge for a couple of hours or so. Keep cool until ready to cook.

To cook, brush the barbecue rack thoroughly with olive oil or oil from the tomatoes, lay on the cauli steaks and cook, turning frequently and brushing with the marinade left in the bag, for about 10 minutes until nicely browned but still al dente.

{ *Be sure not to chuck away the rest of the oil from the pack of oak-smoked tomatoes – use it for brushing any meat, seafood or veg items before and during barbecuing, or in a dressing for an accompanying salad.* }

For the coblets, unwrap the cobs from their papery husks, pulling the latter off at the base, then strip off the silky threads left clinging to the kernels. The core of the cob is mighty tough stuff, so with great care, use a heavy-duty knife to cut each into 4 equal lengths – I used a freezer knife to saw through mine. Place in a large resealable plastic bag. Melt the butter with the oil in a small saucepan over a low heat (or warm the oil gently), add the lime zest and seasoning and stir well, then leave to cool. Add to the corn in the plastic bag and then marinate and cook as for the cauli steaks.

For the peppers, cut them lengthways in half, keeping the stalks attached, then remove the core and seeds. Brush with a little oil from the tomatoes, then lay the pepper halves cut side down on the oiled barbecue rack and cook for a few minutes until lightly charred. Use tongs to turn cut side up, then pop a couple of the tomatoes into each half with the oil that clings to them, scatter with oregano leaves and grill for a few more minutes until lightly charred on the underside and the tomatoes have warmed through.

Whole grey mullet with smoked tomato and olive butter

Our inexpensive locally caught grey mullet proved to be fine and plentiful eating with its hunks of meaty, robust-tasting flesh, so it makes an economical choice for a family barbie. I used some heady aromatics to infuse the cooking fish – eucalyptus-like fresh bay leaves (see page 104), aniseedy bulb fennel and piney marjoram (or use the spicier oregano) – lifted by zesty orange.

As an extra flourish, there were discs of sweet, smoky, herby butter for anointing the crispy chargrilled result. Seek out the super-creamy Island butter to sample here, such as that made by Coppid Hall Farm, available from their Friesian-themed Wight Milk Shed at Havenstreet, or by Briddlesford Farm Dairy on sale at their farm shop near Wootton Bridge.

INGREDIENTS | SERVES 4

1 large whole grey mullet (about 1.2kg), gutted, gills removed
   and scaled (your fish supplier will do all this for you)
handful of fresh bay leaves
1 small locally grown fennel bulb, thinly sliced
½ organic (unwaxed) orange, sliced
a few marjoram or oregano sprigs and/or thyme sprigs
sea salt and freshly ground black pepper

For the smoked tomato and olive butter

100g butter, preferably locally produced (see recipe intro),
   softened
6 The Tomato Stall Oak Smoked Vine Ripened Tomatoes,
   drained and finely chopped, oil reserved for drizzling over the
   fish and oiling
10 pitted black olives, finely chopped
small handful of oregano, marjoram or basil leaves,
   finely chopped
1 The Garlic Farm smoked garlic clove, crushed to a paste

For the flavoured butter, beat the butter in a bowl until light and creamy, then beat in the other ingredients, seasoning to taste with salt and pepper. Tip onto a piece of baking parchment, roll up into a sausage shape inside the paper and twist the ends. Pop into the freezer for about 45 minutes–1 hour until very firm, or into the fridge if preparing longer than an hour or so in advance.

For the mullet, carefully cut off its razor-sharp fins with scissors, then rinse well inside and out and pat dry with kitchen paper. Make a series of diagonal slashes in both sides of the fish and insert a bay leaf into each slash. Pack the cavity with the other ingredients and season inside and out. Drizzle over some of the reserved oil from the tomatoes. Wrap in foil and place in a cool bag along with the wrapped sausage of flavoured butter to transport.

Take the fish out of the cool bag while you prepare your barbecue. Brush a suitable-sized fish basket, if you have one, or the barbecue rack with some of the tomato oil. Once the barbecue is ready for cooking (see page 109), cook the fish for 6–8 minutes untouched, then turn over and cook the other side for the same length of time. Meanwhile, cut the sausage of butter into slices. Serve the barbecued fish topped with the slices of the flavoured butter to melt over.

Variation: For a dairy-free alternative to the flavoured butter, use 100ml extra virgin olive oil instead of the butter, add the other ingredients and leave to infuse. Drizzle over the barbecued fish to serve.

The Tomato Stall's oak-smoked tomatoes are far tastier than any sun-dried type of tomato I've ever come across, and they do slow-roasted toms flavoured with garlic and basil, so you could use those instead and omit the other flavourings. But if you can't be fished with making your own flavoured butter, fast forward to The Garlic Farm's Garlic Butter with Parsley, Thyme and Black Pepper or their Oak Smoked Garlic Butter.

Barbecued fruit fest

No matter how carefully you judge the lighting of your barbecue, the coals always seem to reach their optimum state after you've dished up the main event. So at the very least, this is one way of making the most of that potent heat, but even if it's starting to diminish, it will be up to the task here. Along with locally grown plums and hopefully still apricots (or use imported peaches or nectarines), late summer on the Island sees the appearance of the first of the new-season apples – the rich red Discovery with its crisp, juicy, often pink-tinged flesh that has a twang of strawberry about it. The earliest of the crop may have a little tartness, which will be mellowed with this treatment.

For chocolate options, check out the Chocolate Factory at Rectory Mansion, Brading or Chocolate Island, Godshill, or the charming Chocolate Apothecary café/shop, Ryde, or Mad Chocolate Cowes, while you will find Splendid brittle at Farmer Jack's Farm Shop, Arreton.

INGREDIENTS | SERVES 4–6

sunflower oil, for oiling

For the marinated apple slices
grated zest of 1 and juice of 2 organic (unwaxed) oranges
3 tbsp Island clear honey
½ vanilla pod, split lengthways and seeds scraped out
piece of cinnamon stick
3 locally grown Discovery or other dessert apples

For the plums
4 locally grown ripe plums, halved and stoned
about 1 heaped tbsp finely chopped crystallized ginger

For the apricots
4 ripe apricots, preferably locally grown, halved and stoned
4 squares of dark chocolate or pieces of Splendid Whole Almond Brittle, or a mixture

For the apple slices, put all the ingredients except the apples into a large resealable plastic bag, seal and massage together. Core the apples, slice into rings about 1cm thick and add to the marinade. Reseal the bag and careful turn and gently massage to coat the apple slices thoroughly in the marinade. Leave to marinate in the fridge for a couple of hours or so, then keep cool until ready to cook.

To cook, pour the marinade into an old small saucepan and stand on the barbecue rack to heat up. If you can get it bubbling away and turning a bit syrupy, all to the good, but otherwise just heat it up, then move to the edge of the barbecue. Brush the rest of the rack thoroughly with sunflower oil, lay on the apple slices and cook, turning a few times and brushing with the marinade, for about 10 minutes until softened and caramelized. Transfer to a serving dish.

For the plums and apricots, add them to the oiled barbecue rack cut side down and cook for a few minutes until nicely charred, then carefully turn and add the crystallized ginger to the plum cavities and the chocolate and/or brittle to the apricot cavities. Continue cooking for a few minutes until the chocolate has melted.

To serve, transfer the plums and apricots to the dish containing the apple slices and pour over the hot marinade.

Barbecue-baked Wight cheese with herbs and honey

This is the Island's answer to the classic French concept of baking a whole cheese in its wooden box, the traditional cheese being the seasonal Vacherin Mont d'Or but often replaced with the more common Camembert. Since it's somewhat similar in character to the latter, Isle of Wight Soft makes the ideal candidate for this oh so simple yet hedonistic treatment, the cheese able to be quickly prepared in advance ready to pop on the barbecue and leave to do its own thing. The idea of using honey and oregano particularly appealed in this summer holiday context given their Greek connotations, but you can use an extra virgin olive oil or the Island's cold pressed rapeseed oil and rosemary instead.

We enjoyed this as a finale in the way of a cheese course, but it would work equally well as a starter for a hungry horde. Alternatively, serve as a main event with crudités as well as the toast, or with wedges of Discovery apple or other dessert apples for dipping.

INGREDIENTS | SERVES 4–6

1 whole Isle of Wight Cheese Co. Soft cheese
1 small The Garlic Farm garlic clove, thinly sliced
a few thyme sprigs and/or oregano or marjoram sprigs
Island clear honey, for drizzling
sea salt and coarsely ground mixed peppercorns
The Island Bakers ciabatta bread or other freshly baked local bread, sliced, to serve

Sit the cheese on a sheet of foil. Slice the top in a crisscross pattern, cutting about halfway down into the cheese. Tuck the garlic slivers and herb sprigs into the cuts, then drizzle with honey. Season with salt and the mixed pepper. Wrap the cheese up in the foil and keep cool until ready to cook.

To cook, sit the foil parcel on the barbecue rack for about 15–20 minutes, depending on how hot the barbecue is, until the cheese has begun to ooze (use an oven glove to unwrap the foil). Add the bread slices to the barbecue rack and toast lightly on either side, then lather on the molten cheese.

{ *If you're ever stuck for a good choice of fresh herbs, why not drop into one of the Island's garden centres or nurseries and pick up a growing pot. You will undoubtedly find a wider and more interesting selection on offer and often not much more expensive than the supermarket option yet much longer lasting.* }

Cherry cola and ice cream float

More of a dessert than a soft drink, this is the essence of nostalgic endless, carefree beach days – just what the Isle of Wight is traditionally renowned for – captured in a glass. It's a great way to enjoy the local luscious late-season cherries (see page 81), but if you should miss the last of the crop, you can still buy into the local produce by sourcing the bottled juice, available from Farmer Jack's Farm Shop in Arreton. Most of all, though, this is a vehicle designed for indulging in your Island ice cream of choice, for which you are hugely spoilt. In this instance, I sampled the Isle of Wight Ice Cream Company's Whippingham White Chocolate and Raspberry, which was suitably wicked, but the matter cannot be decided without further personal, exhaustive research being undertaken. So happy scooping!

INGREDIENTS | SERVES 1

*2 tbsp Godshill Orchards Cherry Juice,
    or purée a few stoned cherries (or use
    raspberry juice or purée)*
cola, to top up
*scoop of your favourite locally produced
    ice cream*
*cherries, to decorate, if available (or use
    raspberries)*

Spoon the cherry juice or purée into a tall glass, top up with cola and stir to mix.

Add a scoop of ice cream and garnish with the cherries. Eat with a spoon and use a straw to suck up, noisily, every last bit.

Abbey ale and moonshine refresher

'Apple pie' somehow makes the moonshine here – i.e. high-proof and historically illicit hooch – sound innocuous, wholesome even, and it is indeed tempered with the Island's quality apple juice and mellowed with sweet spice to smooth out any rough edges. But rather than drowning the liquor out, I've matched it with the hefty, hoppy, malty Quarr Abbey Ale brewed by Goddards, which also has herby, spicy notes thanks to the addition of sweet gale and coriander from the Abbey's own gardens (see page 130). The result is a darkly fruity, warmly spicy yet laid-back beverage – just the thing for chilling out in a deckchair.

INGREDIENTS | SERVES 1

2 tbsp Isle of Wight Distillery Apple Pie Moonshine
1 tbsp freshly squeezed lime juice
1 tsp ground ginger
1 locally grown dessert apple slice, such as Discovery (see page 114)
chilled 330ml bottle Quarr Abbey Ale
1 long cinnamon stick, to serve

Put all the ingredients except the ale and cinnamon stick into a well-washed lidded jar, about 400ml in capacity, and seal to transport.

To serve, top up with the chilled ale, add the long cinnamon stick to the jar and give it a good stir.

A Harvest Supper

Autumn is when we traditionally celebrate and give thanks for nature's life-sustaining bounty, safely gathered in from field and orchard – one that is especially rich and diverse here on the Island. And there is no better place to count our collective Island harvest blessings than Quarr Abbey, home to a small community of Benedictine monks and where a never-ending source of spiritual nourishment is to be found in parallel with an abundance of quality produce from its grounds. It was Quarr's matchless mix of serene beauty, quiet vitality and creative purpose, combined with the Benedictine values of hospitality and sharing, that provided the perfect inspiration and ingredients for my harvest 'supper' – more like lunch for our photo shoot in order to catch this magical setting in all its seasonal glory.

Only the picturesque remnants of the ancient Cistercian Quarr Abbey, founded in 1132 and dissolved by Henry VIII in 1536, remain visible beside the coastal path from Ryde, but nearby towers the remarkable, architecturally revered modern Abbey. As you stroll down the pathway towards its exotic Moorish-influenced buildings, you may need to pinch yourself to remember that you are but a conker's throw from the Wightlink Fishbourne car ferry terminal as you lift your gaze to take in the Abbey's nigh-on two million red bricks radiating a welcoming warmth in the mellow sunshine. But spare a moment to peek through the handsome wrought-iron gate into the fruit-laden walled garden belonging to the Benedictine community's original home, the mainly Victorian Quarr Abbey House, whose buildings monk architect Dom Paul Bellot largely retained in his masterly design for the new monastery, which was completed in 1914. The walls continue their sterling service of providing protection for the many plants, shrubs and trees flourishing within and also support for espalier, fan and cordon-trained pear and apple trees as well as figs and loganberries.

Continue on down to the verdant tea garden, if you can resist the squeals of titbit anticipation from the resident pigs penned nearby, and you will find a cornucopia of fresh produce on sale in the farm shop area whatever the season. On the peerless autumn day of our visit, we were met with a picturesque pile of winter squash along with jewel-coloured carrots; a tray of freshly dug, outrageously plump mooli alongside a lucky-dip cache of mixed-variety apples. And it was hard not to miss the stash of ornamental gourds and stripy squash dazzling from their maturing quarters of the sun-drenched greenhouse, despite being viewed through a gently stirring haze of feathery asparagus foliage.

Before you head for the tea shop, be sure to steal a spy through the adjacent gate into the working heart of the kitchen garden to witness a hub of horticultural activity among the neatly tended beds, guarded by quirky scarecrows. Then it's time to sit in peace and sample the fruits of those labours – in our case in the attentive (to the food at least) company of Frieda, the most free-ranging of Quarr's sorority of rescued hens.

Fresh crab and sweetcorn chowder

A Wight twist on the traditional New England speciality, this chunky soup features the sweetest sweetcorn you ever did taste bought on the cob from Farmer Jack's Farm Shop at Arreton and cultivated by Ben Brown, matched with that Island seafood star the crab purchased from Captain Stan's in Bembridge. The latter individual was a monster (autumn and winter is the best time of year for crab) and yielded buckets of both brown and white crabmeat, which will keep for up to 3 days in the fridge (or freeze for up to 3 months). Plus the trimmings went to make a rich-tasting stock. However, you don't have to wrestle with the brown beastie yourself – it also comes pre-picked in cartons – and you can use a ready-made fresh stock, or a cube or bouillon powder. Serve with a superior crusty bread like The Island Bakers rye sourdough.

INGREDIENTS | SERVES 4

knob of butter and drizzle of olive oil
2 shallots or baby onions, finely chopped
a few thyme sprigs, leaves picked
2 locally grown leeks, sliced and well washed
3 locally grown carrots, scrubbed and sliced
3 medium locally grown waxy potatoes, such as Harlequin,
  scrubbed and cut into bite-sized chunks
1 small locally grown fennel bulb, thinly sliced, fronds reserved
  for the garnish (or use 2 celery sticks)
2 locally grown sweetcorn cobs, kernels sliced off
350ml hot Homemade Crab Stock (see below), or chicken or
  vegetable stock
250ml locally produced whole or semi-skimmed milk
grating of nutmeg
200g picked mixed brown and white crabmeat from a locally
  caught whole cooked crab (see page 91 for how to prep;
  reserve the weedy legs and trimmings for the stock) or
  ready-picked
sea salt and freshly ground black pepper

For the homemade crab stock (optional – makes about 1.5 litres)

knob of butter
weedy legs and other trimmings of locally caught whole cooked
  crab, if using
drizzle of olive oil
½ large Spanish onion, finely chopped
1 celery stick, chopped
3 small locally grown carrots or 1 large, scrubbed and chopped
1 The Garlic Farm garlic clove, crushed
a few parsley stems
1 tsp black peppercorns
1 bay leaf, preferably fresh
a few thyme sprigs, leaves picked
1.5 litres water

For the stock, if making, melt the butter in a large saucepan and cook up the crab legs and trimmings for a few minutes. Remove from the pan. Add the oil and then the onion and gently sauté for a few minutes until softened. Add the rest of the ingredients except the water with salt to taste and cook over a medium heat for about 10 minutes until the vegetables are softened. Add the water and bring to the boil. Skim off the foam, then simmer, covered, for about 30 minutes. Strain, then leave to cool. Cover and refrigerate (for up to 2 days) what you need until ready to use; the surplus can be frozen.

To make the chowder, melt the butter with the oil in a saucepan and gently sauté the shallots or baby onions with the thyme for a few minutes until softened. Add the leeks, carrots, potatoes and fennel (or celery) and sauté over a medium heat for about 8 minutes until softened. Add the corn kernels and cook for a couple of minutes. Stir in the hot stock and milk and bring to the boil. Season with the nutmeg, salt to taste and plenty of pepper. Cover and simmer for about 20 minutes or until the potatoes are tender. Add the crabmeat and heat through gently.

To serve, ladle the chowder into warmed bowls and scatter with chopped fennel fronds, if you have them.

Variation: For a dairy-free alternative, use organic coconut oil or dairy-free spread in place of the butter and soya milk instead of cows' milk.

{ *Make a luxurious crab pasta sauce in the same way as for the Lobster and Vine-ripened Tomato Tagliatelle on page 93 by reducing the surplus crab stock and then combining it with the leftover picked crabmeat.* }

Marinated spiced pheasant stew pot

Autumn sees the firing off of the shooting season and the opportunity to purchase locally reared plump pheasant (as well as small, sweet partridge). Depending on the timing of the shoots, you will be certain to bag a brace from Hamiltons Fine Foods/Hamiltons Butchers in Newport and Cowes, Island Foods in Ryde, Paul Murphy in Shanklin or P J Thorne in Freshwater, but I was lucky to nab mine closer to home and for a snip at Delysia Farm near St Helens.

Like the Abbey itself, this piquant treatment displays North African influences, being based on a traditional rabbit dish from Tenerife, so you could opt for using local wild rabbit instead (try Paul Murphy). But if sticking with the bird, as the pheasant is a sedentary slob compared with the original gym bunny, you needn't worry if you have to cut the marinating time short.

INGREDIENTS | SERVES 4–6

brace of oven-ready locally raised pheasant, prepped and
    jointed (see panel), or buy ready-prepared joints
olive oil, for browning and sautéeing
1 tbsp cumin seeds, roughly crushed
1 tbsp sweet paprika
1 tsp hot paprika
250ml homemade pheasant stock (see panel), or
    chicken stock
12 evenly sized shallots
knob of butter or dairy-free spread
large pinch of brown sugar, any kind
sea salt and freshly ground black pepper

For the marinade

250–300ml locally produced medium dry cider, such as
    Godshill Cider Company Rumpy Pumpy Scrumpy
3 tbsp Godshill Cider Company cider vinegar
1 large bay leaf, preferably fresh, torn in half
3 The Garlic Farm garlic cloves, peeled and bashed
1 tsp black peppercorns
1 cinnamon stick, broken in half

Put the pheasant portions with all the marinade ingredients
into a deep glass or ceramic bowl and squish around. Cover
and leave to marinate in the fridge for 3–8 hours or overnight.

Remove the pheasant from the marinade and pat dry,
reserving the marinade. Heat a drizzle of oil in a large,
flameproof casserole or heavy-based saucepan over a
medium-high heat and brown the pheasant joints all over, in
batches, removing to a plate. Add a little more oil to the pan
and cook up the cumin seeds briefly over a medium heat until
fragrant, then add both sorts of paprika and cook, stirring, for
a minute. Stir in the stock. Return all the pheasant and any
accumulated juices to the pan with the marinade and bring to
the boil. Season with salt and pepper, cover and either simmer
gently on the hob for an hour until tender, or transfer to an
oven preheated to 150°C/Gas Mark 2 and cook for 1–1½
hours. Taste and adjust the seasoning.

Meanwhile, pour boiling water over the shallots in a
heatproof bowl and leave for about 15 minutes, then drain.
Peel carefully, without cutting off the root base, to keep intact.
Melt the butter or spread with a little oil in a shallow saucepan
large enough to fit them in a single layer, add the shallots and
cook over a low heat, covered and turning occasionally, for
about 30 minutes until browned and completely tender but
still intact, sprinkling over the sugar for the last 10 minutes.

Serve the pheasant on the bone – or off, in which case you
can divi it up between 5 or 6 people – in its spiced gravy along
with the candied shallots.

*I dished this up with rainbow baby carrots and
slim parsnips along with chunky lengths of leeks
and courgettes, all tossed with olive oil, lemon
juice, clear honey and crushed, toasted coriander
seeds, and roasted in a hot oven for about 25
minutes, with a last-minute sprinkling of
sesame seeds.*

TO PREP AND JOINT WHOLE PHEASANT

1. Your birds may look a bit blackened where they've been
shot, but they will be full of flavour nonetheless. Check for
and pluck out any remnants of feathers, then give them a
good rinse inside and out and pat dry with kitchen paper.
If using whole, they're now ready to go.

2. To joint each bird into 2 leg and 2 breast/wing portions
(the wings are often meagre stumps), sit the bird on a
chopping board, legs pointing towards you. Using a sharp
knife, slice through the skin between the body and one
leg, bend the leg outwards and almost backwards and you
should see the ball socket where the leg joins the body, so
twist and pull away the leg at that point (you can loosen
at the socket with the tip of the knife), cutting through
the skin on the underside. Repeat to cut away the other
leg portion.

3. For the breast/wing portions, insert your knife as close
as you can to the bird's bony central ridge on one side
and slice down along its length. Turn the bird around,
head nearest to you, and continue cutting downwards,
following the contour of the wishbone. Once you've cut
a good way through, grab the portion with your hand and
twist to release, cutting through the skin on the underside.
Repeat on the bird's other side.

4. To make a stock from the carcasses, roast them up in
an oven preheated to 190°C/Gas Mark 5 for about 40
minutes, then leave to cool, break up roughly and place
in a large saucepan with a few black peppercorns and
thyme sprigs and a bay leaf. Add cold water to cover and
bring to the boil, skimming off any scum. Simmer, covered,
for at least 2 hours, several if you can, or use a pressure
cooker to save time. Strain and leave to cool, then cover
and refrigerate until the fat solidifies on the surface and
you can remove it. Keep chilled and use within 2 days, or
freeze for up to 6 months.

Winter squash, beetroot and chestnut braise

Besides Halloween pumpkins, butternut squash is often the only winter squash on offer, but visit the Quarr Abbey, Farmer Jack's, Briddlesford or Bembridge farm shops and you can take your pick of an exciting variety – I used the sweet, nutty red kabocha.

This dish offers foraging opportunities, too, not only for hard-to-miss bay leaves (see page 104) but something a little more challenging – sweet chestnuts. The best place I know to source these is in Beech Copse near Godshill, and the quest will also make for a lovely autumnal ramble. Park in the main car park opposite The Griffin pub, take the GL58 footpath that runs alongside the pub garden and follow it uphill until you reach woodland. Keep your eyes on the ground and you will soon start to spot the finely spiked outer casing of the desired nut (unlike those of the inedible horse chestnut/conker that have a smooth green casing with hard, spaced-out spines). The ripe ones will have mercifully split open to reveal a clutch of nuts, usually a decent one along with two or three pathetic ones best left for our red squirrel friends. Even the bigger ones are a lot smaller than the imported variety, but prepare them in the same way – pierce each one with the tip of a knife, cover with boiling water in a saucepan and boil for 5–10 minutes, then leave until cool enough to peel, removing the inner brown skin along with the outer shell. If you lose patience, simply slice in half and scoop the flesh out with a teaspoon.

INGREDIENTS | SERVES 4

Oil of Wight or Wild Island cold pressed rapeseed oil or olive oil, for brushing and sautéeing

1 medium locally grown winter squash, such as red kabocha, peeled, deseeded and cut into 4cm chunks (about 600g prepared weight)

2 medium locally grown beetroot, peeled and cut into 2cm chunks (reserve the greens if intact for cooking as an accompaniment in the same way as chard – see page 95)

1 large red onion, cut into wedges

250g flat field, Portobello, chestnut or Paris Brown mushrooms, wiped and thickly sliced

2 The Garlic Farm smoked garlic cloves, roughly crushed

a few rosemary sprigs, chopped, plus extra to garnish

2 bay leaves, preferably fresh, torn in half

2 allspice berries, crushed (available from Farmer Jack's Farm Shop)

1 heaped tbsp ground ginger

600ml vegetable stock

2 tsp Wild Island Bay & Juniper Balsamic Dressing and Dip or balsamic vinegar, or to taste

1 tsp molasses sugar or other brown sugar, or to taste

175g sweet chestnuts, foraged or shop-bought, cooked and peeled (see recipe intro)

sea salt and freshly ground black pepper

Heat a ridged griddle pan, griddle plate or heavy-based cast-iron frying pan over a medium-high heat until very hot. Brush lightly with oil, add the squash chunks and give them a light sprinkling of salt, then chargrill, turning occasionally, until nicely browned on all sides. Remove and set aside.

Brush the pan or plate again lightly with oil, add the beetroot and onion and chargrill for a few minutes, turning occasionally, until the onion is softened and browned. Remove and set aside with the squash.

Heat a drizzle of oil in a large sauté or frying pan and sauté the mushrooms over a medium-high heat until the moisture they release has evaporated and they are beginning to brown. Add the garlic, rosemary, bay and allspice and cook, stirring, for a couple of minutes. Stir in the griddled veg, then sprinkle over the ginger and cook, stirring, for a minute or so. Stir in the stock, balsamic, sugar and salt and pepper to taste. Bring to the boil and stir in the chestnuts, then simmer, partially covered, for about 35 minutes until the squash and beetroot are tender but still al dente. Taste and adjust the seasoning, adding more balsamic and/or sugar to taste.

Garnish with extra rosemary before serving with the lightly cooked beet tops, or local Hispi cabbage with a sprinkling of caraway seeds, or kale.

Once harvested, winter squash (except Acorn) need to be 'cured' in a warm, dry, environment for a couple of weeks to fully mature, and some are put into store for about a month for their flavour to develop and sweeten. One drawback of the maturing process is that the skins turn almost impenetrably tough, which makes preparation a challenge. Grower Ben Brown suggests dropping your squash onto a hard surface in order to split it open and make inroads. However, the skin is technically edible if you can roast it into submission.

Hedgerow syrup

You will just have to go a-foraging here for the elderberries, and you will need to make it snappy to beat the birds, but it provides added purpose to a walk over the Downs in the mature autumn sunshine. The lane up to Culver Down, for instance, has many elder trees along its verge, with the most scenic car park you could wish for on the other side of the hedgerow. And while you're at it, you can bag some wild blackberries as well (or instead), along with some sloes, or *winter-keckseys* in Old Wightish, for making your own sloe gin or vodka (see below). Remember to take some bags and look out for a branch with a forked end for hooking down those prize berries always just out of reach. Make sure you have correctly identified the elderberries, and avoid munching them as you pick, since they are mildly toxic in their raw state.

INGREDIENTS | MAKES ABOUT 180ML

about 500g heads of foraged elderberries (to yield about 275g berries) or 275g wild blackberries, or a mixture of both
150ml water
50g brown sugar, any kind (30–40g if using blackberries or a mixture)
2 tbsp clear Island honey (1–1½ tbsp if using blackberries or a mixture)
1 star anise
1 cinnamon stick, broken in half
a few black peppercorns, crushed
2 thick slices of fresh root ginger, peeled

Think therapy as you use a fork to pluck the often weeny elderberries from their stems. Give the elderberries (or blackberries) a thorough rinse, then drain and put into a saucepan with the water and bring to a simmer. Keep simmering for about 15 minutes, stirring energetically with a wooden spoon to help break the berries down. Leave until cool, then tip into a sieve over a bowl and give the berries a good pressing with the spoon to get the best out of them. Don't be put off at this stage (as I nearly was) by the earthy smell (and taste) of the berries and juice; some kind of alchemical process takes place when you add the sugar.

Return the berry purée to the rinsed-out pan, add the rest of the ingredients and bring to the boil, stirring. Let the liquid bubble away for another 15 minutes or so until it becomes slightly syrupy. Then leave to cool again before straining out the spices (keep the star anise and cinnamon for poaching the pears – see opposite). Pour into a well-washed small plastic drinks bottle or, if you want to store it for longer, a small glass screw-top bottle scalded out with boiling water from the kettle, and store in the fridge (it will keep for a couple of months at least). Leave your pan and bowl for swilling out with ginger beer for poaching the pears.

> *You could be waiting some time for a frost on the Island to split your sloes to release their juices for infusing spirit, so freeze them for 12 hours or so before half-filling a scalded-out, large glass bottle. Add a couple of tablespoons of caster sugar, top up with Wight Mermaids Gin or Rock Sea Vodka, seal and shake well. Store in a cool, dark place for at least 3 months, giving it the odd turn, before supping.*

Ginger beer poached pears

The Wight Crystal ginger beer I used is a nifty low-sugar option here, and as a bonus you can be happy in the knowledge that the profits from your purchase will be going to a worthy local community charity (see page 33). But the Godshill Cider Company also does one in a traditional resealable stoppered stone bottle as well as in a regular glass bottle. Serve with a scoop of your favourite Island ice cream such as Calbourne Classics Vanilla or Honey and Stem Ginger flavour or their frozen yogurt, or go for a dairy-free gourmet sorbet from Minghella, and finish with a drizzle of the Hedgerow Syrup.

INGREDIENTS | SERVES 4

4 locally grown firm but ripe pears
½ lemon, for squeezing
500ml bottle of Wight Crystal Traditional Style Ginger Beer or
    other locally produced ginger beer
star anise and broken cinnamon stick saved from the
    Hedgerow Syrup (see opposite)
a little clear Island honey, to taste

Peel your pears neatly, keeping the stalks intact. Excavate and remove the woody base and core with a small sharp knife, teaspoon or corer, at the same time levelling the base, if necessary, so that the fruit will sit upright for serving. While prepping, squeeze a little lemon juice over the pears to prevent them from discolouring.

> *Look out for quince, resembling a chubby, knobbly pear but with a beautiful golden yellow colour and as tough as old boots. Which means you will need a large sharp knife to cut them into quarters for peeling and removing all the woody core, squeezing with lemon juice as you go. Simmer in the spiced ginger beer for about 25 minutes, covered, then uncover and cook for another 15 minutes or until tender.*

Swill out the pan and bowl you used for the syrup with a little of the ginger beer and pour into a saucepan large enough to accommodate your whole pears (or just add a dash of the syrup). Add the rest of the ginger beer and the recycled spices, then slide the pears in gently. Bring to a brisk simmer and cook, uncovered, for 10–20 minutes, depending on the size, variety and ripeness of your pears, but err on the side of caution lest they start to fall apart. Test for doneness by inserting a cocktail stick into the base, which should meet with a slight resistance. Turn off the heat and leave to cool in the poaching liquid, when they will soften a little more (stick the lid on if they were on the firm side when tested). Carefully lift the pears out into a bowl.

Add a little honey to the poaching liquid, bring to the boil and bubble away for a few minutes to reduce slightly. Leave to cool, then pour over the pears, cover and chill before serving.

Apple and wild blackberry frangipane tarts

This is the ideal opportunity to sample a locally grown seasonal apple variety or maybe an Isle of Wight heirloom apple, such as those grown at Quarr Abbey (see overleaf), or drop into The Farm Shop, Bembridge or Briddlesford Lodge Farm shop for the chance to buy into the fine crop cultivated at St Cecilia's Abbey, a cloistered community of Benedictine nuns in Ryde. And check out the Apple Weekend at Osborne House (see page 159) where you can learn about and taste the Victorian orchard fruit varieties grown on the estate, such as Lane's Prince Albert cooking apple.

INGREDIENTS | MAKES 12

50g unsulphured dried apricots, snipped into pieces
sunflower oil, for oiling
70g ground almonds
70g golden caster sugar
a few drops of almond extract
1 large locally produced free-range egg, lightly beaten
1 locally grown dessert apple, peeled, cored and finely chopped
2 handfuls of blackberries, preferably foraged wild ones,
*   mashed with a sprinkling of caster sugar*
flaked almonds, for scattering
icing sugar, for dusting

For the almond pastry
120g plain flour or a gluten-free plain flour mix such as Doves
*   Farm with ½ tsp xanthan gum added, plus extra for dusting*
½ tsp baking powder or gluten-free baking powder
60g ground almonds
2 tsp golden caster sugar
about 5 tbsp Quarr Abbey pressed apple juice or other locally
*   produced apple juice*

Place the apricots in a Pyrex measuring jug, pour over boiling water to just cover (about 6 tbsp) and leave to soak for about 20 minutes while you make the pastry.

Sift the flour and baking powder into a bowl, add the ground almonds and sugar and mix lightly with your fingertips. Stir in enough apple juice with a table knife for the mixture to start to clump together, then use your hands to gather up and work together to form a dough. Wrap in foil and rest (in the fridge if using ordinary plain flour) while you finish making the almond cream. Meanwhile, preheat the oven to 190°C/Gas Mark 5. Lightly oil a 12-hole patty tin.

Use a stick blender to blitz the apricots and soaking water into a smooth but not too sloppy purée, adding a little more water if needed. Transfer to a bowl, add the ground almonds, caster sugar, almond extract and egg and beat together thoroughly. Fold in the apple.

Knead the pastry a little to soften, then roll out on a lightly floured work surface. Using about an 8cm round fluted cutter, cut out 12 rounds and use to line the patty tin holes. Prick the bases lightly with a fork and bake for 5–8 minutes just until the pastry is no longer raw. Remove from the oven and reduce the temperature to 180°C/Gas Mark 4. Spoon a little of the mashed blackberries into the bottom of each pastry case, top up with the almond cream and scatter lightly with flaked almonds. Bake for about 20 minutes until puffed and golden. Transfer to a wire rack to cool, then dust with icing sugar.

ISLE OF WIGHT HERITAGE APPLES

A wealth of apple varieties has been discovered and developed on the Island, both by individual enthusiasts in the late 19th and early 20th centuries and more recently by Deacon's Nursery in Godshill, *the* experts on orchard and soft fruits. Although these apples aren't generally sold commercially (though see overleaf), many of the trees are available from Deacon's for delivery nationwide.

Alverstone Apple – medium to large; green with reddy brown flush; sharp tasting; winter/early spring-maturing cooker; discovered on edge of Alverstone Marshes, 1993

Deacon's Blushing Beauty – medium; bright yellow with pink flushing; juicy and dual-purpose as cooker in autumn turning to dessert in late autumn

Ernie's Russet – large; deep-red russet; early-autumn dessert

Howgate Wonder – very large to huge, one example weighing 1.67kg, winning the 'world's largest cooking and eating apple' title in 1997; bright green with red-orange flushing/striping; sweet cooker that keeps its shape; late-keeping and great for juicing; raised by Mr George Wratten of Howgate Lane (now Road), Bembridge, 1915

Isle of Wight Pippin – small to medium; yellow flushed with orangey red and some russeting; fairly sharp tasting; spring dessert

Isle of Wight Russet – large; orange and yellow striped with often limited russeting; slightly sweet and fragrant; spring dessert, best left on tree as long as possible

King George V – medium; bright yellowy green with an orange flush and darker striping; crisp, slightly sharp and aromatic flavour; autumn dessert; raised in 1898 by Lady Thorneycroft, wife of Sir John (see below), in Bembridge

Little Pax™ – medium, bell-shaped; yellowy with a speckled and striped deep-red flush, very juicy; crisp with a rich, aromatic flavour; mid-autumn dessert but stores very well; raised by Sister Anselma Scollard of St Cecilia's Abbey, Ryde; launched by producer Frank P Matthews

Mary's Apple – medium; dual-purpose cooker/dessert; late-keeping and prolific; named after the developer

Nettlestone Pippin – medium; yellowy green flushed with deep red and some russeting; relatively sharp tasting but juicy and refreshing; early autumn dessert

Peter's Pippin – medium; gold and red with some russeting; late summer dessert

Peter's Seedling – small; red all over; early-autumn dessert and a heavy cropper

Sir John Thorneycroft – large; turns almost fully red; sweet, crisp and juicy; mid-winter dessert, first raised by Sir John and his head gardener in Bembridge, 1911

Steyne Seedling – large; flavour akin to Cox; spring dessert; raised by Sir John, 1893

Vickey's Delight – medium; pale green speckled red; best eaten straight from tree; late summer dessert

Quarr Business

Quarr (pronounced 'core') is a veritable horticultural hotspot, drawing in partners from all quarters of Island life. Under the enterprising stewardship of Estate Manager and Head Gardener Matthew Noyce, the Abbey veg plots provide not only ample naturally grown staple fresh produce for the monastery refectory, tea shop kitchens and farm shop but an impressive range of speciality crops such as mooli, yams and borlotti beans, plus chillies and Australian cucumbers in polytunnels, besides heritage varieties of beetroot, carrot, potato and tomato. All of which have increasingly caught the attention of local hotels, restaurants and caterers, as well as the wider food-loving public. The veg and fruit are also used to make a range of preserves and chutneys on sale at the farm shop, together with the Abbey's own high-welfare bacon and pork and ethical eggs from its ex-commercial hens. Quarr was awarded the National Farmers Union (NFU) Conservation Award for its exemplary land management in 2015.

The Abbey has pioneered a successful land use scheme whereby it leases plots of its land, at a peppercorn rent, to various Island community groups and charities to grow produce, the saleable proportion of which Quarr undertakes to purchase from each group and then sells on through the farm shop, or uses in the monastery and tea shop kitchens. This way, both partners benefit and a sustainable future for the project is secured.

Among the 190 or so fruit trees in the Abbey's orchards are recently established local and old varieties of apple supplied by the Island's Deacon's Nursery such as Isle of Wight Pippin, Sir John Thorneycroft, Peter's Pippin, Steyne Seedling and Nettlestone Pippin (see previous page), and some of the hand-picked crop goes to make Quarr's own hand-pressed apple juice and still and sparkling dry ciders, produced and bottled by Rosemary Vineyard.

Tapping into the long tradition of monastic brewing, which began as a way of producing a safer alternative to drinking insanitary water and to sustain the monks with 'liquid bread' when consumption of solid food was prohibited, the Abbey's Operations Manager Dean Pascall forged a working partnership with the oldest and largest Island brewer Goddards to produce Quarr Abbey Ale. The unique flavouring for this complex, top-fermented dark amber ale is delivered by Quarr's home-grown botanicals of coriander and sweet gale (or bog myrtle, *Myrica gale*), harking back to when a herb mixture known as *gruit* was used to embitter and flavour beer prior to the widespread use of hops.

Beekeeping, another traditional aspect of monastic life, is also a thriving enterprise at Quarr, where a wildflower meadow has been created to provide a pollen and nectar source for its many beehives, from which honey is harvested and available year round from the farm shop. And in yet another joint initiative, the Abbey has established a teaching apiary in conjunction with the Isle of Wight Bee Keeping Association (IWBKA) to help meet the demand for beekeeping training, both theoretical and practical, on the Island and to support the need for an increase in population of healthy local bees.

Hedgerow and orchard kir royale

This is a twist on the classic Kir Royale combo of crème de cassis and Champagne using your homemade foraged-berry syrup with sparkling cider. In the latter role, I chose Quarr Abbey's best, but there are many other Island ciders to try such as those made by the Godshill Cider Company. The Beer and Cider Festival held at the Winter Gardens in Ventnor (see page 158) is the ideal opportunity to get sampling and pick your favourite. You won't have to look far to bag the very few blackberries you need to garnish your cocktail, and even into November you should find the odd cluster of latecomers.

INGREDIENTS | SERVES 1

glug of Hedgerow Syrup (see page 126)
chilled Quarr Abbey sparkling cider or other locally produced sparkling cider, to top up
a few foraged wild blackberries, to garnish

Pour the syrup into a small Champagne flute and top up with the chilled sparkling cider.

As a final flourish, thread a few wild blackberries onto a wooden cocktail stick and lay across the top of the glass, or add to the drink.

Abbey apple and fennel cooler

Since the sun and warmth lingers late on the Island, a long, refreshing drink will be welcome, as it was for us after a glorious day spent in the grounds of Quarr Abbey. The liquoricy notes of the fennel in the chilled tea bring a spicy, aromatic edge to the seasonal apple juice, further enhanced by a hint of cloves, and I've pepped up its freshening quality with a touch of lemon zest. Combining the apple juice with tea also means you're going easier on the sugar intake.

INGREDIENTS | MAKES 1.5 LITRES

2 Pukka Three Fennel tea bags
2 strips of organic (unwaxed) lemon zest
3–4 cloves, lightly crushed
chilled 750ml bottle Quarr Abbey pressed apple juice or other locally produced apple juice
dessert apple slices, plus fennel fronds if available, to garnish

Bring a kettleful of water to the boil, pour about 750ml over the fennel tea bags, lemon zest and cloves in a large teapot and stir well. Leave to infuse until completely cool. Remove the tea bags and strain out the flavourings, then cover and chill well.

To serve, mix the fennel tea infusion with the apple juice in a glass pitcher and drop in a couple of apple slices, plus the odd feathery fennel frond if you have some.

{ *Look out for bargain buys of less-than-perfect or windfall apples on sale, or even ones for free that you may find outside Island folk's homes if there's a glut, which you could juice yourself if you have access to a juicer.* }

Christmas Fare

We have Prince Albert's vision to thank for the impressive Italianate design of Queen Victoria's summer residence and retreat Osborne House, as well as the landscaping and planting of its gardens and woodland. But the Prince Regent and the Queen together are also credited with popularizing our modern-day Christmas traditions, such as the sending of cards, the giving of substantial gifts and the decorating of a fir tree, both of them drawing on their German family customs.

What kicked off the Christmas craze as we know it was an engraving of the royal couple and their children at Windsor Castle gathered around a Yule tree bedecked with lighted candles and other decorations and with assorted toys assembled beneath, which appeared in the *Illustrated London News* (the 19th-century equivalent of *Hello!* magazine) in 1848. Throughout Prince Albert's lifetime the royal family would continue to return to Windsor from Osborne for Christmas itself, but Victoria was to withdraw to her Island sanctuary a few days after Albert's untimely death on 14 December 1861 and thereafter preferred to spend her Christmases there, where the Durbar Room would be piled high with lavish gifts for the royal household and ceremoniously distributed by the Queen on Christmas Eve.

The festive feast took place on Christmas Day at 9pm, and a menu from 1894 features roast beef and Yorkshire pud for mains, plus roast turkey with braised chestnuts and chine of pork. A supplementary side table would be groaning with cold cuts including a humungous game pie, a whole stuffed wild boar's head and a baron of beef – the entire backside of an ox, too large for any range at Osborne to accommodate and so was roasted at Windsor and shipped to the Island on the royal yacht, along with much of the other Christmas fare. And for afters? Mince pies and plum pudding, so no changes there, although the royal version of the latter was of appropriately empire proportions.

You can still enjoy a taste of the authentic Victorian Christmas experience at English Heritage's various seasonal events held at Osborne from around mid-November into December. And for the chance to feast on contemporary Christmas fare, there are all sorts of festive fairs and markets held across the Island, while hampers of Island foodie goodies are available from the farm shops and other outlets.

Our festive table was more modest in scale than the Osborne banquet but nevertheless a fitting celebration of locally produced seasonal specialities. We were warm enough, with the aid of a glass of mulled mead and a pre-prandial nibble, to linger a while in happy anticipation of the feast to come on the twinkly light-festooned patio of our neighbours' Nonsuch Cottage in Bembridge, before a light drizzle blew in off the incoming tide. Originally a humble fisherman's abode, it has been transformed into a stylish and commodious holiday home/let with a kitchen–diner amply equipped to handle a major Yuletide event. Which was to where we thankfully decamped for the gorging proper to commence.

Festive bites

Wild mushroom and thyme

Kick off the yuletide proceedings with a warm-up mini feast of mushrooms both fresh and dried. I bagged a pack (at the Red Funnel Cowes Christmas Festival – see page 159) of Ventnor Botanic Garden's finest fungi, a dried mix of oysters and shiitake grown in their underground mushroom fruiting chamber, which you can view on a visit to the garden. I've teamed the mushrooms with the wonderfully candied black garlic (see page 109), which makes sense since it was originally an Asian health food. The toasts can be prepared a couple of days in advance and kept in an airtight container.

INGREDIENTS | MAKES 12

15g Ventnor Botanic Garden Exotic Gourmet Dried Mushrooms
drizzle of olive oil
1 shallot, finely chopped
100g chestnut mushrooms, sliced
3 The Garlic Farm black garlic cloves, mashed to a paste
1 tsp chopped thyme leaves, plus extra sprigs to garnish
2½–3 tbsp Calbourne Classics Whole Milk Yogurt, or dairy-free natural yogurt with a squeeze of lemon juice to taste
sea salt and freshly ground black pepper

For the toasts
about 4 medium-thick slices of soft wholemeal bread
olive oil, for brushing

Make the toasts. Preheat the oven to 200°C/Gas Mark 6. Use the rim of a wine glass 5–6cm in diameter to cut out 12 rounds. Flatten out slightly with a rolling pin, place on a baking sheet and brush with olive oil. Bake for about 5 minutes until golden brown and crisp. Cool on a wire rack.

Put the dried mushrooms in a bowl, pour over boiling water from the kettle to cover and leave to soak for 30 minutes, weighting down with a smaller dish to keep them submerged. Strain, reserving the soaking liquid, and squeeze out the excess liquid. Slice any larger mushrooms.

Heat the oil in a frying pan and gentle sauté the shallot with a grinding of salt for 5 minutes until softened. Stir in the chestnut mushrooms and cook for a couple of minutes, then add the dried mushrooms, season to taste with salt and pepper and cook until all the liquid released by the mushrooms has evaporated. Add the garlic and thyme leaves and cook, stirring, for a minute, then moisten with a little of the mushroom soaking liquid. Remove from the heat, then stir in the yogurt and check the seasoning.

Pile onto the toasts, garnish with thyme sprigs and serve warm or at room temperature.

Celeriac and apple remoulade with lobster

Celeriac, in season from the autumn on through the winter, is another of those scary-looking ingredients, scabby and bristling with hairy roots. But crack through that craggy exterior and you will reach its subtly celery-, nutty-flavoured flesh. Remoulade is its classic (French) starring role, but it's also great boiled in small chunks along with potato and then mashed with a little butter or the Island's cold pressed rapeseed oil and seasoning, or used in soups and stews.

INGREDIENTS | MAKES 12

100g locally grown celeriac, peeled and sliced into thin matchsticks
1 small red-skinned dessert apple, cored and sliced into thin matchsticks
½ lemon, for squeezing
½ small–medium freshly cooked locally caught Island lobster, meat picked

For the dressing
3 tbsp (dairy-free) mayonnaise
2 tsp The Island Mustard Company Thyme and Tarragon Mustard or other locally produced wholegrain mustard
pinch of sugar, any kind, to taste if needed
sea salt and freshly ground black pepper

smoked paprika, to garnish
Toasts (see left), to serve

As you prep the celeriac and apple, drop the matchsticks into a bowl and squeeze over some lemon juice to prevent them turning an unappealing brown.

For the dressing, mix all the ingredients together, seasoning to taste with salt and pepper, then stir into the celeriac and apple until well combined.

Pile onto the toasts, top with the lobster meat and garnish each with a little smoked paprika.

{ *If you prefer, use about 100g Island white crabmeat instead of the lobster, and try The Garlic Farm's mellow Toasted Garlic Mayonnaise in place of the mayo, mustard and seasoning. Use a gluten-free bread for the toasts if desired or necessary.* }

Roast goose Dickensian style

Back in Queen Victoria's heyday, the exotic and pricey turkey had become the bird of choice for the Christmas feast among the well heeled, while the poor folk had to make do with goose 'eked out' by trimmings, as illustrated by Charles Dickens in *A Christmas Carol*. Nowadays, the fashion pendulum has swung back towards the trad goose. Not that the Queen would have been bothered either way, as she always preferred the roast beef of old England.

One mighty factor in goose's favour is the copious amounts of curiously lightweight fat it produces, perfect for roasting parboiled floury potatoes, sweet potatoes and parsnips to serve on the side, along with freshly harvested crisp Brussels sprouts or pretty frilly Kalettes, a cross between sprouts and kale, and colour-contrasting carrots. Locally raised goose and other festive birds and special roasts are available from Brownrigg's, or order from the local butcher, as I did from WW Woodford & Son in Bembridge.

INGREDIENTS | SERVES 6

4–5kg locally raised goose
1 whole dessert apple and 1 whole peeled onion, studded
with cloves
handful of fresh bay leaves
sea salt and freshly ground black pepper

For the celebration stuffing

3 locally produced smoked streaky bacon rashers, derinded
and diced
1 large onion, finely chopped
a few thyme sprigs, leaves picked
goose liver (if it came with the bird, optional), chopped
400g locally produced pork sausage meat
90g fresh white breadcrumbs
2 tbsp The Garlic Farm Celebration Chutney or The Borneo
Pantry Christmas Chutney
plain flour, for dusting

For the spiced apples

1 shallot, finely chopped
7 small dessert apples
1 tsp ground allspice or mixed spice
2 tsp Island clear honey

For the gravy

2 tbsp plain flour
600ml chicken stock
1–2 tbsp Quarr Abbey Spiced Apple Jelly or other locally
produced fruit jelly

Remove your goose from the fridge about an hour before cooking while you preheat the oven to 190°C/Gas Mark 5. Remove any giblets plus any large wads of fat from inside the bird. Tuck the apple, onion and bay into the cavity. Sit the bird on a grill/oven rack set over a foal-lined roasting tray (or on a couple of extra peeled onions). Prick down either side with a skewer a few times to help release the fat, then season well.

Roast the goose for about 45 minutes, then carefully pour or spoon off the fat into a heatproof bowl. Continue roasting for about another 1¼ hours, draining off the fat again about halfway through, by which time the skin should be well browned and crisp. Test for doneness by piercing the thickest part of the thigh with a skewer, and if the juices run clear, it's done; if not, return to the oven for 15 minutes. Park the bird on a warmed platter and leave to rest in a warm place for 20 minutes before carving.

Make the stuffing while the bird is roasting. Add the bacon to a hot frying pan and fry over a medium-high heat until the fat has rendered and the bacon has lightly browned. Lift out onto

kitchen paper to drain. Gently sauté the onion in the bacon fat for about 5 minutes until softened, adding the thyme along the way, then stir in the goose liver if you have it or fancy it, season with a little salt and plenty of pepper and cook for a few more minutes until no longer pink. Add to the bacon and leave to cool, then mix with the remaining stuffing ingredients, using your hands to combine thoroughly. Form into 12 balls and refrigerate until ready to cook. Heat a good spoonful of the goose fat in a large frying pan, dust the stuffing balls lightly with flour and cook gently, turning frequently, for about 25 minutes until nicely browned and cooked through.

For the apples, also while the bird is roasting, heat a little of the goose fat in a small frying pan and gently sauté the shallot with a grinding of salt for about 5 minutes until soft. Meanwhile, core 6 of the apples and score around their bellies. Peel, core and finely chop the 7th apple, then stir into the shallot with the spice. Cook briefly, then stir in the honey. Heat a little more goose fat in a shallow saucepan large enough to fit the apples in a single layer, add the apples and spoon the shallot mixture into the centres. Cover and cook over a low heat for about 20 minutes until tender – test with a cocktail stick after 15 minutes, and if almost done, turn off the heat and leave covered.

Make the gravy while the goose rests. Pour off most of the fat from the roasting tray, sprinkle in the flour and work into the pan juices over a medium heat until smooth. Gradually stir in the stock and bring to the boil, stirring constantly. Bubble away until thickened, then stir in the jelly until melted. Taste and season accordingly. Serve with the carved turkey, spiced apples and stuffing balls.

Variations: For a gluten-free version, use gluten-free sausage meat, breadcrumbs and flour for the stuffing, and cornflour for the gravy. If serving the apples with the flan overleaf, replace the butter with Oil of Wight or Wild Island cold pressed rapeseed oil for sautéeing.

Caramelized shallot, carrot and chestnut flan

This vegan festive centrepiece is suitably laden with seasonal flavours of chestnut, citrus and sage, with lots of smoky, complex sweetness delivered by the caramelized shallots, balsamic and black garlic. The pastry can be a bit crumbly due to the coconut oil, but it delivers the requisite rich, short result. And who cares if a bit of the crust comes away in your hand while serving – cook's perk I say.

Serve wedges of the flan with the Spiced Apples (see previous page), along with parboiled heirloom potatoes roasted in Oil of Wight or Wild Island cold pressed rapeseed oil with chopped fresh rosemary leaves, and lightly cooked locally grown cavolo nero, Brussels sprout tops or mustard leaf, or fancy varieties of broccoli such as Cape or purple and white sprouting broccoli.

INGREDIENTS | SERVES 6 WITH ALL THE TRIMMINGS

12 evenly sized round shallots
Oil of Wight or Wild Island cold pressed rapeseed oil or
    olive oil, for sautéeing and oiling
1 tsp brown sugar, any kind
2 tbsp Wild Island Bay & Juniper Balsamic Dressing and Dip or
    balsamic vinegar
150g locally grown baby carrots, scrubbed and halved
    lengthways
salt
1 medium red onion, finely chopped
a few sage leaves, torn, plus extra for scattering
250g chestnut mushrooms, sliced
4 The Garlic Farm black garlic cloves, mashed to a paste
225g cooked peeled chestnuts (see page 124),
    roughly crumbled
grated zest of 1 organic (unwaxed) clementine or tangerine
about 200ml vegetable stock, plus 600ml for the gravy
½ tsp dried thyme
2 tsp Erica's Homemade Onion Marmalade or The Borneo
    Pantry Caramelized Onion Marmalade
sea salt and freshly ground black pepper

For the pastry
220g plain flour, plus extra for dusting
¼ tsp salt
¾ tsp dried thyme
55g chilled (i.e. solid) organic coconut oil
55g chilled dairy-free spread, diced
about 4–5 tbsp ice-cold water

Start the filling. Pour boiling water over the shallots in a heatproof bowl and leave for about 15 minutes, then drain. Peel carefully, without cutting off the root base, to keep intact, then cut in half horizontally. Heat a glug of oil in a lidded heavy-based sauté or frying pan large enough to fit the shallot halves in a single layer, add them cut side down, cover and cook gently for about 25 minutes until tender throughout and lightly browned on the underside. Sprinkle over the sugar, then carefully turn the shallot halves over, drizzle over 1 tbsp of the balsamic and cook for another 5 minutes, uncovered, until caramelized. Carefully remove the shallots from the pan and set aside. You can leave the pan unwashed ready to finish cooking the filling later.

Meanwhile, for the pastry, sift the flour into a bowl with the salt, then stir in the thyme. Scrape out the solid coconut oil from the jar onto the scales, whereupon it should break up into small pieces. Rub this and the spread into the flour lightly with your fingertips until crumbs form. Stir in just enough iced water to bring the mixture together into a dough. Wrap in foil and rest in the fridge for 15 minutes.

Preheat the oven to 190°C/Gas Mark 5 and put in a baking sheet to heat up. Lightly oil a 23cm flan dish. Roll out the pastry on a lightly floured surface and use to line the dish. Line the pastry case with the pastry foil wrapping and fill with dried rice or pasta. Bake on the hot baking sheet for 15 minutes. Remove the foil and its contents and bake for another 5 minutes or until the pastry base is just cooked. Remove the dish, but leave the baking sheet in the oven and turn the heat up to 200°C/Gas Mark 6.

While the pastry is baking, cook the carrots, reserving 2 halves for the gravy, in a saucepan of lightly salted boiling water for about 8–10 minutes, depending on size, until just al dente, then drain. At the same time, gently sauté the red onion, saving 1 heaped tbsp for the gravy, with the torn sage in a little oil in the shallot pan for about 5 minutes until softened. Add the mushrooms, saving a few slices for the gravy, with the black garlic and cook for a few minutes until their liquid has mostly evaporated, then mix in the chestnuts, saving a small handful for the gravy. Add most of the zest and the 200ml stock and simmer for 5 minutes. Season to taste.

When gearing up to serve, turn the mushroom mixture into the pastry case, adding a bit more stock if necessary to make sure it's juicy. Arrange the shallots cut side up (save any broken-up ones for the gravy) and carrots cut side down on top, scatter with a few extra sage leaves and the remaining zest and brush with the remaining balsamic. Bake on the baking sheet for about 15 minutes until piping hot and the pastry and veg are nicely browned.

Meanwhile, make the gravy. Gently sauté the reserved red onion and carrot along with any caramelized shallot casualties, all finely chopped, with the thyme and a grinding of salt in a little oil in a saucepan for about 8 minutes. Add the reserved mushrooms, finely chopped, and sauté for a few minutes. Mash the reserved chestnuts and stir in, then add the 600ml stock with the onion marmalade and gently simmer until ready to serve with the flan, cut into wedges.

Variation: For a gluten-free version, use a gluten-free plain flour mix such as Doves Farm for the pastry and mix in 1 tsp xanthan gum. The dough will be pretty fragile, so roll out and transfer in pieces, then patch together in the dish.

{ *You can use ready-prepped chestnuts in pouches here to save time and effort, although I much prefer to cook up some fresh ones, available from the Island farm shops. Any leftover cooked chestnuts will freeze well for a few months.* }

Chocolate and ginger trifle

If you're not a fan of ginger, you are going to be in trouble here. Having said that, you could always use an alternative-flavoured cookie and simply skip the stem ginger. However, it does contribute a warming spicy festive flavour and pairs famously well with dark chocolate as well as prunes and dates. The dairy-free version of the topping, as pictured, produces more of an airy foam than a whipped cream effect, which makes a welcome light contrast to the dense body of the trifle.

Godshill Cider Company produces a range of country wines in miniature bottles, so you could sample other seasonal favourites such as cranberry or sloe, or buy an assorted gift pack. And should you be a total ginger nutcase like me, serve the pud with a glass of Adgestone Vineyard's ginger wine made from their home-grown fresh ginger.

INGREDIENTS | SERVES 4–6

150g packet Isle of Wight Biscuit Company Ginger-flavoured Farmhouse Cookies (dairy free) or Ginger Butter Crunch
50ml bottle Godshill Cider Company Damson Wine or other locally produced country wine
2 x 250ml cartons soya single cream, or 250ml dairy single cream plus 250ml locally produced whipping cream for the topping
125ml locally produced semi-skimmed cows' milk or soya or other plant-based milk
4 large locally produced free-range egg yolks
50g golden caster sugar
1 tsp syrup from the stem ginger jar, plus extra to flavour the topping
30g plain flour
100g bar (dairy-free) dark chocolate (about 70% cocoa solids), finely chopped, plus extra, grated, to decorate
4.5g sachet egg white powder, for those potentially vulnerable to raw egg, or 1 large locally produced free-range egg white (for the topping if using soya cream)

For the fruit and spice mix
120g pitted prunes, halved
80g pitted dried dates, quartered
grated zest of 2 and juice of 4 organic (unwaxed) clementines or tangerines, plus extra grated zest to decorate
1 stem ginger ball, finely chopped, plus (optional) extra to decorate
piece of cinnamon stick
¼ tsp ground cloves

Put the fruit and spice mix ingredients into a saucepan and simmer, covered, for 10 minutes, then leave to cool.

Meanwhile, place the cookies in the base of a largish handsome bowl to form a single layer, sprinkle over the booze and leave to soak.

Make the chocolate custard. Put 1 carton soya cream or the dairy single cream with the cows' or plant-based milk in a saucepan. Fish out the cinnamon stick from the fruit and spice mix and add it to the pan. Heat to just below boiling point, while you whisk the egg yolks, sugar, ginger syrup and flour together with a balloon whisk in a bowl until smooth. Strain (to remove the cinnamon) the hot cream mixture onto the egg mixture, whisking constantly. Return to the pan and add the chopped chocolate. Cook over a medium-low heat, continuing to stir steadily, until the custard thickens nicely. This could take a good 20 minutes, so stick on some carols and enjoy a festive sing-song, but do resist getting impatient and whacking the heat up, as you will end up with choccy scrambled eggs. However, should the custard fail to start thickening up after 10 minutes or so, tweak the heat up a notch. Pour into a bowl, cover the surface with clingfilm and leave to cool completely.

Spoon your fruit mix over the soaked cookies and top with the chocolate custard. Cover and chill in the fridge for at least a couple of hours or until ready to serve.

For the dairy-free topping, either reconstitute the egg white powder according to the sachet instructions, then whisk in a bowl until stiff, or simply whisk the fresh egg white until stiff. Then gently fold the remaining carton of soya cream, flavoured with a little ginger syrup, into the egg white and spoon over the trifle. Alternatively, top the trifle with the softly whipped dairy whipping cream flavoured with the ginger syrup. Decorate with grated chocolate and zest, plus extra stem ginger shards if you like.

Variations: For a booze-free alternative, soak the cookies in 50ml freshly squeezed clementine or tangerine juice, or local apple juice. For a gluten-free version, use gluten-free cookies and chocolate, and cornflour in place of plain flour. For the topping, instead of the egg white powder and soya cream, try whipped Soyatoo Soya or Coconut Topping Cream.

Wight Xmas ale cake

This can hardly be described as virtuous – what cake can be given its high-sugar nature – but as Christmas cakes go, it is definitely on the lighter side with no added fat, which also makes it easy on effort and cake-making kit. It is best, though, if the dried fruit and spices are allowed to steep in the ale overnight, but even that doesn't actually involve any extra work. And for the decoration, the marzipan and icing of tradition are forsaken for a country-style glazed fruit and nut topping, which also involves considerably less hassle. For a truly quick and inexpensive cake-decorating fix, buy a 60g pack of Raisins, Nuts and Cherries from a Southern Co-operative store, then artfully arrange and glaze as instructed.

It seemed only fitting to use one of the Island's special festive ales for the soaking, namely Santa's Ale from Yates' Brewery, but there are plenty of hefty ale options to choose from – see the panel opposite.

INGREDIENTS | MAKES I MEDIUM CAKE (SERVES 8–10)

a few cloves
piece of cinnamon stick
350ml Yates' Brewery Santa's Ale or other Island winter ale (see panel)
pared zest of 1 organic (unwaxed) clementine or tangerine and a little freshly squeezed juice if needed
125g mixed dried fruit
100g dried figs, hard stalks removed, snipped into small pieces with kitchen scissors
60g dark muscovado or soft dark brown sugar
2 tbsp The Island Mustard Company Marmalade with Ginger or other locally produced marmalade, plus extra for glazing
grated zest of 1 organic (unwaxed) lemon
sunflower oil, for oiling
2 large locally produced free-range eggs, beaten
80g walnut halves or whole blanched almonds, toasted (see page 57) and chopped, plus extra whole nuts for decorating
140g Calbourne Water Mill Fine Wholemeal Flour or chestnut flour
150g white self-raising flour
1 tbsp ground mixed spice
strips cut from whole candied citrus peel and natural glacé cherries, for decorating

Heat the whole spices in a heavy-based saucepan over a medium heat until they smell nicely aromatic. Add the ale and pared clementine or tangerine zest and stir well. Heat to a gentle simmer and simmer for about 15 minutes. Turn off the heat and leave to cool for a few minutes.

Put all the dried fruit, the sugar, marmalade and grated lemon zest in a bowl. Strain the cooled ale mixture to remove the pared zest and whole spices into a measuring jug and make up to 300ml with clementine or tangerine juice if necessary. Pour onto the dried fruit mix and stir well. Cover the bowl with clingfilm and leave to soak at room temperature overnight or for however long you have to spare.

Preheat the oven to 180°C/Gas Mark 4. Lightly oil and then line the side and base of an 18cm round cake tin with baking parchment. Beat the eggs into the soaked fruit mixture and stir in the chopped nuts. Sift the flours and ground spice together, then fold into the mixture. Dollop the mixture into the lined tin and level the surface. Bake for about 1 hour 5–15 minutes until a skewer inserted into the centre comes out clean, but check after 45 minutes and cover the top loosely with baking parchment to prevent overbrowning. Leave to cool completely in the tin on a wire rack, then turn out and remove the lining paper.

Heat a little extra marmalade in a small saucepan with a splash of cold water. Paint over the top of the cake, then arrange extra nuts and the candied peel and glacé cherries on top. Brush with more of the marmalade mixture to glaze and leave to cool. The cake will keep, wrapped in foil in an airtight container in a cool place, for up to 4 days.

Variation: For an alcohol- and gluten-free version, replace the ale with a fruity tea infusion, using a Teapigs Super Fruit tea bag for instance, and use 140g chestnut flour or gluten-free buckwheat flour and 150g white gluten-free self-raising flour mix such as Doves Farm.

WIGHT WINTER ALES

The beers below are those available in bottles, with the exception of Mocha Stout; more are available in cask, such as Goddards' Winter Warmer (5.2% ABV), a rich, fruity, malty ruby black beer.

Dark Side of the Wight 5.0% ABV– a dark ruby ale with malty milk chocolate in the nose leading to plenty of orange fruit and a bitter, roasted, perfumed finish (Yates)
Duck's Folly 5.2% ABV – a dark amber, traditionally brewed strong English ale hopped with Goldings and Fuggles hops to give a spicy, full-bodied aroma, with a complex sweetness and a hoppy, dry finish (Goddards)
Mocha Stout 4.2% ABV – a smooth stout with dark chocolate notes and a coffee aroma, brewed with Island Roasted coffee beans; available in a 5-litre mini cask (Goddards)
Santa's Ale 4.9% ABV – a deep amber ale brewed with festive ingredients such as cinnamon and clove spices and zesty fruits, generously hopped with Cascade and Columbus hops to give a spicy and slightly toasted finish; used by master butcher Paul Murphy of Shanklin to flavour his special-edition Xmas sausages (Yates)
Wight Christmas 4.4% ABV – a red to amber ale brewed using speciality Munich and malted oats with a touch of British Goldings and Bramling Cross hops, plus chocolate malt; gold medal winner in the flavoured beer category of the World Beer Awards 2015 (Island Brewery)
Yule Be Sorry 7.6% ABV – a richer, dark-coloured ale prepared using pale and roasted malts with terrified wheat; three hops are used to give a rich, full-bodied result (Yates)

The Wight cheeseboard and sweetmeats

Round off your Christmas feast the traditional way but on an all-Wight theme with a selection of the Island's handmade local cheeses. I served mine with the Island Biscuit Company's Celery Seed Ryes (available in other flavours), along with The Taverners Pub Damson Paste (see opposite for other preserve options) and locally produced butter (see page 112).

Isle of Wight Cheese Co. Blue – *handmade naturally rinded, blue-veined, 3–5-week-aged pasteurized cheese; multi-award winning, including Best English Cheese, World Cheese Awards*

Isle of Wight Cheese Co. Soft – *a soft white, surface mould, 2–4-week-aged pasteurized cheese, somewhere between a Brie and Camembert type*

Isle of Wight Cheese Co. Gallybagger Mature – *available in December only, unpasteurized Cheddar type made, pressed into Dutch Gouda moulds and aged for 12 months on Lawson Cypress wooden shelves (standard Gallybagger is aged for 4–5 months and made all year round in small quantities)*

The Green Barn Soft Goats' Cheese with Mixed Herbs – *mild and creamy, made using fresh pasteurized milk from the farm's dairy goat herd using vegetarian rennet (also Plain; with Chives; with Garlic)*

Applewood smoked cheese – *a locally made hard cheese smoked at Delysia Farm shop near St Helens.*

{ *'Tis not the season for Isle of Wight Cheese Co. Old Gaffer Blue, but do catch it when you can – a special-edition unpasteurized soft blue cheese aged for a couple of weeks longer than the Blue, available in late May only for the biennial Yarmouth Old Gaffer's Festival held in June.* }

If you're in the market (and who wouldn't be) for a gourmet sweet treat to serve with an after-dinner cup of freshly brewed locally craft-roasted coffee (see page 97) or perhaps tea specially blended for the Island's chalky water (see page 21), make your choice from the following delicacies, if you can, available from the farm shops and other retail outlets, farmers' markets and Christmas fairs.

The Green Barn *Goats' Milk Fudge special festive Mixed Spice flavour (but also Chocolate, Coffee, Vanilla, Sea Salt and Cinnamon for Easter) or the award-winning* **Mrs Bucketts** *Homemade Tablet fudge in a variety of flavours including Cointreau and Rum and Raisin; or* **Chocolate Mad Fudge** *from the Chocolate Mad Cowes shop in Cowes or look out for* **Isle of Fudge** *homemade clotted cream fudge at festive fairs*

Rachel's Confectionery *Winter Toffee or* **Splendid** *brittle*

Chocolate Apothecary *handmade salted peanut chocolate slab and chocolate-dipped candied orange peel, available from their Ryde café/shop*

Ocean Creed *(formerly the Seaforth Chocolate Co.) collection of eco-friendly dark and milk chocolate developed by Abraham Seaforth, relaunched and rebranded in 2017, made using the finest organic cocoa beans harvested in the Dominican Republic and transported across the Atlantic on the emission-free brigantine sailing ship Tres Hombres to be roasted, refined and conched in Switzerland and then moulded in Belgium before release in Cowes*

Pick of the Preserves

The **PINK'S** family business of making preserves has its origins way back in the late 1880s, and now Fiona Pink has picked up the spoon and stirred up a storming range of award-winning contemporary products like the fiery yet fragrant Green or Red Chilli Jelly, or twists on tradition such as the aromatic tomato-based Empire Chutney, plus flavour-packed pestos.

The Fruit Bowl makes a wide variety of Wight Marque-accredited luscious fruit jams (used to fill The Island Bakers' legendary doughnuts), such as Gooseberry and Elderflower and Loganberry and Cherry, with 90% of the fruit coming from its own three-acre smallholding in Newchurch. While time-honoured methods are used for the jam-making, cutting-edge green technology including solar voltaic panels for electricity and solar thermal panels for hot water, plus rainwater harvesting for irrigation, ensures that the 'jam factory' is self-sufficient in energy.

'Nothing grizzly added' growls the bear from the **Bear Preserves** label, so fear not the bite of artificial additives in these jars of chutneys, pickles, relishes, jams and jellies. Local produce is, however, high on the list of ingredients including seasonal specials such as Island asparagus for a chutney, Godshill Orchards' apricots flavoured with their home-grown herb for Apricot and Lavender Jam, and Bonchurch figs picked nearby for Autumn Spiced Fig Relish, plus strawberries from the family farm in Titchfield, Hampshire for Harris Strawberry Jam. Check out their handy picnic (also perfect for a festive breakfast or gift) pack of four small jars.

Erica's Homemade collection of preserves boasts over 52 varieties, handmade by the lady herself in small batches using fresh produce from her own Horringford Gardens in the Arreton Valley, together with other local fresh produce.

Among the many interesting chutneys is Apple Ginger Beer and Spiced Plum, while the conserves include the 3Rs – a summery melange of rhubarb, redcurrant and raspberry – as well as the alternative-coloured Greengage. The marmalade range features Tawny, inspired by an accidentally burnt batch of marmalade, which tasted so good that burnt sugar is now purposefully added.

The Borneo Pantry produces a range of homemade chutneys and relishes, featuring some new takes on old favourites like Proper Piccalilli and Spicy Sweetcorn Relish, and trendsetters such as Pickled Watermelon or Caramelized Onion and Cranberry Marmalade. You can buy as a mini selection box of nine flavours or three in a cute jute gift bag.

If creamy fruit curds are your particular weakness, then a trip to **Isle of Wight Lavender** at Staplehurst Grange on the way to Newport will reward you with a lovely selection including orange, banana and ginger, along with edible and cosmetic lavender goodies aplenty.

Wight toast

The special ingredient here is the Spiced Pear Vodka Liqueur, one of a range of flavoured vodka liqueurs and vodkas produced by the Tipsy Wight family business using entirely locally grown ingredients for steeping, or seasonally foraged ones in the case of their Hedgerow, Elderflower, Sloe and Wild Plum Vodka Liqueurs and their Wild Garlic Vodka. What's more, they come in quirky squiffy-shaped bottles, with glasses to match, making ideal Xmas gifts.

You might think ready-made almond milk would save you the trouble here, but first, despite the name, it hardly contains any almonds (2% if you're lucky), and second, the toasting step is key to hitting that extra festive note. If you're not planning on downing this in one or at least swiftly, it's a good idea to serve it with a swizzle stick (cinnamon sticks are the obvious seasonal choice), as the almond milk tends to separate if left to stand, though this is a pretty unlikely scenario.

INGREDIENTS | SERVES 4

70g raw almonds in their skins
250ml chilled Wight Crystal Still Spring Water
20cl bottle Tipsy Wight Spiced Pear Vodka Liqueur
120ml freshly squeezed clementine or tangerine juice
ice cubes
freshly grated nutmeg and/or spiral of clementine or tangerine
*   peel, to garnish*

For the toasted almond milk, preheat the oven to 180°C/ Gas Mark 4. Spread the almonds out on a baking sheet and toast in the oven for about 15 minutes. Leave to cool, then cover with cold water to a depth of about 2.5cm in a bowl. Cover the bowl with clingfilm and leave to soak in the fridge overnight and then some – about 12 hours. Strain and rinse, then whizz the almonds in a blender or food processor with the water until smooth. Strain through a nut milk bag or fine-mesh sieve lined with muslin (or improvise with a large clean cotton hanky), gathering the bag or cloth around the solids and squeezing out all the liquid (save the almond sludge to make a korma curry sauce, or add to a smoothie or a biscuit dough) into a measuring jug – you will need 200ml in total for the 4 cocktails.

To serve, either briefly stir the toasted almond milk with the other ingredients and some ice cubes in a mixing glass, or shake in a cocktail shaker with ice, then strain over ice in cocktail glasses. Garnish with grated nutmeg and/or a citrus peel spiral and serve straight away.

{ *If you can't be bothered to make the toasted almond milk or don't have the necessary kit, substitute 200ml locally produced whipping cream and garnish instead with finely grated toasted blanched almonds.* }

Island mulled mead

Mead – yes, it tastes as good as it sounds, being produced by fermenting honey with water. And from the Godshill Cider Company, it comes with a bag of spices for mulling, to make, as labelled, 'a perfect fireside drink'. But that didn't stop me tickling it up with some additional seasonal ingredients for a truly festive cup of cheer.

INGREDIENTS | SERVES 4

37.5cl bottle Godshill Cider Company Christmas Mead
  (with whole spices) or use any other mead and add the spices
  specified for the alcohol-free spiced hot punch right
250ml Adgestone Vineyard or Rosemary Vineyard dry white wine
250ml locally produced pressed apple juice such as
  Quarr Abbey or Rosemary Vineyard
125ml freshly squeezed orange juice, plus 1 organic
  (unwaxed) orange studded with cloves and cut into
  slices to garnish
juice of ½ lemon
1 tbsp Island clear honey, or to taste
star anise and/or whole pieces of cinnamon stick,
  to garnish (optional)

Put all the ingredients (except the garnish items) in a saucepan and gently heat, stirring, for a few minutes until hot.

Pour into a punch bowl, add the orange slices, along with extra whole spices if you like, to garnish, then ladle into heatproof glasses while still hot.

For an alcohol-free spiced hot punch, use 500ml Wight Crystal Traditional Style Ginger Beer and 350ml locally produced pressed apple juice along with the orange juice, lemon juice and honey as above, and adding ½ cinnamon stick, broken in half, a few cloves, bruised with a pestle and mortar or the base of a heavy pan, and 2 star anise. Heat as above, then add dessert apple and organic (unwaxed) orange slices to garnish.

Pick of the Season

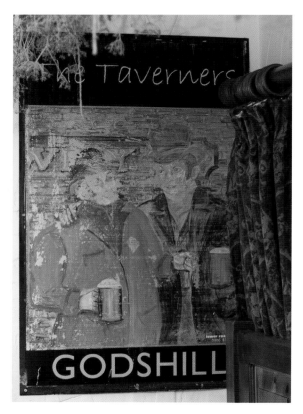

The seasonal produce charts that adorn the walls of The Taverners in the heart of picture-perfect Godshill village, reproduced here by kind permission of proprietors Lisa and Roger Serjent, reflect the ethos behind this Michelin-awarded pub and eating house (with adjoining produce and kitchen shop), namely the tireless pursuit of ultimate freshness and quality. The Taverners team source their produce according to what is available on the day locally, whether harvested, caught, foraged or shot. Veg patches in the pub garden yield home-grown specialities such as artichokes, courgettes, beans and herbs under the expert guidance of Living Larder's Will Steward (see page 17), while their own fruit trees and those in a small orchard they have established nearby are there for the raiding by the chefs. So follow The Taverners lead and go seasonal…

Key ● = at its best   ● = very good

Vegetables

	DEC	JAN	FEB	MAR	APR	MAY	JUN	JUL	AUG	SEP	OCT	NOV
ASPARAGUS						●	●					
BEANS							●	●	●	●		
BEETROOT	●	●	●	●	●	●				●	●	●
BROCCOLI			●	●	●				●	●		
BRUSSELS SPROUTS	●	●	●									●
BUTTERNUT SQUASH												●
CABBAGES	●	●	●							●	●	●
CARROTS	●	●	●							●	●	●
CAULIFLOWER	●	●	●						●	●	●	●
CELERIAC	●	●	●	●								
CHICORY	●	●	●	●	●							●
COURGETTES								●	●	●	●	
ELDERFLOWERS						●						
FENNEL	●	●	●	●						●	●	●
GLOBE ARTICHOKES					●	●	●	●				
HORSERADISH							●	●	●			
JERUSALEM ARTICHOKES		●	●									
KALE	●										●	●
LEEKS	●	●	●	●					●	●	●	●
LETTUCE						●	●	●	●	●		
NETTLES				●	●							
PARSNIPS	●	●	●								●	●
PEAS							●	●				
POTATOES, JERSEY ROYAL					●							
POTATOES, RATTE						●	●					
PUMPKINS	●									●	●	●
SALSIFY	●	●	●									
SAMPHIRE							●	●	●			
SORREL												
SPINACH	●	●	●						●	●	●	
SPRING GREENS				●	●	●						
SQUASH, SUMMER									●			
SWEDE	●	●	●	●	●					●	●	●
SWEETCORN									●	●		
SWISS CHARD									●			
TOMATOES								●	●	●	●	
TRUFFLES, SUMMER									●	●		
TURNIPS	●	●	●	●						●	●	●
WATERCRESS							●	●	●	●	●	●
WILD GARLIC				●	●							
WILD MUSHROOMS											●	●

Game

	DEC	JAN	FEB	MAR	APR	MAY	JUN	JUL	AUG	SEP	OCT	NOV
GROUSE	•								•	•	•	•
HARE	•	•	•	•						•	•	•
PARTRIDGE	•	•								•	•	•
PHEASANT	•	•									•	•
PIGEON				•	•	•	•	•				
RABBIT										•	•	•
RED HIND (VENISON)	•	•	•									
RED STAG (VENISON)								•	•			
ROE BUCK (VENISON)										•		
ROE DOE (VENISON)	•	•			•							
SNIPE	•	•							•	•	•	•
WILD BOAR	•	•	•							•	•	•
WILD DUCK	•	•	•	•						•	•	•
WOODCOCK	•										•	•

Fish and Shellfish

	DEC	JAN	FEB	MAR	APR	MAY	JUN	JUL	AUG	SEP	OCT	NOV
ANCHOVIES	•	•	•				•	•	•	•	•	•
BLACK SEA BREAM							•	•	•	•		
BRILL					•	•	•	•				
CLAMS	•	•	•	•							•	•
CUTTLEFISH							•	•	•	•	•	•
DAB					•	•	•	•				
DOVER SOLE	•	•	•	•	•	•					•	•
FLOUNDER				•	•	•	•	•	•	•	•	•
GREY MULLET				•	•	•	•	•	•	•	•	•
GURNARD				•	•	•	•					
HAKE							•	•	•			
HALIBUT					•	•						
HERRING	•								•	•	•	•
JOHN DORY								•	•	•		
LOBSTER					•	•	•	•	•	•	•	•
MACKEREL				•	•	•	•	•	•			
MONKFISH				•	•	•	•	•				
MUSSELS	•	•	•	•	•	•				•	•	•
OYSTERS, NATIVE	•	•	•	•	•					•	•	•
RAZOR CLAMS				•	•							
RED MULLET							•	•	•	•		
RED SEA BREAM	•	•	•									
SALMON, WILD				•	•	•						
SARDINES							•	•	•			
SCALLOPS	•	•	•								•	•
SEA BASS				•					•	•	•	•
SEA URCHIN	•	•	•	•							•	•
TURBOT					•	•	•	•	•	•	•	•
WHELKS										•	•	•
WHITEBAIT	•	•	•	•	•	•						
WHITING							•	•	•		•	•
WINKLES				•	•					•	•	•

Fruit and Nuts

	DEC	JAN	FEB	MAR	APR	MAY	JUN	JUL	AUG	SEP	OCT	NOV
APPLES, BRAEBURN											•	•
APPLES, COX'S	•	•	•	•							•	•
APPLES, CRAB										•		
APPLES, ROYAL GALA									•	•	•	
APRICOTS							•	•	•	•		
BLACKBERRIES								•	•	•	•	•
BLUEBERRIES								•	•	•	•	
CHERRIES							•	•	•			
CRANBERRIES		•	•									
DAMSONS										•	•	•
ELDERBERRIES										•	•	
FIGS, BLACK									•	•	•	
GOOSEBERRIES							•	•				
GREENGAGES									•			
MELONS							•	•	•	•	•	
NECTARINES							•	•	•			
PEACHES							•	•	•			
PEARS, CONFERENCE	•	•	•	•								•
PEARS, WILLIAMS				•	•							
PLUMS, RED									•	•	•	
QUINCE											•	•
RASPBERRIES								•	•	•	•	
REDCURRANTS							•	•				
RHUBARB		•	•	•							•	•
SLOES											•	•
STRAWBERRIES						•	•	•	•	•		
WILD STRAWBERRIES								•				
CHESTNUTS											•	•
COBNUTS										•	•	
HAZELNUTS		•										
WALNUTS												•

Directory of Island Retailers, Products and Producers

FARM AND PRODUCE SHOPS

Adgestone Vineyard shop (and Cabin Café) (page 156) Besides selling its own range of table wines, country wines and liqueurs, plus its Arson Fire chilli-flavoured preserves, dipping sauce and liqueur, the shop stocks other locally produced preserves and pestos, Isle of Wight Cheese, honey and chocolates.

Ale House Family Gift Shop, 24a Holyrood Street, Newport PO30 5AZ 01983 559356; www.alehousefamily.co.uk/shop/
A mini off-licence and gift shop, alongside the Island's smallest pub the Newport Ale House, selling a wide range of local products including ales from all three Island breweries, Goddards, Island Brewery and Yates', Isle of Wight Distillery spirits, Tipsy Wight range of flavoured vodkas and vodka liqueurs, Adgestone Vineyard wines and Rosemary Vineyard wines, cider and apple juice, The Garlic Farm and Wild Island bottled items, The Fruit Bowl jams, Island Roasted coffee, Calbourne Water Mill porridge oats in a variety of flavours and Isle of Wight Biscuit Company biscuits, plus a range of their own Ale House-branded preserves, condiments and gifts. Products also available online.

Barrow Boys, 154–155 High Street, Ryde PO33 2HT 01983 566636; www.facebook.com/Barrow-Boys-293415734123406
Impressive selection of fresh fruit and veg and herbs, including both seasonal locally grown produce and more exotic imports.

Bliss Ice Cream Parlour, 12 Bath Road, Cowes PO31 7QN 01983 295400; www.blissicecreamparlour.com
Sells tubs of gourmet Minghella ice cream, sorbet and frozen yogurt to take away for self-catering, plus Slab Artisan Isle of Wight Fudge in a variety of flavours handmade by its sister company.

*Briddlesford Lodge Farm Shop (and Bluebells Café), Wootton (page 156)
Sells a range of dairy products from Briddlesford's own Guernsey herd: skimmed, semi-skimmed and whole pasteurized milk as well as unpasteurized, plus double and clotted cream, butter and halloumi-style cheese, and Minghella gourmet ice cream produced using their milk and cream on the farm. Also stocks a wide variety of Island produce such as fresh fruit and veg, baked items, preserves, drinks and meats from the in-house butchery, including the farm's own rose veal.

Brighstone Village Shop, Main Road, Brighstone PO30 4AH 01983 740843; info@brighstonevillageshop.co.uk; www.brighstonevillageshop.co.uk
Sells Island-grown veg, Scarrots Lane Bakery and Grace's freshly baked bread and cakes, Briddlesford Farm Dairy milk and Hazelgrove Farm Eggs, Isle of Wight Cheese, fresh and cooked locally produced meat (e.g. Mottistone sausages and lamb) and fish, Calbourne Water Mill range of flours and muesli and Adgestone Vineyard wine. Hampers available.

*Brownrigg's Farm Shop & Butchery (with café), Newport Road near Godshill (page 156)
Extensive premises stocking the full range of Island produce including dry goods, fresh fruit and veg and Isle of Wight Cheese. The butchery sells the full range of its own meat including beef from their Ruby Red Devon cattle and lamb, along with free-range pork and their own dry-cured and smoked bacon, fresh and smoked gammon and cooked ham from the Isle of Wight Bacon Company, which it also incorporates; plus their own free-range chicken (and eggs), duck, seasonal bronze turkey and goose, and game; and handmade meat and poultry pies. Online shop and Island/mainland delivery service. Products also on sale at the farmers' markets (page 153).

Calbourne Water Mill Café and Gift Shop, Calbourne (page 156)
Sells their full range of stoneground flour, porridge and rolled oats and muesli, plus their own freshly baked bread and Millers Shortbread Rounds, and homemade jams and chutneys. Products also available online.

Chale Green Stores (and café), Chale Green PO38 2JN 01983 551201; shop@chalegreenstores.co.uk; www.chalegreenstores.co.uk
Sells a range of Island products including Calbourne Water Mill flour, Wild Island and The Tomato Stall products, Erica's Homemade preserves, mustards and honey; and its deli section includes Isle of Wight Cheese.

Chocolate Mad Cowes, 13 Bath Road, Cowes PO31 7QN 01983 242296; shop@chocolatemadcowes.co.uk; www.facebook.com/chocolatemadcowes
As well as selling their own range of exclusive chocolates hand-dipped in Valrhona chocolate and their Chocolate Mad Fudge, the shop sells the locally created Ocean Creed chocolate range among other luxury chocolate.

The Cider Barn, High Street, Godshill (see Godshill Cider Company, page 156); 103 High Street, Shanklin PO37 6NS 01983 866366
Both shops stock the full range of Godshill Cider Company products including apple and pear cider and cider vinegar, mead, country wines, liqueurs and ginger beer, their own cider mustard plus The Island Mustard Company flavoured mustards, various preserves, Wild Island dressings, Goddards and other Island ales and Isle of Wight Biscuit Company cookies. Products also available online.

*The Dairy Deli Farm Shop, Shalfleet (see Calbourne Classics, page 156)
Sells the range of Calbourne Classics dairy products including ice cream and frozen yogurt and whole milk and Greek-style yogurt, plus their own pies and quiches, cakes and scones, desserts and cheesecakes (cakes also available from their online shop). Also stocks Isle of Wight Cheese and local free-range eggs, frozen meats and bacon. A wide range of fresh local produce plus Calbourne Classics products also on offer online at www.realislandfood.co.uk for delivery Islandwide. Hampers available.

Delysia Farm shop, Carpenters Road (next to Oasis), Brading PO36 0QA
Hand-harvested fruit and veg from the farm; freshly laid duck, goose and rare-breed chickens' eggs; game when in season; proprietor John Day's own locally caught crab, lobster and large prawns; plus on-site smoked fish and shellfish, game (fresh and smoked) and cheese.

*The Farm Shop, Bembridge (with vegetarian/ gluten-free café), 8 High Street, Bembridge PO35 5SD 01983 874236; janeannga@aol.com; www.facebook.com/ TheFarmShop
Specializing in 'farm to fork' local fresh seasonal produce from Living Larder and A E Brown Farms and other, smaller growers including specialities such as rainbow chard and heritage carrots, mustard leaf, Kalettes, courgette flowers and quince, plus heirloom apples from St Cecilia's Abbey, Ryde. Also stocks Isle of Wight Cheese, The Green Barn Soft Goats' Cheese, Briddlesford Farm Dairy double cream, Minghella ice cream and sorbet and local free-range duck and chickens' eggs, The Island Bakers breads and brownies and other sweet bakes; full range of Island dry goods such as Jasper's Artisan Coffee, Wild Island oils and dressings, Oil of Wight, PINK'S pestos and The Garlic Farm products; plus homemade soups using fresh local ingredients. Hampers available.

Farmer Jack's Farm Shop, Arreton Barns, Main Road, Arreton, Newport PO30 3AA 01983 527530; hello@ farmerjacks.co.uk; www.farmerjacks.co.uk
Wide variety of fresh Island fruit and veg, much of it grown by owner families the Browns (of A E Brown Farms) and the Pierces (of Godshill Orchards), most notably asparagus, sweetcorn, pumpkins and winter squash, speciality brassicas, and cherries and apricots and their juice/coulis, wine and preserves. Plus the full range of Island bottled and packaged products including ales; The Island Bakers artisanal breads, and Scarrots Lane Bakery and Splendid Cakes bakes and brittle; Isle of Wight Ice Cream Company ice cream. Also has a deli stocking Isle of Wight Cheese and The Garlic Farm garlic butters, plus extensive butchery featuring Island-produced meats and poultry.

Five a Day, 34 High Street, Ventnor PO38 1RZ 07891 083806
Sells a selection of fresh seasonal produce from local growers, including tomatoes and asparagus.

The Food Hamper, 116 High Street, Cowes PO31 JAX 01983 295680; thefoodhamper_iow@yahoo.co.uk; www.facebook.com/thefoodhamper; www.thefoodhamper-cowes.com
Stocks a wide variety of Island dry goods such as PINK'S, Wild Island, The Tomato Stall, The Garlic Farm and Calbourne Water Mill products; Catch Isle of Wight fish cakes and pâté and tartare sauce; Isle of Wight Cheese and The Green Barn Soft Goats' Cheese; J. Wilkinson's savoury pies; plus their own homemade specialities such as canapés, quiches, pâtés and cakes, suppers and desserts to order and a range of ready-meals for the freezer. Hampers available.

The Garlic Farm Shop and Restaurant, Newchurch (page 156)
Stocks the full range of The Garlic Farm products including dressings and sauces, chutneys and condiments, snacks and garlic purée, butter, beer and vodka; all forms of bulb garlic including green garlic, scapes and garlic spring onions in season, elephant garlic, smoked and black garlic, garlic plaits and grappes; garlic for growing and fertilizer; various gift items, kitchen gadgets and books; plus other Island produce. The products can also be ordered online or by phone; website gives details of mainland and Islandwide stockists. Hampers available.

*The Green Barn Shop – Isle of Wight Dairy Goats, Bouldnor, Yarmouth (page 156)
Sells a range of goat dairy products from their own mixed-breed herd including pasteurized whole milk, cheese (soft plain and flavoured) and fudge in a variety of flavours (with seasonal specials), plus other selected Island produce such as Mrs Bucketts Kitchen cookies and preserves.

House of Chilli, Holliers Farm, Branstone PO36 0LT 01983 866313; www.facebook.com/Houseofchilli
Sells all things chilli related, including their own range of chilli sauces, plus chilli-flavoured chocolate made by

Chocolate Apothecary, Ryde (page 156), preserves, beers and different varieties of dried chilli, spice mixes and chilli seeds for growing.

Mottistone Farm Shop, Mottistone Manor Farm, Mottistone, Newport PO30 4ED 01983 741560
Stocks beef products from its own herd of Aberdeen Angus cattle bred on the Island, as well as their own pork and lamb, plus homemade pasties and pies. Also sells locally and home-grown fruit and veg when in season, plus Wild Island products.

*Quarr Abbey Tea and Farm Shop, Ryde (page 156)
The shop adjoining the café sells the Abbey's range of products using their own produce including ale, cider, apple juice, clear and soft-set honey, jams and jelly and chutneys, plus their unique blend of roasted coffee. They also sell pork cuts, bacon and sausages from their own pigs and eggs from their rescued free-range hens. Outside, a wide range of fresh, naturally grown produce is on sale from the Abbey's own grounds including heritage varieties of apple, carrot, potato and tomato and more exotic items such as mooli, fresh borlotti beans and chillies, plus asparagus, fennel and squash according to the season.

Rectory Mansion, 46–48 High Street, Brading PO36 0DQ 01983 300828; enquiries@rectorymansion.co.uk; www.rectorymansion.co.uk
The produce shop, adjoining the coffee shop, stocks a variety of Island products including ales, fruit juices, the Tipsy Wight range of flavoured vodkas and vodka liqueurs, Isle of Wight Distillery spirits, Adgestone Vineyard wine, Wild Island, The Garlic Farm, PINK'S and

The Tomato Stall's sauces and dressings, and the Island Mustard Company's flavoured mustards. Adjacent is the Chocolate Factory selling all kinds of fancy chocolate bars and confections that can be crafted to order, plus luxury chocolates and fudge.

Rosalie's of Cowes, 49 High Street, Cowes PO31 7RR 01983 298672; www.rosaliesofcowes.co.uk
Sells The Garlic Farm garlic bulbs and black garlic and their bottled products; PINK'S pestos and preserves; Wild Island's oils, dressings and marinades; Greeff's Biltong; Isle of Wight Biscuit Company's cookies and shortbread; Isle of Wight Clotted Cream Fudge; and local honey. Products also available online.

*Rosemary Vineyard Gift Shop (and Vineleaf Coffee Shop), Ashey, near Ryde (page 156)
Stocks the vineyard's full range of table wines, plus its own country wines and liqueurs, cider and apple juice, as well as the Isle of Wight Distillery's craft gin, vodka and moonshine. Also sells a wide selection of Island products including The Island Mustard Company's mustards and preserves, Island of Wight Biscuit Company cookies, Goddards ales and The Needles Isle of Wight Sweet Manufactory confectionery. Products also available online.

Sharon Orchard Cider Press Shop (and Coffee House), Ashey, near Ryde (page 156)
The shop stocks Sharon Orchard's own ciders and unpasteurized cider vinegar, their range of single-variety apple juices and cherry juice, country wines and liqueurs and traditional lemonade, plus Island honey, cakes and various preserves and mustards. The range of products varies according to season, and many are available for sampling before purchase.

Tapnell Farm Gift Shop, Tapnell Farm, Newport Road, Yarmouth PO41 0YJ 01983 758722; hello@tapnellfarm.com; www.tapnellfarm.com
As well as selling its own The Cow Co-branded range of sauces (BBQ, Tomato and Brown) and relish, coffee beans and milk chocolate, the shop stocks bottled products by The Garlic Farm, The Tomato Stall, Wild Island and PINK'S, plus Ventnor Botanic Garden's ale, dried mushrooms, jam and marmalade, Godshill Cider Company cider, the Island Biscuit Company's cookies and Bloody Hell Hot Sauce.

The Taverners Pub, High Street, Godshill PO38 3HZ 01983 840707; www.thetavernersgodshill.co.uk
The shop attached to the pub sells a range of its own food products including freshly baked bread and pies, preserves, sauces and condiments, spice blends and cordials. It also stocks other locally made jams, honey, Isle of Wight Cheese and ice cream.

Twins Gluten Free, Brading (page 156)
Sells a range of hand-baked gluten-free items including breads, cakes, scones, pies and pastries, plus bake-your-own mixes and ready-to-roll gluten-, dairy- and soya-free pastry. Products also on sale at the Island's farmers' markets (page 153).

Ventnor Botanic Garden gift shop, Ventnor
(page 156)
The gift shop within the Visitor Centre stocks a variety of Island products including its own VBG-branded ales using hops grown in the botanic garden, packs of mixed exotic dried mushrooms cultivated in its underground mushroom fruiting chambers and chutneys. Products can also be ordered online, including Dr. Hill Hassall's Botanics Eucalyptus Mixer, a made-to-order cordial using eucalyptus leaves handpicked from the garden.

Wight Milk Shed, CHF Wight Milk, Havenstreet
(page 156)
A Friesian cow-painted shed on the edge of Coppin Hall Farm on the roadside selling its own whole, semi-skimmed and skimmed Wight Milk, double and whipping cream and butter; plus free-range chickens' eggs, and duck eggs when available, and potatoes; Glebe Farm jelly, marmalade and chutney; and Greeff's Biltong.

Yarmouth Deli, 1 The Square, Yarmouth PO41 0NS
01983 761196
Stocks some local seasonal fruit and veg and Island bottled products such as PINK'S, Wild Island and Erica's Homemade preserves, Isle of Wight Cheese, plus freshly baked bread, home-cooked pies and other savouries, soups, cakes and desserts.

BAKERIES

The Bakery (and café), 33 High Street, Bembridge
PO35 5SD 01983 872644
Good variety of cakes, biscuits and pastries, both sweet and savoury, as well as breads, rolls and buns.

*Cantina (café/restaurant), 20 High Street, Ventnor
PO38 1RZ 01983 855988; info@cantinaventnor.co.uk; www.cantinaventnor.co.uk
The in-house bakery bakes not only speciality breads but also sweet and savoury pastries daily.

Grace's Bakery, 31 High Street, Cowes PO31 7RS
01983 566868; 114a Pyle Street, Newport PO30 1XA 01983 525636; 178 High Street, Ryde PO33 2HW 10983 566868; 20A Regent Street, Shanklin PO37 7AA; 1 The Quay, Yarmouth PO41 0PG 01983 760190; www.gracesbakery.co.uk

Breads and cakes are made the traditional way in this long-established family business without the use of additives or bleached flours.

The Island Bakers, Newport and other outlets
(page 156)
Award-winning bakers producing top-quality artisanal breads including sourdough, fougasse, focaccia, pumpernickel and ciabatta, as well as brown and other daily breads, baguettes and rolls. Also brownies and other sweet treats.

Scarrots Lane Bakery (Market Bakery), 35 Scarrots Lane, Newport PO30 1JD 01983 521187; www.facebook.com/Scarrots-Lane-Bakery-558368354252063
Wide selection of cakes and bakes all made from scratch on the premises, including traditional favourites such as lardy cakes, doughnuts, cheese scones, treacle tarts and seasonal fruit pies, plus a variety of breads and rolls.

BUTCHERS

Hamiltons Fine Foods/Hamiltons Butchers,
1 Daish Way, Newport PO30 5XB 01983 526098; 67 Pyle Street, Newport PO30 1UL 01983 821017; 23 High Street, Cowes PO31 7RY 01983 293129; www.hamiltonsfinefoods.co.uk; www.hamiltonsbutchers.co.uk
Produces its own dry-cured and smoked bacon, homemade sausages and chipolatas and cooked meats, plus made-to-order meat and poultry pies and pasties. Also stocks seasonal game and New Forest venison. Products also available online, plus delivery service.

Island Foods, Units 6 & 8 Cypress Court, 6 Cothey Way, Ryde PO33 1QT 01983 717606; info@islandfoodsiow.co.uk; www.islandfoodsiow.co.uk
Cures its own bacon and makes its own sausages and chipolatas, plus burgers, meatballs, chicken skewers and other barbecue items; sells fresh duck, plus a wide variety of game when in season including rabbit and wild duck; also stocks The Garlic Farm condiments and sauces. Products also available online.

Norris & Knight, 23 High Street, Ventnor PO38 1RZ
01983 854330
In addition to the butchery, it includes a deli counter selling a range of shop-baked pies and pasties, plus Isle of Wight Cheese.

Paul Murphy Butchers, 17 Regent Street, Shanklin
PO37 7AF 01983 864245
Sells game (including rabbit) when in season, and makes his own renowned sausages, plus croquettes and faggots.

P J Thorne Butchers, Avenue Road, Freshwater PO40
9UT 01983 754955
Specializes in game when in season.

WW Woodford & Son, 26 High Street, Bembridge
PO35 5SE 01983 872717; www.woodfordandson.co.uk
Sells a wide range of prepared meat and poultry items for home-cooking and barbecuing including sausages in

an array of flavours, chipolatas, burgers, marinated kebabs and other speciality items, plus seasonal game; freshly baked raised pork pies and other meat and poultry pies, pasties, puddings and Scotch eggs and sausage rolls; also has a deli that stocks shop-cooked ham and other cooked meats and Isle of Wight Cheese. Delivery service available.

Many Island butchers also sell locally produced free-range eggs and other local products.

FISH SHOPS AND SUPPLIERS

The Best Dressed Crab Limited (floating café and shop), Fisherman's Wharf, Embankment Road, Bembridge PO35 5NS 01983 874758; www.thebestdressedcrabintown.co.uk
The shop of this lifeboatmen family business sells crab, lobster and prawns, live or cooked, straight off what was their own-built boat, but now owned by a master fisherman colleague.

Captain Stan's Bembridge Fish Store, 5 High Street, Bembridge PO35 5SD 01983 875572; **Captain Stan's Ryde Fish Store,** 27 Cross Street, Ryde PO33 2AA; 01983 611611; info@bembridgefish.co.uk; www.bembridgefish.co.uk
Sells Bembridge Ledge crab and lobster, and Bembridge prawns when available, plus a wide variety of their own locally caught fish; seafood platters available. Also sells handmade prepared items such as fish cakes and crab cakes, pasties, ramekins and soup, fish curries, taramasalata and hummus, plus other deli items and authentic Spanish ingredients for making paella and other specialist ingredients; frozen shellfish and other freezer items; and marsh samphire. Mainland delivery service.

Hancock's Fishmongers, 88 Upper St James' Street, Newport PO30 1LB 01983 533707
Range of locally sourced fresh fish on offer, and cooked Island crab and lobster, plus marsh samphire and ready-made chilled sauces to accompany.

Island Fish Farm Shop, Punthouse Lane, Limerstone, Brighstone PO30 4PL 01983 740941; meadowlakesiow@gmail.com; www.islandfishfarm.co.uk
Sells its own freshly caught rainbow trout, plus whole

or filleted hot-smoked trout and smoked trout pâté to order. Open April–October.

J & B Fisheries, Avenue Road, Freshwater PO40 9UT 01983 752269; jbfisheries@btinternet.com; www. jbfisheries.com
An impressive selection of fresh fish caught from their own boat moored at Yarmouth Harbour, plus crab, lobster and prawns. They also smoke fish on the premises, and prepare gravadlax and fish pâté.

Phillips Seafood and Smokehouse, 111 High Street, Cowes PO31 7AT 01983 245247; 339 Newport Road, Northwood, Cowes PO31 8PG 01983 282200; www. phillipsseafoodandsmokehouse.co.uk
Besides locally caught fresh fish, Phillips produces its own cold-smoked salmon and other smoked fish products, and crab cakes, plus a range of frozen fish and seafood, including cockles. Delivery service available.

*Ventnor Haven Fishery (with fish or crab/lobster and chips takeaway), Eastern Esplanade, East Street, Ventnor PO38 1JR (contact details as follows); *Seafood Corner, High Street, Newport PO30 1SR 01983 852176; info@ ventnorhavenfishery.co.uk; ventnorhavenfish@btconnect. com; www.facebook.com/pages/Ventnor-Haven-Fishery/206565562710506
Sells both a range of its own freshly landed fish and shellfish, including crab, lobster and whelks, and cooked and prepared crab and lobster; plus crab cakes, turnovers and pâté and other ready-made items.

FARMERS' MARKETS

Newport
07800 727903; info@islandfarmersmarket.co.uk; www. islandfarmersmarket.co.uk
St Thomas Square – held every Friday 9am–2pm

Ryde
Contact details as above
The Co-operative Food car park, 4 Anglesea Street – held every Saturday 8.30am–12.30pm

Seaview
Pier Road car park – held once a month during the summer

I Love Wight stages local food and craft markets at The Garlic Farm and in Brading's main car park. Follow them on www.facebook.com/realilovewight

For details of **Country Markets** held around the Island, check out www.country-markets.co.uk

FRUIT AND VEGETABLE BOXES

Horringford Gardens, Middle Barn, Horringford, Newport PO30 3AP 01983 865720; www.horringford.com

The Isle of Wight Veg Box Company, Stoneshells Nursery, Bathingbourne Lane, Sandown PO36 0LU 01983 865761; 07812607109; info@iowvegboxdelivery. co.uk; www.iowvegboxdelivery.co.uk

*Living Larder, Apse Heath (page 156)

WAYSIDE HONESTY STALLS

Look out for these Islandwide, selling freshly laid free-range eggs, home-grown fruit and vegetables and home-cooked preserves.

ONLINE ISLAND PRODUCE SUPPLIERS

www.farmerschoice.co.uk
Dedicated to delivering free-range meat and quality fresh produce 'from dirt to doorstep' throughout the UK, including that of many Island producers.

www.realislandfood.co.uk
Set up by The Dairy Deli team (page 150), the full range of Calbourne Classics products are on offer including yogurt and ice cream, homemade cakes and other sweet bakes and savoury pies, plus locally produced fresh meat and poultry and other fresh produce.

SUPERMARKETS AND FOOD STORES

The Co-operative Food
Southern Co-operative supports Isle of Wight producers through its 'Local Flavours' programme, with dedicated displays in all its Island branches, and an especially extensive range available in its flagship Freshwater store. It also hosts a pavilion under the same banner at the Royal Isle of Wight County Show (page 158).

Welcome Store, Bembridge
This Southern Co-operative franchise store carries a good range of locally produced items, including bottled products from The Garlic Farm, The Island Mustard Company, Wight Crystal soft drinks and Island ales, ciders and fruit juices; Oil of Wight; Isle of Wight Biscuit Company cookies and crackers and Calbourne Water Mill muesli; fresh produce such as The Tomato Stall tomatoes and The Garlic Farm bulb garlic; Island honey; and Calbourne Classics yogurt and Isle of Wight Cheese.

Tesco
Stocks The Tomato Stall tomatoes during the summer months and some other local fresh seasonal produce, plus a selection of bottled Island ales, Wight Crystal spring water and ginger beer and Isle of Wight Biscuit Company biscuits.

Waitrose
Their East Cowes store carries a range of Wight produce including bottled preserves and mustards from local suppliers such as The Garlic Farm, plus Quarr Abbey Ale and other Goddards craft beers.

You will also find selected leading Island brands in many other convenience stores, gift shops, pubs and other eateries and tourist outlets around the Island.

You can even bag them while travelling on **Wightlink's Portsmouth–Fishbourne car ferry,** St Clare.

PROFESSIONAL FORAGER

Fruit of the Land, Paul Noakes 07964772689/01983 873059; fruitoftheland.wordpress.com

*Members of the Royal Isle of Wight Agricultural Society's Wight Marque scheme – see page 11

A–Z of Island food and drink

ale The Garlic Farm; *Goddards Brewery; *Island Brewery; *Quarr Abbey; Ventnor Botanic Garden; Yates' Brewery

apple juice *Quarr Abbey; *Rosemary Vineyard; Sharon Orchard

apricot
– coulis Godshill Orchards
– liqueur Godshill Cider Company
– preserves Godshill Orchards
– wine Godshill Cider Company; Godshill Orchards

apricots, fresh Godshill Orchards

artichokes
– globe *Living Larder
– Jerusalem *Living Larder; *Quarr Abbey

asparagus *A E Brown Farms; The Garlic Farm; *Quarr Abbey

aubergines *Living Larder

bacon *Brownrigg's Farm Shop & Butchery (Isle of Wight Bacon Company); Hamiltons Fine Foods/Hamiltons Butchers; Island Foods; Mottistone Farm Shop; *Quarr Abbey

balsamic, dressings and dips *The Tomato Stall *Wild Island

barbecue
– charcoal Woodworks Wight
– foods *Briddlesford Lodge Farm Shop; *Brownrigg's Farm Shop & Butchery; Farmer Jack's Farm Shop; Mottistone Farm Shop; see also Butchers
– sauces and relishes The Cow Co, Tapnell Farm; The Garlic Farm; House of Chilli

beef *Briddlesford Lodge Farm Shop; *Brownrigg's Farm Shop & Butchery; Farmer Jack's Farm Shop; Mottistone Farm Shop; see also Butchers

beer see Ale
– ginger Godshill Cider Company; Wight Crystal

beetroot, heritage *Living Larder; *Quarr Abbey

biltong, beef The Garlic Farm; Greeff's Biltong

biscuits, savoury see Crackers, savoury

biscuits, sweet see also Cookies; Shortbread CFO Foods; Isle of Wight Biscuit Company; The Rock Shop; see also Bakeries

black pudding WW Woodford & Son

borlotti beans *Living Larder; *Quarr Abbey

brandy, flavoured Godshill Cider Company; Hedgerow Harvest; Sharon Orchard

brassicas, winter speciality *A E Brown Farms; *Living Larder

bread see Bakeries
– gluten-free Twins Gluten Free

brittle Splendid Cakes

brownies The Island Bakers; Say It With Brownies; Splendid Cakes; Twins Gluten Free

butter *Briddlesford Farm Dairy; CHF Wight Milk
– garlic The Garlic Farm

cakes *Calbourne Classics; Mrs Bucketts Kitchen; Splendid Cakes; see also Bakeries
– gluten-free Twins Gluten Free

carrots, heritage *Living Larder; *Quarr Abbey

celeriac *Living Larder; *Quarr Abbey

celery *Quarr Abbey

chard *Living Larder; *Quarr Abbey

cheese *Isle of Wight Cheese Company
– goats' *The Green Barn – Isle of Wight Dairy Goats
– halloumi-style *Briddlesford Farm Dairy
– smoked Delysia Farm shop

cheesecake *Calbourne Classics

cherries, fresh Godshill Orchards

cherry juice Godshill Orchards; Sharon Orchard
– brandy Sharon Orchard
– liqueur Adgestone Vineyard; Godshill Cider Company; *Rosemary Vineyard
– preserves; wine Godshill Orchards

chicken *Brownrigg's Farm Shop & Butchery

chillies, dried House of Chilli

chillies, fresh *Medham Farm; *Quarr Abbey

chilli products Arson Fire, Adgestone Vineyard; Bloody Hell Hot Sauce; Chocolate Apothecary; The Garlic Farm; Greeff's Biltong; House of Chilli; The Island Mustard Company; Isle of Wight Biscuit Company; PINK'S; *Tipsy Wight; *The Tomato Stall; *Wild Island

chipolatas see Sausages

chocolate Chocolate Apothecary (including dairy- and gluten-free); Chocolate Island; Chocolate Mad Cowes; House of Chilli (produced by Chocolate Apothecary); Ocean Creed; Rectory Mansion Chocolate Factory

chutney see Preserves

cider Godshill Cider Company; *Quarr Abbey; *Rosemary Vineyard; Sharon Orchard

coffee Betapak; The Break Lever; *Island Roasted; *Jasper's Artisan Coffee; *Quarr Abbey (produced by Island Roasted)

confectionery see Sweets

cookies Isle of Wight Biscuit Company; Mrs Bucketts Kitchen

cordials The Taverners Pub

country wines see Wine

courgette flowers *Living Larder

crab see Shellfish

crackers, savoury Isle of Wight Biscuit Company

cream
– clotted *Briddlesford Farm Dairy
– double *Briddlesford Farm Dairy; untreated *Queen Bower Dairy; CHF Wight Milk
– whipping CHF Wight Milk

crosnes (Chinese artichokes) *Living Larder

curd, fruit Isle of Wight Lavender

curry paste, Thai The Garlic Farm

dressings and dips Arson Fire, Adgestone Vineyard; The Garlic Farm; House of Chilli; *The Tomato Stall; *Wild Island

duck breasts; legs; whole *Brownrigg's Farm Shop & Butchery
– eggs *Hazelgrove Farm Eggs; *Medham Farm
– wild Hamiltons Fine Foods/Hamiltons Butchers; Island Foods

edible flowers *Bartletts Farm Flowers; *Living Larder

edible plants The Coastal Gardener

eggs, free-range chickens' *Brownrigg's Farm Shop & Butchery; Delysia Farm shop; *Hazelgrove Farm Eggs; *Medham Farm; *Quarr Abbey

– duck *Hazelgrove Farm Eggs; *Medham Farm
– goose Delysia Farm shop

elderberry liqueur *Rosemary Vineyard; *Tipsy Wight
– wine Adgestone Vineyard; Godshill Cider Company; *Rosemary Vineyard

fennel, bulb *Living Larder; *Quarr Abbey

fish, fresh see Fish shops and suppliers
– fish and shellfish products; Catch Isle of Wight; see also Fish shops and suppliers
– locally smoked fish and shellfish Delysia Farm shop; Island Fish Farm Shop; J & B Fisheries; Phillips Seafood and Smokehouse

flour, stoneground Calbourne Water Mill

fruit, fresh * Briddlesford Lodge Farm Shop; *A E Brown Farms; *Brownrigg's Farm Shop & Butchery; Delysia Farm shop; The Farm Shop, Bembridge; Farmer Jack's Farm Shop; *Living Larder; *Quarr Abbey; see also separate entries for specialist individual vegetables

fudge Chocolate Mad Cowes; *The Green Barn – Isle of Wight Dairy Goats; Isle of Fudge; ; Mrs Bucketts Kitchen; Slab. Artisan Isle of Wight Fudge; Sweet Memories

game *Brownrigg's Farm Shop & Butchery; Delysia Farm shop; see also Butchers

gammon *Brownrigg's Farm Shop & Butchery (Isle of Wight Bacon Company); see also Butchers

garlic, black; bulb (plus grappes and plaits); elephant; green; scapes; seeds for growing; smoked; spring onions The Garlic Farm
– products The Garlic Farm; The Island Mustard Company; *Wild Island

gin *Isle of Wight Distillery
– flavoured Godshill Cider Company; Hedgerow Harvest; Sharon Orchard

ginger beer Godshill Cider Company; Wight Crystal

ginger wine Adgestone Vineyard

goats' cheese; fudge; milk *The Green Barn – Isle of Wight Dairy Goats

goose *Brownrigg's Farm Shop & Butchery
– eggs Delysia Farm shop

ham *Brownrigg's Farm Shop & Butchery (Isle of Wight Bacon Company); Hamiltons Fine Foods/Hamiltons Butchers; WW Woodford & Son

herbs, growing The Coastal Gardener; Isle of Wight Lavender; *The Tomato Stall

honey
– clear *Bunbury Bees; Mary Case Honey; *Medham Farm; Sharon Orchard
– cut honeycomb Mary Case Honey; *Medham Farm
– set/soft set Mary Case Honey; *Medham Farm; *Quarr Abbey

horseradish
– condiments with garlic The Garlic Farm
– pesto with beetroot PINK'S

hummus Captain Stan's Bembridge/Ryde Fish Stores

ice cream *Calbourne Classics; *Isle of Wight Ice Cream Company; *Minghella

jam see Preserves
jelly see Preserves
juices, cold-pressed raw Made by Krista

Kalettes *Living Larder
kidney, lambs'; pigs' *Brownrigg's Farm Shop & Butchery;
    see also Butchers
kippers Delysia Farm shop; Phillips Seafood and
    Smokehouse

lamb *Briddlesford Lodge Farm Shop; *Brownrigg's Farm
    Shop & Butchery; Farmer Jack's Farm Shop; Mottistone
    Farm Shop; see also Butchers
lemonade Sharon Orchard; Wight Crystal
liqueurs Arson Fire, Adgestone Vineyard; Godshill Cider
    Company; Hedgerow Harvest; *Rosemary Vineyard;
    Sharon Orchard; *Tipsy Wight
liver, chicken; duck *Brownrigg's Farm Shop & Butchery
– lambs'; pigs' *Brownrigg's Farm Shop & Butchery; see
    also Butchers
lobster see Shellfish

mallard see Wild duck
marinades and rubs *Wild Island
marmalade see Preserves
mayonnaise, with garlic The Garlic Farm
mead Godshill Cider Company; Rosemary Vineyard
– Christmas (with spices) Godshill Cider Company
milk
– cows', pasteurized semi-skimmed; skimmed; whole
    *Briddlesford Farm Dairy; CHF Wight Milk; *Queen
    Bower Dairy
– cows', unpasteurized *Briddlesford Farm Dairy;
    *Queen Bower Dairy
– goats', pasteurized *The Green Barn – Isle of Wight
    Dairy Goats
mooli *Quarr Abbey
Moonshine, Apple Pie *Isle of Wight Distillery
muesli Calbourne Water Mill
mushrooms
– dried Natural Wight Mushrooms; Ventnor Botanic
    Garden
– fresh Natural Wight Mushrooms
mustard The Garlic Farm; Godshill Cider Company; The
    Island Mustard Company; Sharon Orchard
mustard leaf *Living Larder

nuts, mixed, flavoured with garlic The Garlic Farm

oats, porridge; rolled Calbourne Water Mill
oil, cold pressed rapeseed; olive, infused The Garlic Farm;
    *Oil of Wight; *Wild Island
olives, green stuffed with garlic The Garlic Farm

partridge see Game
pasties and pies, savoury *Briddlesford Lodge Farm Shop;
    *Brownrigg's Farm Shop & Butchery; *Calbourne
    Classics; Isle of Wight Pies; Mottistone Farm Shop;
    Twins Gluten Free; J. Wilkinson's; see also Butchers
pastries, pies and tarts, sweet see Bakeries
patty pan squash *Living Larder
peanut butter; chocolate PINK'S

pear cider Godshill Cider Company
peppers, Romano/Romero *Living Larder
pesto The Garlic Farm; PINK'S
pheasant see Game
pickle see Preserves
popcorn, garlic and herb; chilli, garlic and herb The Garlic
    Farm
pork *Briddlesford Lodge Farm Shop; *Brownrigg's Farm
    Shop & Butchery (Isle of Wight Bacon Company);
    Farmer Jack's Farm Shop; Mottistone Farm Shop;
    *Quarr Abbey; see also Butchers
pork scratchings The Garlic Farm; Hamiltons Fine Foods/
    Hamiltons Butchers
– with garlic and chilli The Garlic Farm
potatoes, heritage *Living Larder; *Quarr Abbey
preserves Arson Fire, Adgestone Vineyard; Bear
    Preserves; The Borneo Pantry; Erica's Homemade;
    *The Fruit Bowl; The Garlic Farm; Glebe Farm, available
    from the Wight Milk Shed (page 152); The Island
    Mustard Company; *Medham Farm; PINK'S; *Quarr
    Abbey; Sharon Orchard; *The Tomato Stall; Ventnor
    Botanic Garden
pumpkins *Briddlesford Lodge Farm Shop; *A E Brown
    Farms; *Quarr Abbey

quail Island Foods
– eggs Farmer Jack's Farm Shop
quiches *Calbourne Classics; The Food Hamper;
    Scarrots Lane Bakery; J. Wilkinson's
– gluten-free Twins Gluten Free
quince *Briddlesford Lodge Farm Shop; *The Farm
    Shop, Bembridge; Mary Case Honey

rabbit Hamiltons Fine Foods/Hamiltons Butchers; Island
    Foods; Paul Murphy Butchers; WW Woodford & Son
radish, rainbow *Living Larder; *Quarr Abbey
relish The Cow Co, Tapnell Farm; see also Preserves

salad fruit and vegetables *Living Larder; *Quarr Abbey;
    *The Tomato Stall
salsify *Living Larder
salt, sea, with garlic The Garlic Farm
sauces Arson Fire, Adgestone Vineyard; The Cow Co,
    Tapnell Farm; House of Chilli; The Garlic Farm; *The
    Tomato Stall
– tartare Catch Isle of Wight
sausage rolls Hamiltons Fine Foods/Hamiltons Butchers;
    J. Wilkinson's; WW Woodford & Son
sausages *Briddlesford Lodge Farm Shop; *Brownrigg's
    Farm Shop & Butchery; Farmer Jack's Farm Shop;
    Mottistone Farm Shop; see also Butchers
scones *Briddlesford Lodge Farm Shop; *Calbourne
    Classics; Mrs Bucketts Kitchen; Twins Gluten Free; see
    also Bakeries
Scotch eggs J. Wilkinson's; WW Woodford & Son
shellfish Delysia Farm shop; see also Fish shops and
    suppliers
shortbread Calbourne Water Mill; CFO Foods; The Rock
    Shop
smoothies, raw Made by Krista
sorbet *Isle of Wight Ice Cream Company; *Minghella
soup Catch Isle of Wight; Captain Stan's Bembridge/Ryde

Fish Stores; *The Farm Shop, Bembridge; *Ventnor
    Haven Fishery; Yarmouth Deli
sourdough bread The Island Bakers
squash, summer and winter *Briddlesford Lodge Farm
    Shop; *A E Brown Farms; *Living Larder; *Quarr
    Abbey
sweetcorn *A E Brown Farms; *Quarr Abbey
sweets The Needles Isle of Wight Sweet Manufactory;
    The Rock Shop; Sweet Memories; see also Fudge;
    Toffee

taramasalata Captain Stan's Bembridge/Ryde Fish Stores
tea All About Tea; Betapak
toffee Rachel's Confectionery
tomato
– cordial; juice *The Tomato Stall
– pesto PINK'S
– preserves The Garlic Farm, *The Tomato Stall
– smoked/roasted *The Tomato Stall
tomatoes, heritage *Quarr Abbey; *The Tomato Stall
turkey *Brownrigg's Farm Shop & Butchery

veal, rose *Briddlesford Lodge Farm Shop; *Brownrigg's
    Farm Shop & Butchery
vegetables *Briddlesford Lodge Farm Shop; *A E Brown
    Farms; Brownrigg's Farm Shop & Butchery; Delysia
    Farm shop; The Farm Shop, Bembridge; Farmer Jack's
    Farm Shop; *Living Larder; *Quarr Abbey; see
    also separate entries for specialist individual vegetables
venison Delysia Farm shop; Hamiltons Fine Foods/
    Hamiltons Butchers; Island Foods
vinegar
– balsamic; fruit *Wild Island
– cider Godshill Cider Company; Sharon Orchard
    (unpasteurized)
vodka *Isle of Wight Distillery
– flavoured liqueur *Tipsy Wight
– infused The Garlic Farm; *Tipsy Wight

water, spring, sparkling; still Wight Crystal
whisky *Isle of Wight Distillery
wild boar Delysia Farm shop; Island Foods
wild duck Hamiltons Fine Foods/Hamiltons Butchers;
    Island Foods
wine Adgestone Vineyard; *Rosemary Vineyard
– country Godshill Cider Company; *Rosemary Vineyard;
    Sharon Orchard

yogurt, Greek-style; whole milk *Calbourne Classics
– frozen *Calbourne Classics; *Minghella

*Members of the Royal Isle of Wight Agricultural
Society's Wight Marque scheme – see page 11

Index of Island producers

Many of the producers have online shops, mainland stockists and/or Island delivery services. Please see websites for these details.

Adgestone Vineyard, Upper Road, Brading PO36 0ES 01983 402882; www.adgestonevineyard.co.uk

All About Tea Ltd, 56 Middle Street, Southsea, Hampshire PO5 4BP 023 92750122; www.allabouttea.co.uk

*Bartletts Farm Flowers, Bartletts Green Farm, Brading Road, Ryde PO33 1QQ 07581006234; www.bartlettsfarmflowers.co.uk

Betapak Ltd, Rookley Industrial Park, Pritchett's Way, Rookley PO38 3LT; 01983 721100; www.betapak.co.uk

Bloody Hell Hot Sauce, bloodyhellhotsauce@yahoo.com; www.bloodyhellhotsauce.com

The Borneo Pantry, Oakleigh, Ryde 07809 707837; theborneopantry@gmail.com; www.facebook.com/borneopantry

The Break Lever 07803042730; mat@thebreaklever.co.uk; www.thebreaklever.co.uk

*Briddlesford Lodge Farm, Briddlesford Road, Wootton, Ryde PO33 4RY; 01983 884650; info@briddlesfordlodgefarm.com; www.briddlesfordlodgefarm.com

*A E Brown (Farms) Ltd, Hale Manor Farm, Hale Common, Arreton PO30 3AR 01983 865204; info@aebrownfarms.co.uk

*Brownrigg's Farm Shop & Butchery, Newport Road, Godshill PO38 3LY 01983 840191; info@brownriggfarmmeats.co.uk; www.brownriggfarmmeats.co.uk; www.brownriggpoultry.co.uk

*Bunbury Bees, 34 New Street, Newport katebucci@gmail.com; www.bunburybees.co.uk

*Calbourne Classics, Three Gates Farm, Shalfleet PO30 4NA 01983 531204; info@calbourneclassics.co.uk; www.calbourneclassics.co.uk

Calbourne Water Mill, Newport Road, Calbourne PO30 4JN 01983 531227; info@calbournewatermill.co.uk; www.calbournewatermill.co.uk

Catch Isle of Wight, The Old Dairy, Kings Manor Farm, Copse Lane, Freshwater PO40 9TL; 01983 755551; 07710352750; hello@catchisleofwight.co.uk; www.catchisleofwight.co.uk; products available on the Island from The Co-operative Food, Freshwater; The Food Hamper, Cowes

CFO Foods, 48 Well Street, Ryde PO33 2RZ; 01983 614639; admin@cfofoods.co.uk; www.cfofoods.co.uk

CHF Wight Milk, Coppid Hall Farm, Main Road, Havenstreet, Ryde PO33 4DH 01983 882489; wightmilk@btconnect.com; www.chfwightmilk.iofw.co.uk

Chocolate Apothecary, 7 Esplanade, Ryde PO33 2DY 01983 718292; sue@chocolateapothecary.co.uk

Chocolate Island, High Street, Godshill PO38 3HH 01983 840090; info@islelovechocolate.co.uk; www.islelovechocolate.co.uk

The Coastal Gardener, Fakenham Farm, Eddington Road, St Helens, PO33 1XS 07977 550050; thecoastalgardener@icloud.com; www.thecoastalgardener.co.uk

Deacon's Nursery, Moor View, Godshill PO38 3HW 01983 840750/522243; www.deaconsnurseryfruits.co.uk

Erica's Homemade, Middle Barn Lane, Newport PO30 3AP 01983 865720; www.ericashomemade.co.uk

*The Fruit Bowl, The Laurels, High Street, Newchurch PO36 0NJ 01983 867613; www.chessell.plus.com/fruitbowl

The Garlic Farm, Mersley Lane, Newchurch PO36 0NR 01983 865378; contact@thegarlicfarm.co.uk; www.thegarlicfarm.co.uk

*Goddards Brewery, Barnsley Farm, Bullen Road, Ryde PO33 1QF 01983 611011; info@goddardsbrewery.com; www.goddardsbrewery.com

Godshill Cider Company, High Street, Godshill PO38 3HZ 01983 840680; rob@godshillcider.co.uk; www.godshillisleofwight.co.uk

Godshill Orchards, Hollow Lane, Godshill PO38 3JA 07973 382965; 07919 406418; robert@godshillcherries.co.uk; www.godshillcherries.co.uk; produce/products available from Farmer Jack's Farm Shop

Greeff's Biltong 01983 611288; sales@isleofwightbiltong.co.uk; www.isleofwightbiltong.co.uk

*The Green Barn – Isle of Wight Dairy Goats, Main Road, Bouldnor, Yarmouth PO41 0XN; 01983 761310; iowgreenbarn@outlook.com; www.thegreenbarn-isleofwight.co.uk

*Hazelgrove Farm Eggs, Hazelgrove Farm, Ashey PO33 4BD 07875650948; sales@hazelgrovefarm.co.uk; www.facebook.com/Hazelgrove-Farm-Eggs-249597511884355

Hedgerow Harvest, Aldermoor Farm, Upton Road, Ryde PO33 3LA 01983 566009; liqueursATaldermoor-farm.co.uk; www.hedgerow-harvest-liqueurs.co.uk

The Island Bakers, 89 St James' Street, Newport PO30 1LB 01983 400450; info@theislandbakers.com; www.theislandbakers.com

*Island Brewery, Dinglers Farm, Yarmouth Road, Shalfleet PO30 4LZ 01983 821731; info@islandales.co.uk; www.islandbrewery.co.uk

The Island Mustard Company, 27 Sandown Road, Lake PO36 9JL 01983 506528; theislandmustardco@btconnect.com; www.theislandmustardcompany.co.uk

*Island Roasted, Caffe Isola, 59 Pyle Street, Newport 01983 857670/524800; info@islandroasted.co.uk; www.islandroasted.co.uk

Isle of Fudge, 7, Shide Villa, Medina Avenue, Newport PO30 1HH; 07877 745283; isleoffudge@yahoo.co.uk; www.facebook.com/IsleOfFudge

Isle of Wight Bacon Company, *Brownrigg's Farm Shop & Butchery, Newport Road, Godshilll PO38 3LY 07980 158183 (catering enquiries); info@isleofwightbacon.co.uk; www.isleofwightbacon.co.uk

Isle of Wight Biscuit Company, Macketts Farm, Macketts Lane, Hale Common PO30 3AS 01983 865555; islandbiscuits@aol.co.uk; www.islandbiscuits.co.uk

*Isle of Wight Cheese Company, Queen Bower Dairy, Alverstone Road, Sandown PO36 0NZ 01983 402736; rich@isleofwightcheese.co.uk; www.isleofwightcheese.co.uk

*Isle of Wight Distillery, Rosemary Vineyard, Smallbrook Lane, Ryde, Newport PO33 4BE 01983 811084; xavier@isleofwightdistillery.com; www.isleofwightdistillery.com

*Isle of Wight Ice Cream Company, Riverway, Newport PO30 5UX 01983 539238; sales@isleofwighticecream.co.uk; www.isleofwighticecream.co.uk

Isle of Wight Lavender, Staplehurst Grange, Staplers Road, Newport PO30 2LU 01983 825272

*Jasper's Artisan Coffee, Yarcroft, Brading; 07855 754495; info@jasperscoffee.co.uk; www.jasperscoffee.co.uk

*Living Larder, Ventnor Road, Apse Heath PO36 0JT 01983 717164; aimee@livinglarder.co.uk; www.livinglarder.co.uk

Made by Krista, Hill Top House, High Street, Newchurch PO36 0NN; 07886 243885; kladenton@hotmail.com; www.madebykrista.com

Mary Case Honey, Limerstone Farm, Limerstone, Newport PO30 4AB; 07739 475664; marycaseiow@gmail.com; www.islandfarmersmarket.co.uk/1220-Mary_Case_Honey-farmer/

*Medham Farm, Medham Farm Lane, Cowes PO31 8PH; 01983 299088; michael@medhamfarm.com; www.medhamfarm.com

*Minghella, Briddlesford Lodge Farm, Briddlesford Road, Wootton PO33 4RY; 01983 883545; icecream@minghella.co.uk; www.minghella.co.uk

Mrs Bucketts Kitchen 01983 405951; mrsbuckettskitchen@tesco.net; www.facebook.com/mrsbuckettskitchen

Natural Wight Mushrooms Ltd, Godshill PO38 3LY; themushroomfarmer.co.uk

The Needles Isle of Wight Sweet Manufactory, The Needles, Alum Bay PO39 0JD 01983 752401; www.theneedles.co.uk/pages/sweet-manufactory

Ocean Creed, 5 Somerton Estate, Cowes PO31 8PB; info@oceancreed.com; www.oceancreed.com

*Oil of Wight, Broadfields, Chapel Lane, Merstone PO30 3DA; 07970 572154; info@oilofwight.co.uk

PINK'S, Perreton Farm, North Barn, Merstone PO30 3DL; 01983 632032; 07712288168; fiona@pinksfoods.co.uk; www.pinks-online.co.uk

*Quarr Abbey, Quarr Hill, Ryde PO33 4ES 01983 882420; admin@quarr.org; www.quarrabbey.org

*Queen Bower Dairy, Alverstone Road, Sandown, PO36 0NZ 01983 403840; queenbowerdairy@btconnect.com; www.queenbowerdairy.co.uk

Rachel's Confectionery, Albert Road, Gurnard PO31 8JU; www.rachelsconfectionery.com

The Rock Shop, 91–93 High Street, Old Village, Shanklin PO37 6NR 01983 862950; 29, Beachfield Road, Sandown PO36 8LT 01983 402005; info@therockshopiow.co.uk; www.therockshopiow.co.uk

*Rosemary Vineyard, Smallbrook Lane, Ryde PO33 4BE 01983 811084; info@rosemaryvineyard.co.uk; www.rosemaryvineyard.co.uk

Say It With Brownies, 38 Horestone Drive, Seaview PO34 5DD 01983 568064; hello@sayitwithbrownies.co.uk; www.sayitwithbrownies.co.uk

Sharon Orchard, Smallbrook Lane, Ryde PO33 4BE 01983 564595; sharon@sharonorchard.com; www.sharonordhard.co.uk

Slab. Artisan Isle of Wight Fudge, sold through Bliss Ice Cream Parlour (page 150); info@slabfudge.com; www.slabfudge.co.uk

Splendid Cakes, Lavender Cottage, Farriers Way, Shorwell 07762 935953; amy@splendidcake.co.uk; www.splendidcake.co.uk

Sweet Memories, Arreton Barns, Main Road, Arreton PO30 3AA 01983 528353; info@arretonbarns.co.uk; www.arretonbarns.co.uk/sweet-memories

*Tipsy Wight, Medham Farm, Medham Farm Lane, Cowes PO31 8PH; 01983 299088; ruth@tipsywight.com; www.tipsywight.com

*The Tomato Stall Ltd, Wight Salads Nursery, Main Road, Hale Common, Arreton PO30 3AR T 01983 866907; hello@thetomatostall.co.uk; www.thetomatostall.co.uk

Twins Gluten Free, 60/61 High Street, Brading PO36 0DQ 01983 609379/07817 627764; info@twinsglutenfree.co.uk; www.twinsglutenfree.co.uk

Ventnor Botanic Garden, Undercliff Drive, Ventnor PO38 1UL 01983 855397; info@botanic.co.uk; www.botanic.co.uk

Wight Crystal Spring Water, 7 Daish Way, Dodnor Industrial Estate, Newport PO30 5XJ; 01983 520128; enquiries@oseliow.org.uk; www.wightcrystal.org.uk

*Wild Island, Unit A, Langbridge Rural Business Park, Newchurch PO36 0NP 01983 868305/07740 825561; www.wildislandstore.co.uk

J. Wilkinson's, 1 High Street, Sandown PO36 8JW; 07763119476; info@wilkinsonsclassicpies.co.uk; www.wilkinsonsclassicpies.co.uk

Woodworks Wight, Natural Enterprise Ltd, Northwood House, Ward Avenue, Cowes PO31 8AZ; www.woodworkswight.co.uk

Yates' Brewery, Unit 4, Langbridge Business Centre, Newchurch PO36 0NP 01983 867878; www.yates-brewery.co.uk

Useful websites

www.english-heritage.org.uk – full details of the English Heritage historic buildings on the Island, including Osborne House and Carisbrooke Castle

www.gardenappleid.co.uk for more on Isle of Wight apple varieties including information about those grown at St Cecilia's Abbey, Ryde, and Osborne House; see also **www.suttonelms.org.uk/apple50.html**

www.go-fish.co.uk/isleofwight.htm – details of freshwater fishing opportunities on the Island

www.greattasteawards.co.uk – details the winners of the Guild of Fine Foods Great Taste awards including those on the Island, the acknowledged benchmark for fine food and drink

www.hampshirefare.co.uk – a not-for-profit community organization dedicated to championing local food and drink in Hampshire, and which stages the annual Hampshire Food Festival throughout July showcasing the county's food and farming

www.iowramblers.com – offering a programme of group walks on the Island throughout the year, plus details of the main walking events

www.iwcp.co.uk – online version of the must-have Island's weekly newspaper (also available in print), the *Isle of Wight County Press*

www.mattandcat.co.uk – a highly rated independent guide to eating out on the Island

www.myisleofwight.com – supported by Red Funnel Ferries yet an independently produced, authoritative insiders' guide to Island life, including local food and drink

www.nationaltrust.org.uk – full details of the Trust's properties and places to visit on the Island, such as the only surviving windmill, in Bembridge, Newtown Old Town Hall and The Needles Headland and Tennyson Down, plus lots of ideas for interesting things to do

www.realisleofwight.co.uk – podcast and website hosted by Tony and Ali; 'a full, frank and funny guide to all things Isle of Wight'

www.styleofwight.co.uk – the Island's inspirational lifestyle mag, available in print or online, which is strong on Island food and drink features, recipes and tips

www.tasteofthewight.co.uk – free local guide to food and drink published in three editions Spring/Summer, Summer/Autumn and Christmas available both online and in a printed version at outlets throughout the Island and onboard many ferry services, plus news, features, recipes and competitions available on the website

www.vipcottages.com – award-winning holiday accommodation website

www.visitisleofwight.co.uk – the Island's official tourism website, with bags of info on Island activities and events including local food-related items of interest

www.wightconservation.co.uk – although no longer updated, the website offers much interesting information about Island wildlife and habitats, and conservation strategies

www.wightfarmholidays.co.uk – specializing in B&B and self-catering accommodation in countryside locations around the Island

www.wightlink.co.uk/do/wightlife-brochure/ – Wightlink Isle of Wight Ferries' free guide to the Island including accommodation, food and drink, events and places of interest (also available in print)

www.wightlocations.co.uk – offering a range of quality self-catering cottages and homes for short breaks and holidays both coastal and rural, with a finger on the pulse of the Island food and drink vibe

www.wightmarque.tasteofthewight.co.uk – detailing the Wight Marque scheme set up by the Royal Isle of Wight Agricultural Society to identify through the Wight Marque logo individual products, producers and establishments that support local Isle of Wight produce, including a full list of Wight Marque members and products

www.wightwash.org.uk – website for the Island branch of CAMRA (Campaign for Real Ale), which publishes a seasonal magazine in print and online

www.wildonwight.co.uk – the Island's biodiversity website

FURTHER READING

Garlic: The Mighty Bulb by Natasha Edwards, Kyle Books
The Garlic Farm Cookbook by Natasha Edwards and Colin Boswell, The Garlic Press
The Goodness of Garlic by Natasha Edwards, Kyle Books
The Last Great Event with Jimi Hendrix and Jim Morrison: When the World Came to the Isle of Wight, Volume II by Ray Foulk with Caroline Foulk, Medina Publishing Ltd
Stealing Bob Dylan from Woodstock: When the World Came to the Isle of Wight, Volume I by Ray Foulk with Caroline Foulk, Medina Publishing Ltd
Taste of the Wight Isle of Wight Recipe Book, Solent; profits from sales of the book go to Bite the Wight (bitethewight.com), an initiative of the Isle of Wight Youth Trust
V is for Vegan by Kerstin Rodgers, Quadrille Publishing Ltd
Wild Cocktails from the Midnight Apothecary by Lottie Muir, CICO Books

Island food and drink events

Royal Hotel Ventnor's Gastronomic Weekends
www.royalhoteliow.co.uk/gastronomic-weekend-tour.aspx
Not exactly a normal foodie event, but an exceptional treat staged several times a year. The weekend includes transport to the Island, gourmet meals in the hotel, cookery demonstrations and visits to Island producers, including The Garlic Farm, Goddards Brewery, the Isle of Wight Distillery, Living Larder and The Tomato Stall.

APRIL / MAY

Real Ale Festival
www.iwsteamrailway.co.uk/events/real-ale-festival.aspx
Staged at Havenstreet Station with a full service of steam trains operating, an extensive range of interesting ales are on tap for sampling, including a wide variety of Island-brewed beers. Musical and other entertainments such as falconry displays as well as hot and cold food are laid on.

JUNE

Festival of the Sea
www.visitisleofwight.co.uk/whats-on/events/festival-of-the-sea
A series of events in late June and early July celebrating the Island's links with the sea, including the famous Round the Island Race and other sailing, cycling, eating and drinking happenings with a maritime theme.

Open Farm Sunday
www.farmsunday.org
A national event strongly supported on the Island with participants including The Tomato Stall and Wight Salads, Living Larder and Briddlesford Lodge Farm. Farm gates are thrown open to visitors so that they can learn, at first hand, about how our food is grown. Opportunities to buy the produce on site.

Royal Isle of Wight County Show
www.riwas.org.uk
Still in the traditional country show mode, with a food pavilion created by Taste of the Wight in 2014 and now sponsored by Southern Co-operative, stalwart supporters of local producers, under their banner of 'Local Flavours'. Plus equine, canine and livestock displays and competitions.

JULY

The Isle of Wight Vegan Festival
www.iowveganfestival.com
Featuring delicious vegan and raw food, along with holistic therapies, live music and children's entertainments.

Real Ale Train
www.iwsteamrailway.co.uk/events/real-ale-train.aspx
Billed as a summer evening of trains and fine ale, take a tour of the stations along the steam railway line, supping a glass or two at each, and enjoy a hearty supper of bangers and mash dished up halfway through the round trip.

AUGUST

The Chale Show
www.thechaleshow.co.uk
A favourite summer event on the Island, the show boasts one of the largest horticultural marquees on the South Coast with over 1,200 exhibits including vegetables, fruit and flowers. A bustling farmers' market selling local produce is also on offer, plus traditional village fete events as well as large-scale displays and activities in the main arena. A fun-packed kids area keeps the children fully occupied.

The Garlic Festival
www.garlic-festival.co.uk
The Island's largest summer show staged near Newchurch with not just garlic from the renowned Garlic Farm but a feast of food stalls showcasing the whole range of local fresh produce and products, along with cooking demos from top Island chefs. Plus live music, archery, animal events, fun fair and bags of entertainment specially designed for kids.

V-Dub Island
www.v-dubisland.com
The Island's 'family-friendly Volkswagen festival with a chilled-out music vibe' that also offers a chance to shop for produce from a selection of top Island producers. Plus Taste of the Wight stage and sponsor various fun food-related activities such as a Cooking in a Camper competition and a Pie-eating Extravaganza.

Ventnor Fringe
www.ventnorexchange.co.uk/vfringe
A uniquely Wight take on the famous Edinburgh Fringe attracting an exciting, eclectic mix of creative endeavour, including that of various enterprising Island food and drink producers.

SEPTEMBER

Beer and Cider Festival
www.theventnorwintergardens.com/beerfest.html
The Winter Gardens source a great range of Island beers and ciders and other selected local artisanal drinks and specially prepared cocktails for visitors to try and buy. Plus there are lots of Island foods to enjoy as accompaniments.

Bembridge Harbour Food Festival
www.bembridgefestivals.co.uk
An independent food and drink festival (free entry) with exhibitors representing a wide variety of quality local products. Participating eateries in the East Wight villages of Bembridge and St Helens cook up special menus to make the most of the local produce including Bembridge Ledge lobsters and crabs.

Hops Festival

www.botanic.co.uk/whats_upcoming
Held at the Ventnor Botanic Garden to celebrate the hops harvest, with a chance to sup some local ales including the garden's own Original Botanic Ale and Botanic Pale Ale. Plus lots of entertaining challenges for both children and adults.

Isle of Wight Sweetcorn Fayre

www.arretonbarns.co.uk/sweetcorn-fayre
Heaps of the Island's super-sweet sweetcorn cobs freshly harvested from the fertile land surrounding Arreton Old Village are barbecued, frittered, popped and even steam-milled, with related family fun activities, and all in the aid of local charities. Plus there are stalls selling other local produce along with crafts various, live music and children's fun fair entertainments.

Sausage and Cider Festival

The Griffin, Godshill
www.thegriffiniow.co.uk/events
A lively event held every September to celebrate what it says. There is an extra twist because this traditional pub boasts a complex maze in its delightful garden, backed by a lovely old wood, in one of the Island's favourite villages for visitors, with many outlets selling Island produce.

Wolverton Manor Garden Fair

www.gardenfair.org.uk
A charitable event set in the grounds of a beautiful Jacobean manor house not far from Newport. Besides nurseries and other plantspeople, among the exhibitors is a range of Island food and drink producers, as well as arts and crafts various.

SEPTEMBER / OCTOBER

Apple Weekend

www.english-heritage.org.uk/visit/places/osborne/events
An opportunity to sample the harvest from the apple and other fruit trees growing in the grounds of Osborne House, and to learn about Victorian fruit varieties. Offers activities for the whole family.

OCTOBER

Beer and Buses Weekend

www.iwbeerandbuses.co.uk
The Isle of Wight branch of CAMRA (Campaign for Real Ale) and the IW Bus Museum come together to stage this Islandwide event where they put on a fleet of characterful retro and vintage buses to visit various participating pubs and sample local ales and produce at special deals. Travel is free, although you are encouraged to purchase the inexpensive printed programme that details all the routes, timetables and pubs involved.

DECEMBER

Cowes Christmas Festival

www.redfunnel.co.uk/coweschristmas
A wide variety of Island food and drink producers exhibiting their wares, including seasonal specialities ideal for gifts or to ensure that the festivities go off in foodie style. Sampling opportunities are to be had, plus live cookery demos from talented local chefs staged at the ferry company Red Funnel's Interactive Cookery Theatre.

Acknowledgements

My heartfelt thanks go to all the following people who have helped immeasurably in the making of this book.

THE CONTRIBUTORS

Paul Richardson, publisher of Foreland Books, whom I am also blessed to count as my partner in epicureanism and life.
Ben Wood, not only for his superb photography but for sharing his unrivalled network of contacts, as well as his tireless support for the project.
Christian Warren and Laura Boynton, Style of Wight, for their inspired design and creative enthusiasm.
Georgina Moore for her consummate marketing contribution.
Anne Sheasby, cookery writer and editor, for her forensic proof-reading of the recipes and main text of the book.
Gerry and Steve Price for much invaluable help both on the creative side and with practical graft, and moral support.

THE MODELS AND EATING COMPANIONS

Mandy, Esther and Helena Bartholomew; Gerry, Steve and Alfie Price; Anna, Sol and Rufus Wood, and dog friends Noodle and Lula; Luca and Jude Wallis; Izzy and John Chudleigh; Jeremy Gully and Penny Walford.

ADVICE, INFORMATION, PROPS, ADDITIONAL PHOTOGRAPHY AND ALL SORTS OF OTHER HELP AND ENCOURAGEMENT

Barnes Edwards, The Garlic Farm; Josephine Boswell, The Garlic Farm Field Kitchen; Mark Curtis, Wight Locations; Matthew Noyce, Dean Pascall and Lucy Sutton, Quarr Abbey; Esther Bartholomew and Johnny Mitchell, photographic assistants; Simone Drinkwater, Simon Kingsley and Elisa Rosolin of Casemate UK; John Day, Delysia Farm; Russ Broughton, Adgestone Vineyard; Ben Brown, A E Brown Farms; Cedric and Bernice Grieve, Cranmore, Yarmouth; Jane 'the veg' Holman, The Farm Shop, Bembridge; Graham Hawkins, WW Woodford & Son,

Bembridge; Clare Warren-Monroe and Izzy Jensen, Bembridge Flower Shop; Sarah and Nick McChesney; Bill Attrill; John Scott; Stonecastle Graphics; Mat Tucker, The Break Lever; James Chastney, IT consultant; Mark Coucher, Short Run Press; Roger Serjent and Lisa Choi, The Taverners, Godshill; many other producers, retailers and consumers of Isle of Wight food and drink, sadly too numerous to mention individually, but to whom I am also very grateful.

Some of the props featured in the photos are my own, including precious family items of much sentimental value, but many were treasures mined from the Earl Mountbatten Hospice charity shops around the Island. Also pictured were Christmas decorations sourced from Pomegranate, Bembridge, and pieces from the Tregear Pottery, Niton, and Bonchurch Pottery.

THE LOCATIONS

'The Full Wight' was photographed at and around Jo and Paul Richardson's beach hut at the Foreland, Bembridge.
The 'Dinner for the Crew' was enjoyed on the houseboat Sturdy in Bembridge Harbour, courtesy of Georgina Moore and James du Cann (Sturdy can be rented via www.theharbourhouseboat.co.uk and www.

canopyandstars.co.uk/harbourhouseboat).
The 'Picnic on the Downs' was shot on St Boniface Down above Ventnor.
'Festival Nammet' happened on location and at an impromptu campsite.
'A Victorian Tea Party' was staged in the garden of Seaview House, courtesy of Mark Curtis of Wight Locations (2 Seaview House can be rented via www.wightlocations.co.uk).
The 'Fisherman's Feast' was thrown at Beachside Cottage, Steephill Cove, courtesy of Juliette Elkins (Beachside Cottage can be rented via www.mulberrycottages.com).
'Barbie on the Beach' ran and ran around Ben Wood's beach hut on St Helens Duver on a sunny high-summer Saturday.
'A Harvest Supper' was celebrated in the gardens of the Quarr Abbey Tearoom, courtesy of the Prior.
'Christmas Fare' was indulged in at Nonsuch Cottage, Bembridge, courtesy of Helen and Mark Turnbull (Nonsuch Cottage can be rented via www.wightcoastholidays.com).

BACK COVER QUOTATIONS

These are courtesy of, in order of appearance:
Jamie Magazine; Quadrille Publishing Ltd; Octopus Publishing Group Ltd; and Robin Courage.